Committees in Congress

SECOND EDITION

Committees in Congress

SECOND EDITION

Steven S. Smith and Christopher J. Deering

A Division of Congressional Quarterly Inc.
1414 22nd Street N.W., Washington, D.C. 20037

Printed in the United States of America

Library of Congress Cataloging-in-Publication Data

Smith, Steven S., 1953-
    Committees in Congress/Steven S. Smith and Christopher J.
Deering.--2nd ed.
    p. cm.
    Includes index.
    ISBN 0-87187-559-4
    1. United States. Congress--Committees. 2. United States.
Congress--Reform. 3. United States--Politics and government--1945-
I. Deering, Christopher J., 1951-. II. Title.
JK1029.S64 1990   90-39237
328.73′0765--dc20   CIP

To Barbara and Ty
s.s.s.

To the Mary Deerings
c.j.d.

Contents

TABLES

FIGURES

Preface

Committees are central to congressional policy making. The vast majority of legislation is discussed, amended, and reported by committees.
The daily routines—indeed, the careers—of nearly all members are
structured by committee duties. And committees are the most important
point of access to Congress for outsiders—interest groups, the administration, and the general public. The vital role of congressional committees motivated the first edition of *Committees in Congress* and continues to
do so in the second.

Readers familiar with the first edition will notice that the second
edition is a very different book. The emphasis in the first volume fell
upon a comparison of decision-making practices *within* individual committees. It emphasized differences in committee composition, structure,
and environment. And it gave special attention to changes in decision-
making patterns that resulted from reforms in the 1970s.

In this edition, the analysis of committee differences and change are
updated and extended. For example, we include new discussion and
analysis of member goals and the role of subcommittees. But we go
beyond those concerns to address the *committee systems* of Congress.
Sources of committee power and the changing relationship between
committees and their parent chambers and parties also are examined.
Most important, perhaps, we argue that two decades of change have
produced committees that are less powerful and autonomous. The place
of committees in the legislative process has changed in ways that are just
as remarkable as the changes in the distribution of power within
committees.

At the same time, this edition is more helpful to new students of
congressional politics. Additional background material is provided that
is necessary for understanding the operation of the committee systems.
There is less detail about individual committees but greater attention to

committee experiences on the floor, conference committee politics, the consequences of developments in the budget process, and new reform proposals.

Second editions inevitably accrue additional intellectual debts and this one is no exception. To that end we gratefully acknowledge the assistance and advice of Stanley Bach, Bill Connelly, Paul Herrnson, George Kundanis, Walter Oleszek, Jack Pitney, Judy Schneider, Barbara Sinclair, and Don Wolfensberger. In addition, Paul Joyce, Forest Maltzman, James Owens, Priscilla Regan, Marcia Sleight, Morton Soerensen, and Mark Watts provided assistance.

Both editions have been enhanced by experiences and contacts established through the Congressional Fellowship Program of the American Political Science Association. We also benefited from the support of the Dirksen Congressional Leadership Research Center.

In addition, we continue our debt of gratitude to Jean Woy whose faith in the project during its earliest stages remains primarily responsible for its continuance. At CQ Press David Tarr, Joanne Daniels, Nancy Lammers, Kathryn Suárez, and Ellen Loerke provided abundant support for this second edition. Lys Ann Shore provided editorial guidance that has made this edition a clearer presentation of our ideas. Pat Ruggiero produced a thorough index. Finally, we are grateful to Ann O'Malley who guided the manuscript through the final stages of production with unstinting energy and skill.

As with the first edition, numerous members of Congress and their staff offered their time to answer our questions about committee politics. This book is about the patterns of their activities, and we are grateful for their forbearance and for their responsiveness to our questions.

Steven S. Smith and Christopher J. Deering

CHAPTER 1

Committees in Congress

Committees long have been the central structural components of Congress. Their history, in many respects, is a reflection of the history of the nation and of Congress. They have been called petty baronies and fiefdoms, the little legislatures, the nerve ends, and the workshops and laboratories of Congress. In the contemporary Congress, the vast majority of policy disputes on Capitol Hill are resolved during committee consideration of bills. Legislation is seldom considered on the House or Senate floor without a committee's stamp of approval. The careers and reputations of individual members of Congress also are molded by their committee activities. It is through committees that members most frequently contribute to policy, gain media and constituency attention for their involvement with an issue, and develop their closest working relationships with colleagues, executive officials, and lobbyists.

Our primary purposes in this book are to introduce the major features of the congressional committee systems and to describe how they have changed in recent decades. In so doing, we place committees in relation to other features of legislative politics, compare the House and Senate committee systems, and assess the ever-changing balance of power within the two chambers. We begin in this chapter by explaining why committees are important in understanding congressional politics. We chart the current committee system, describe the formal sources of committee structure and procedure, and outline the foundations of congressional committee power. We conclude the chapter by discussing briefly the central themes of the book: variation among and change in congressional committees and the two committee systems.

TYPES OF COMMITTEES

Other than providing for a bicameral Congress and presiding officers, the U.S. Constitution is silent on the issue of how Congress should organize itself to make public policy. Throughout its history Congress has invented an array of committees for this purpose: ad hoc, conference, select, special, standing, and joint committees, for example. The House of Representatives routinely uses the Committee of the Whole and the Committee of the Whole House on the State of the Union to facilitate its work. And both chambers have used many committees by other names—task forces, for example. In fact, the formal names of committees often do not indicate the role they play. Two characteristics distinguish the basic types of committees: whether or not they have *legislative authority* (the right to receive and report measures), and whether or not they are *permanent* (in existence from congress to congress).

In the modern Congress, committees have three primary powers: collecting information through hearings and investigations, drafting the actual language of bills and resolutions, and reporting legislation to their parent chambers for consideration. All committees have the power to collect information. But some committees do not have the formal authority to draft *and* report legislation to their parent chamber. Thus, the first key characteristic of committees is whether they have the power to report legislation.

Furthermore, not all committees are permanent or *standing committees*. Standing committees carry over from one congress to the next by virtue of being written into the rules of the House and Senate. These rules (see the box on p. 3 for an example) name the committees, define their formal jurisdictions or responsibilities, establish procedures, and (in the Senate) prescribe their sizes. Nonstanding committees may carry over for more than one congress but, at least formally, cease to exist after a period of time specified by the parent chamber. Thus, the second key characteristic of committees is whether they are permanent or temporary.

Committees can be legislative or nonlegislative and permanent or temporary, as Table 1-1 shows. The most important committees (and the primary focus of this book) are the standing committees, along with their subcommittees. These committees are both legislative and permanent, and they are the point of origin for most legislation.

Arguably the next most important committees are those that have legislative jurisdiction but lack permanent status. During the early congresses nearly all committees were of this type. After a bill or resolution had been debated, a small group of members was appointed as an *ad hoc committee* to draft final language and report back to the chamber. During most of its history Congress did not use ad hoc committees, instead preferring to create standing committees when new issues arose that required legislative action. In 1975, after an absence of nearly a hundred years, the House amended its rules to permit the

Rule 10

ESTABLISHMENT AND JURISDICTION OF STANDING COMMITTEES
THE COMMITTEES AND THEIR JURISDICTIONS

1. There shall be in the House the following standing committees, each of which shall have the jurisdiction and related functions assigned to it by this clause and clauses 2, 3, and 4;. . .

   (c) Committee on Armed Services.

   (1) Common defense generally.
   (2) The Department of Defense generally, including the Departments of the Army, Navy, and Air Force generally.
   (3) Ammunition depots; forts; arsenals; Army, Navy, and Air Force reservations and establishments.
   (4) Conservation, development, and use of naval petroleum and oil shale reserves.
   (5) Pay, promotion, retirement, and other benefits and privileges of members of the armed forces.
   (6) Scientific research and development in support of the armed services.
   (7) Selective service.
   (8) Size and composition of the Army, Navy, and Air Force.
   (9) Soldiers' and sailors' homes.
   (10) Strategic and critical materials necessary for the common defense.
   (11) Military applications of nuclear energy.

In addition to its legislative jurisdiction under the preceding provisions of this paragraph (and its general oversight function under clause 2(b)(1)), the committee shall have the special oversight function provided for in clause 3(a) with respect to international arms control and disarmament, and military dependents education.

Speaker, on his or her own initiative but subject to House approval, to create ad hoc or select committees. But they are rarely used.

Conference committees and, very rarely, *select committees* also fall into the category of legislative, temporary committees. Conference committees are appointed to resolve the differences between House and Senate versions of legislation. Because the Constitution, in effect, requires that the House and Senate pass identical legislation before it is sent to the president, conference committees often are crucial to policy outcomes. (See Chapter 5 for more discussion of this role.) Within certain limits, these committees have the power to consider, alter, and report legislation. Conference committees dissolve as soon as a chamber acts on the

TABLE 1-1   Types of Congressional Committees

	Legislative authority?	
Permanent?	Yes	No
Yes	standing committees most subcommittees	joint committees
No	conference committees ad hoc committees some select committees	most select and special committees task forces

conference report. It is also worth noting that they are bicameral committees, composed of a delegation of senators and a delegation of representatives.

Only four committees have permanent status but lack legislative authority; they are the four *joint committees*—Economic, Taxation, Library, and Printing—whose membership comprises both representatives and senators, with the chairmanship rotating between members of the two chambers. The Joint Taxation and Joint Economic committees have some importance in policy making. As nonlegislative committees, the only "power" of these panels is an ability to analyze and to publicize findings regarding current public policy issues. But Joint Taxation maintains a large expert staff that serves the two revenue committees— House Ways and Means and Senate Finance. And the Joint Economic Committee conducts hearings and studies on economic policy problems that often receive considerable attention. Library and Printing focus entirely on matters internal to Congress by overseeing, respectively, the Library of Congress and the Government Printing Office.

The final group of committees—typically designated *select* or *special committees*—is neither permanent nor legislative. Select and special committees may be used for several purposes: to highlight important policy issues, to study or investigate pressing problems, to coordinate the development of policy that overlaps the jurisdictions of several standing committees, or simply as a reward to particular legislators. Select committees have been used on several occasions to examine and recommend reforms for the House and Senate. Two of these, the Bolling Committee and the Stevenson Committee, were instrumental in proposing House and Senate reforms during the 1970s. The best-known committees sometimes have been select committees. The Senate's Watergate Committee of 1973 (formally the Select Committee on Presidential

---

Creating Select Committees: The Select Committees on the Iran–Contra Affair

With the House and Senate launching their special investigations into the Reagan administration's secret Iran arms deals, there are signs pointing to increasing partisan rifts over Congress' handling of the scandal.

These divisions did not prevent the two chambers from overwhelmingly approving broadly worded resolutions (S Res 23, H Res 12) the week of Jan. 5 [,1987] to establish separate select committees that will probe the sale of weapons to Iran and possible diversion of funds to the Nicaraguan contras. . . .

The Senate on Jan. 6 voted 88-4 to establish its special panel, formally named the Select Committee on Secret Military Assistance to Iran and the Nicaraguan Opposition. The 11-member panel, six Democrats and five Republicans, is chaired by Daniel K. Inouye, D-Hawaii.

The next day, the House created its 15-member Select Committee to Investigate Covert Arms Transactions with Iran on a 416-2 vote. The committee of nine Democrats and six Republicans is being chaired by Lee H. Hamilton, D-Ind. . . .

The special committees each could begin hearings in February. The Senate panel is scheduled to conclude its work by Aug. 1, although its charter would allow the Senate to vote to continue through October. The House panel has until Oct. 30 to wrap up unless the House extends the deadline.

The select committees will have broad mandates, allowing them to go far beyond the Iran-contra connection. . . . The House committee's charter contains virtually no limits.

Source: Steven Pressman, "Partisanship Marks Launching of Iran Panels," *Congressional Quarterly Weekly Report*, January 10, 1987, 87 and 89.

Campaign Activities) and more recently House and Senate select committees to investigate the Iran-Contra affair are prominent examples (see the box on this page).

Unfortunately, the names of committees can be misleading. Good examples are the House and Senate Select Intelligence Committees. As the label *select* suggests, at one time these committees were temporary and lacked legislative jurisdiction. Neither is true today, however. Both committees are permanent even though they are not established in the standing rules of the two chambers; instead, they appear without time limit in the standing orders. And both committees have legislative and

TABLE 1-2   A Numerical Portrait of the Committee Systems of the 101st Congress (1989-1990)

Committees	House	Senate
Standing committees	23	18
Subcommittees	139	86
Special committees	0	1
Select committees	4	1
Ad hoc committees	0	— a
Joint committees	4	
Conference committees	76 b	

Source: "Committees and Subcommittees of the 101st Congress," *Congressional Quarterly Weekly Report,* May 6, 1989.

a Senate rules do not permit ad hoc committees.

b This figure is for the 100th Congress, (1987-1988). Data for the 101st Congress are not yet available.

budget authority over the Central Intelligence Agency, the Defense Intelligence Agency, the National Security Agency, and some activities of the Federal Bureau of Investigation.

Subcommittees also can fall into each of these permanent/temporary, legislative/nonlegislative categories. With very few exceptions, Congress's standing committees all have created more or less permanent subcommittees.[1] In addition, the House Budget Committee has a set of standing nonlegislative subcommittees called *task forces.*[2] Conference committees provide a third variant: temporary, joint, legislative subcommittees. For example, during recent congresses, conference committees have been formed to consider large "temporary" appropriations measures, called *continuing resolutions.* These committees have been so large (as many as two hundred members) that they have broken up into numerous subcommittees. Finally, committees have frequently created select or special subcommittees to study particular problems and report back to the full committees.[3]

Not surprisingly, this armada of committees tends to increase in any given congress (see Table 1-2) and there is no feasible way to consider each type fully, let alone each committee at great length. Therefore, while we occasionally consider other committees, our primary focus is upon committees that share these two important traits—they are standing committees, and they have legislative powers. A list of these panels appears in Table 1-3.

TABLE 1-3 Senate and House Standing Committees of the 101st Congress (1989-1990)

Senate	House
Agriculture, Nutrition, and Forestry	Agriculture
Appropriations	Appropriations
Armed Services	Armed Services
Banking, Housing, and Urban Affairs	Banking, Finance, and Urban Affairs
Budget	Budget
Commerce, Science, and Transportation	Energy and Commerce Merchant Marine and Fisheries Science, Space, and Technology
Energy and Natural Resources	Interior and Insular Affairs
Environment and Public Works	Public Works and Transportation
Finance	Ways and Means
Foreign Relations	Foreign Affairs
Governmental Affairs	District of Columbia Government Operations Post Office and Civil Service
Judiciary	Judiciary
Labor and Human Resources	Education and Labor
Rules and Administration	Rules House Administration Standards of Official Conduct [a]
Select Committee on Indian Affairs [b]	
Select Committee on Intelligence [b]	Select Committee on Intelligence [b]
Small Business	Small Business
Veterans' Affairs	Veterans' Affairs

Source: "Committees and Subcommittees of the 101st Congress," *Congressional Quarterly Weekly Report,* Special Report, May 6, 1989.

Note: Senate committees listed alphabetically, with corresponding House committees listed adjacent. Senate committees with broader jurisdictions have each of the relevant House committees adjacent.

[a] The House Standards of Official Conduct Committee is permanent and has legislative jurisdiction, while the Senate Ethics Committee does not; hence the latter is not listed.

[b] In spite of the word *Select* in their names, the House and Senate Select Intelligence Committees and the Senate Select Committee on Indian Affairs are permanent and have legislative jurisdiction. Thus, they are included in this list.

SOURCES OF COMMITTEE PROCEDURE AND STRUCTURE

The procedures and organizational arrangements associated with the committee systems have varied a great deal during the two-hundred-year history of Congress. Indeed, they tend to change to some small degree at the beginning of each congress. More rarely, dramatic changes in structure and procedures of the committee systems have fundamentally altered the character of the two systems. These changes may be achieved through a variety of mechanisms.

Article I, Section 5 of the Constitution states that "each house may determine the rules of its proceedings." As a result, House and Senate committees are principally, but not solely, the creatures of the separate sets of standing rules maintained by the two chambers—primarily Rules 10 and 11 in the House and Rules 24 to 28 in the Senate.[4] These two sets of rules are roughly parallel. Each prescribes about the same number, jurisdiction, and procedures for the committees of its chamber. But nothing requires the House and Senate to adopt identical rules in creating and regulating their committee systems. In fact, House and Senate rules governing their committee systems differ in important ways, as will be explored later in the book.

Chamber rules are not the only source of guidance for committee structure and procedures. Federal statutes, rules of the party caucuses in each chamber, individual committees' written rules, and informal norms and folkways all help to define the House and Senate committee systems.

Statutes, such as the Legislative Reorganization Acts of 1946 and 1970, helped to shape the committee systems by creating new panels and legislative procedures. The old Joint Committee on Atomic Energy, each of the current joint committees, the two Small Business committees, the two Budget committees, and the Senate Veterans' Affairs Committee all were created by statute. Indeed, in retrospect it may well be judged that the Budget and Impoundment Control Act of 1974, which created the two budget committees and is the source of much of the very complicated budget process now used by Congress, had a much bigger impact on Congress than any one or perhaps all of the other reforms enacted during the 1970s. This act, and follow-up reforms in the 1980s, fundamentally altered the relationship of the various committees of Congress, as Chapters 2 and 5 explain.

While some party rules concern the organization of committees—limiting the number of House subcommittees, for example—their primary influence is procedural. These rules establish procedures for assigning members to committees, dictate how committee leaders are selected, limit the powers of full committee chairs, or, as in the case of

House Democrats, even set rules for the use of subcommittees. Party rules remain subordinate to the standing rules of the chamber and may not, therefore, contradict them.

Individual committees also must adopt their own rules. These rules must be consistent with chamber rules, but they often go into greater detail about the chair's privileges and committee procedures. Meeting times, voting procedures, subpoena authority, referral of legislation to subcommittees, staff appointment procedures, and other topics are addressed in committee rules.

Finally, each chamber has evolved a set of recognizable, yet unwritten, norms or folkways that constrain individual members' behavior and, as a result, committees' performances.[5] The best known, and most criticized, of these was the traditional apprenticeship system prescribing that newer members be "seen but not heard" (see Chapter 2). But there are many other norms and standard operating procedures not defined in formal rules. Most conspicuously, seniority is the basis for selecting committee and subcommittee leaders in the vast majority of cases.

These five sets of formal and informal rules—chamber rules, statutes, party rules, committee rules, and norms—define the House and Senate committee systems. Change in any one of them can alter the function or power of committees.

COMMITTEE POWER IN CONGRESS

Whatever its source in formal and informal rules, committee power can be viewed as having two forms, negative and positive.[6] *Negative* committee power is the ability to defend the status quo successfully in the face of others who favor change. In the context of committee relations with a parent chamber, negative power rests on the ability of a committee to restrict the choices available to the chamber. *Positive* committee power is the ability of a committee to change a policy in the face of others who oppose change. In committee-chamber relations, positive power rests on the capacity of a committee to circumvent the floor or to convince some members to vote for the committee position contrary to their true policy preferences. The ability of committees to exercise each form of power rests, in part, on the rules and procedures of Congress, but also involves other resources that committees can bring to bear in a legislative battle.

The negative and positive powers of congressional committees are stronger than those of committees in most other legislatures. Indeed, the special character of committee power in Congress requires careful study. And yet committee power in Congress is not unlimited. Important constraints on committee power exist, which set bounds on the extent to which committees make policy autonomously.

NEGATIVE POWER

Negative committee power has many sources in Congress. The most obvious is the ability to obstruct legislation by refusing to report it to the floor. This "gatekeeping" power is considerably stronger in the House than in the Senate. Since 1880, House rules have featured strict language that compels the referral of legislation introduced in that chamber to *the* committee with appropriate jurisdiction.[7] This rule, in conjunction with written jurisdictions and permanent status, is a long-standing foundation of House committee power; it guarantees committees monopoly jurisdiction over designated policy areas (see the box on p. 11). This foundation of House committee power was weakened by a 1974 rule that allowed the referral of legislation to multiple committees. The Senate has adopted no similar strict requirement. Senate standing committees are permanent and they do have written jurisdictions, but Senate rules simply give them "leave to report" bills and resolutions within that jurisdiction. It is by precedent that nearly all bills and resolutions introduced to the Senate are referred promptly and without quarrel to the committee with appropriate jurisdiction.

Committee gatekeeping power in the House is reinforced by a strict germaneness rule for floor amendments. In the House, but not in the Senate, floor amendments must be directly related to the provisions being amended. The rule makes it difficult to raise issues that are not addressed explicitly in a committee bill. In the Senate there is no limit on the content of amendments for most measures. As a result, senators may incorporate the text of whole bills as amendments to other bills. Indeed, relatively minor pieces of legislation may become the vehicles for the consideration and adoption of much more important legislation. In most situations, nongermane amendments may be prohibited only by unanimous consent.

Even in the House, gatekeeping power is not perfect because of the existence of mechanisms for floor majorities to bring matters to the floor, such as suspension of the rules, discharge petitions, and special rules. And the House Rules Committee may report a resolution that, if adopted by majority vote, can discharge a measure from a committee and bring it to the floor for consideration. However, such mechanisms are difficult to employ without the support of the majority party's leadership.

Negative committee power is reinforced by other features of floor procedure. In both chambers, there are "depth" limitations on the number and degree of amendments to amendments that may be

---

Rules on Bill Referral

House Rule 10, Paragraph 1:

" . . . all bills, resolutions, and other matters relating to subjects within the jurisdiction of any standing committee as listed in this clause shall . . . be referred to such committees. . . ."

Senate Rule 25, Paragraph 1:

"The following standing committees shall be appointed at the commencement of each Congress, and shall continue and have the power to act until their successors are appointed, with leave to report by bill or otherwise matters within their respective jurisdictions."

---

pending at one time, in the absence of a special rule or unanimous consent agreement that provides otherwise. Furthermore, in the House measures are considered for amendment title by title or section by section. Amendment sponsors may offer their amendments only when the appropriate section is debated, and amendments must be germane to that section.

Committee *bill managers*—members who shepherd bills through the final stage of floor consideration—are recognized before other members to offer amendments on behalf of the committee before other amendments are considered, and during the consideration of other amendments they usually are recognized before others to offer second-degree amendments. In combination, depth limitations and recognition privileges order the consideration of alternatives so as to ensure that bill managers have an opportunity to offer alternatives to unfriendly amendments. The procedures often permit bill managers to dilute the effects of unfriendly amendments once they have been offered.[8]

Negative power is fortified by procedures of a more tactical nature, such as House special rules and Senate unanimous consent agreements. House special rules are resolutions from the Rules Committee that, if adopted by a majority vote, bring legislation to the floor and set limits on debate. Committees often seek and receive special rules that restrict amendments in some way. The Senate does not employ a similar procedure, although amendments and debate may be limited by unanimous consent. Because a single senator can prevent a unanimous consent request from being implemented, Senate committees are more vulnerable to unfriendly and unpredictable floor amendments.

Finally, domination of conference delegations by committee members also reinforces committees' ability to block unwanted outcomes and obtain compromises for others. Because of this dominance and because conference reports cannot be amended on the floor, committee members are in a position to reverse decisions made in floor amendments provided that the other chamber's conferees agree and that the final product is acceptable to House and Senate majorities. Reversals of floor decisions may abate the damage done on the floor to a committee's original plan.[9]

Taken together, these elements of congressional procedure confer upon committees considerable negative power. Careful deployment of negative power gives committees important bargaining advantages that may be used to buy support for their legislation. In other words, negative power sometimes yields positive results. For example, a committee may threaten to block a measure important to a member if that member opposes another measure important to the committee. But there are practical limits on the ability of committees to translate negative power into positive power in this way. Among other things, it might be expected that repeated hostage-taking strategies eventually would produce a backlash, perhaps in the form of challenges to the procedures granting the negative powers in the first place.

POSITIVE POWER

Direct sources of positive committee power are weak in Congress, at least when compared with sources of negative power. Since early in the nineteenth century, committees have been able to report legislation at will.[10] The proposal power does not guarantee floor consideration of committee-reported measures, with a few exceptions where legislation has privileged status and may be called up at any time by the committee. Majority party leaders may refuse to schedule the legislation, and floor majorities may oppose motions to take up legislation on the floor. And once a committee gets its bill to the floor, it must fend off unfriendly amendments and garner majority support. Avenues for circumventing the floor are very limited. Committee members sometimes manage to introduce new items at the conference stage, particularly when one of the chambers has adopted an amendment in the nature of a substitute, but even then a majority of both houses must approve the conference report.

To promote their legislative proposals successfully, committees often must employ their extra-procedural resources, which are substantial. First, committees sometimes gain tactical advantages over competitors because of their special role in gathering political and policy *information*. Committee members may selectively reveal that information to their chambers.[11] Committee leaders usually are better informed about the politics and policy substance of issues within their committees' jurisdictions, which often allows them to make more persuasive arguments than their opponents. Their informational advantage also may help them know where to expect support and opposition and the sources of unfriendly floor amendments. Second, committee *staffs* put committees in a better position than most members to anticipate actions of the floor, the other chamber, and conference; to draft defensive amendments strategically and rapidly; and to solicit the assistance of interest groups and others. And third, strong *personal relationships* with party leaders, other colleagues, and outsiders, developed during years of service in Congress, promote trust, help to gain support, and facilitate deal making.

Extraprocedural resources are important when there is some dissent from committee recommendations. Dissent means competition, and many committees' competitors have substantial political resources of their own. The president, party and faction leaders, interest groups, and others have access to large staffs, political and policy expertise, timely and relevant information, a network of political friends, and the ability to attract public attention, just as committee members do. These competitors can alter the policy preferences of members by changing the political costs and benefits of supporting committee recommendations. Thus, in the hunt for majority support in the House and Senate, committees sometimes find themselves outgunned by their opposition.

THE ULTIMATE WEAPON

Committee power, then, is the product of a mix of procedural and extra-procedural resources. Negative committee power stems primarily from the particular sequence and procedures of congressional legislating. In fact, the multiple procedural advantages of committees are often sufficient to block changes in policy, particularly in the House. In contrast, positive power concerns committees' ability to persuade and so must be developed from extra-procedural sources.

The parent chambers retain the ultimate weapon against wayward committees: dissolution of committee jurisdictions and parliamentary privileges. All congressional committees are creations of their parent chambers and may be restructured or abolished by them. Committees are established and retained because they perform valued services for the chambers and individual members. In this light, committees are never truly autonomous decision-making units; rather, they must function in a procedural fashion and with a substantive effect generally consistent with the interests of their parent chambers. When the individual committees or the committee system as a whole become dysfunctional for a majority of members, they can change, and have changed, chamber or party rules to remedy the situation.

Yet, in practice, committees wield real power, often somewhat independently of the preferences of their parent chambers. This is possible because threats to dismantle or reconstitute a committee usually are not credible. For example, a threat to strip a committee of jurisdiction normally is not taken seriously, if for no other reason than that it would set a precedent that members of other committees would not like to see repeated.[12] Other tools of the parent chambers or parties are too unwieldy to be effective. A chamber could reduce a committee's budget, thereby limiting its effectiveness, but that could limit the committee's ability to act in policy areas in which the committee and chamber are in full accord. The parties may strip individual members of their committee assignments in retribution for their activities and policy positions, but even this is not a practice that most members would like to make commonplace. In any event, a committee threatened by the parent chamber and parties would find friends outside of Congress coming to its aid.

The net result is that committees are seldom far out of step with their parent chambers and parties and, when they are, there seldom is a sanction to fear. The most immediate and practical means available for chamber control is simply to reject the legislative measures recommended by a committee.

VARIATION AND CHANGE IN THE COMMITTEE SYSTEMS

The committee systems, along with the parties, are the central organizational features of Congress. In the following chapters, we will see that the House and Senate committee systems differ in important ways, that there is substantial variation in the jurisdictions and roles of individual committees, and that the committee systems change constantly. When viewed in historical perspective, variation and change are conspicuous attributes of congressional committees.

Variation and change in the rules and practices governing the committee systems are generated by the interests of both individual members and the institution as a collectivity. Individual and institutional interests have changed frequently as the political, social, and economic environments in which Congress operates have evolved over two centuries. All three levels—individual, institutional, and environmental—interact to shape the procedural and structural features of Congress.[13] We will discuss them in turn.

INDIVIDUAL INTERESTS

It is reasonable to suppose that congressional procedure and structure in the House and Senate chambers must be consistent with the preferences of at least a majority of the membership. After all, the Constitution allows each chamber to determine its own rules. Thus, if committees vary from each other in their jurisdictions, formal powers, staff resources, or autonomy, it generally is appropriate to assume that a chamber majority supported that arrangement at one time. Of course, past practices have a tendency to outlive their usefulness, so it is not necessarily true that a majority of members would support every aspect of current arrangements if they were asked to vote on each one. The important thing to remember is that if a majority (or perhaps an extraordinary majority in the Senate) is committed to changing current arrangements, they have the power to do so.

Needless to say, not all members are alike. Differences in individuals' backgrounds and ambitions and in constituency interests produce differences among members in their attitudes about how Congress should operate. This is one reason why it is difficult to find a majority of like-minded members in favor of a particular procedural or structural reform. But because not all members want the same results from their service in Congress, it also is possible simultaneously to meet the needs of most members. As a result, substantial variation in the power and jurisdictions of committees has been tolerated during most of the last two centuries.

At most times in the history of Congress, most members had an investment in current arrangements. Some members held positions of authority in the current system, some had devised career plans with the current system in mind, and some members simply preferred to avoid the uncertainties associated with change. Consequently, major procedural and structural changes have occurred only rarely. It sometimes seems as though institutional inertia prevents any meaningful change. An unusual mix of conditions is required to convince a majority of members that their committee systems need a thorough overhaul.

Nevertheless, given time, Congress has proven to be quite capable of implementing great change in its committee systems. Change in the character of the membership has played an important role in motivating or facilitating procedural and structural reform. In the last two centuries, members have gradually taken an interest in serving out their political careers in Congress, have faced ever-changing pressures in the electoral arena, and eventually have become independent political entrepreneurs. All of these developments have influenced members' views about how the institution should operate.

INSTITUTIONAL FORCES

It would be misleading to suggest that individual needs directly determine the rules of the institution. Certain institutional constraints to new directions usually exist to slow, compromise, or redirect reform efforts. In particular, past decisions about procedure and structure affect current decisions. This is most obvious when members who hold powerful positions—positions that were created by past decisions—resist change. Such opponents of change often are able to exact concessions from the proponents as a condition for considering and adopting change, resulting in compromised reforms. One consequence of resistance from entrenched interests is that it is easier to add new procedures and structures than it is to eliminate old ones.

In addition, many past procedural or structural choices become so well accepted that only arrangements consistent with them are considered seriously at present. And when new arrangements are debated, reformers often discover that they have somewhat inconsistent goals for new arrangements. For example, given the House's prior commitment to a system of active committees and subcommittees, it is not possible to devise a highly efficient, centralized decision-making process. To grant great centralized legislative powers to the Speaker would be inconsistent with the expectation that the members and staffs of the dozens of subcommittees will remain devoted to conducting investigations and writing legislative detail. Maximizing efficiency in processing legislation and the quality of information Congress has at its disposal are not fully compatible goals in most institutional settings.

Of course, institutional factors serve as more than constraints on decisions about rules. The interests of individual members sometimes are related directly to the capacities of Congress as an institution. For example, the power of individual members is determined in part by the ability of Congress to compete with the presidency and the courts for control over public policy. A powerless Congress would be of little use to members motivated by their own influence on public policy. To the extent that their individual well-being is tied to the status of the institution, members are compelled to weigh the interests of the institution when making decisions about legislative procedures and structures.

In many cases, however, the interests of individual members are not fully compatible with collective interests. There are many situations in which a majority of members recognize the advantages of a certain reform, but no one sees enough personal benefit in it to formulate a specific proposal and work for its adoption. This constitutes a *collective action problem* that is difficult to resolve. In other situations, as we have noted, opposition can stymie or compromise a reform effort that has overcome the collective action problem. Consequently, congressional decision-making processes, including the role of the committee systems, seldom are designed to maximize the competitiveness of Congress as an institution. Rather, they represent a mix of individual and collective interests that is fully satisfactory to few members.

ENVIRONMENTAL FACTORS

Conflict between members and tensions between individual and collective interests sometimes are temporarily balanced to produce what appears to be a stable decision-making process. Such an equilibrium is likely to remain in place as long as the membership and legislative responsibilities of Congress exhibit little change. But factors that Congress cannot control often produce substantial change in the membership and agenda. This change in turn upsets the balance of preferences about institutional arrangements and stimulates a search for new arrangements to meet the evolving needs of individual members and the shifting demands on the institution. Change in the formal and informal rules governing the committee systems is a common result.

In short, the driving force of most institutional change is environmental change. A downturn in the economy may contribute to electoral results that alter the political balance in Congress and lead the parties and factions within Congress to seek new institutional arrangements to fit their new circumstances. The gradual accumulation of power by the president, perhaps as a result of the increasing importance of international politics, may eventually generate a response from members of Congress concerned about their own influence. Or more generally, an increase in the speed of change and the complexity of Congress's environment may transform the burdens on individual members, alter the institution's work load, and create pressures for change in decision-making processes.

EXAMINING VARIATION AND CHANGE

In the following chapters these themes of variation and change are explored in greater detail. Our primary concern is with variation among and changes in committees and the committee systems during the last three decades. Many observers have argued that the primary effect of changes made in the 1970s has been to exacerbate the fragmented nature of congressional decision making. The increased number and independence of subcommittees have caused the most stir, leading some observers to describe congressional decision making in the 1970s as "decentralized" and as "subcommittee government." Increasingly, it seemed, initial policy decisions were made within the subcommittees of Congress. Rather than complain about dictatorial full committee chairs, members came to decry the lack of "responsible leadership" and the presence of "runaway subcommittees." Decentralized decision making, critics charged, served to undermine further the efficiency and coherence of legislative policy making.

More recently, scholars and observers of Congress have remarked upon a trend toward recentralization.[14] Increased partisanship, larger but fewer major pieces of legislation, the so-called "top down" budgeting process, increased leadership powers, and more assertive leaders are all seen as evidence of this trend. Should this prove true, then much of the conventional wisdom about an irreversibly decentralized Congress must be called into question.

Whether centralized, decentralized, or some other adjective best characterizes Congress as a whole, past experience indicates that it is unwise to be satisfied with sweeping generalizations about congressional committees. This is a central lesson of Richard Fenno's Congressmen in Committees, a study of six House and six Senate committees in the 1960s.[15] Fenno discovered that committees differ in two vital ways: in the nature of their political environments, and in the personal goals of their members. As committee environments differ, so do demands placed on committee members. And members' goals dictate the nature of legislative products that committees seek to create. Together, environments and members' goals shape relations among committee members, especially the formal and informal mechanisms they devise for making committee decisions.

Just as Fenno observed that committees differ in important ways, it also must be noted that committees change in a variety of ways. Changes—particularly in policy agendas, membership composition, and committee members' attitudes and goals—may enhance, moderate, or even counteract the effects of formal alterations in committee structure and procedure. Thus, among other things, patterns of centralization or decentralization among House and Senate committees may be quite varied. This attention to variety requires that we take advantage of previous scholarship, especially that of Fenno, who identifies fundamental ways in which committees and their members differ.[16] It also requires that the study's central components be defined to capture the dynamic quality of political relationships.

Our treatment of committees begins in Chapter 2 with an examination of the historical development of the two committee systems. The discussion is intended to make students of Congress aware that things have not always been as they are today. This may seem prosaic, but even the best of scholars falls prey occasionally to historical short-sightedness. Indeed, after the initial period of House decentralization congressional observers are now wondering if a true "postreform" era has begun.

Issue agendas and the identities of individuals and groups that place demands on committees are closely related and therefore are treated together throughout this study. They are considered explicitly in Chapter 3. The chapter explores the different types of agendas and external actors, outlines the nature of committee members' personal political goals, and considers how those goals have changed as the membership, institutional arrangements, and political environment have changed.

Chapter 4 considers the major components of the decision-making processes within committees: chairs, subcommittees, and staff. The chapter assesses the degree to which "subcommittee government" is an accurate characterization of committees' decision-making practices. The discussion gives special emphasis to variation and change in the internal decision-making practices of committees during the past three decades.

Chapter 5 demonstrates that the relationship between standing committees and their parent chambers and parties is not etched in stone. To the contrary, the relationship has evolved in important ways during the last two decades. Developments in floor activity, the roles of parties and their leaders, and the budget process have changed the distribution of power within Congress. The chapter describes the decline of committee autonomy and the response of committees during the last two decades.

We conclude in Chapter 6 with a summary discussion of the current state of the committee systems, various proposals for reform, and the prospects for change.

NOTES

1. The current exceptions are the ethics committees in the two chambers and the Senate Budget and Select Intelligence committees.
2. It is not the only time task forces have been used, but they are the only ones presently in existence. During the 99th Congress, for example, the House Administration Committee had a Task Force on Libraries and Memorials. It became a standing, presumably legislative, subcommittee in the 100th Congress. For other examples, see Chapter 4.
3. But none currently exist. The House Committee on Education and Labor has a subcommittee called Select Education, but that panel has legislative jurisdiction for miscellaneous education issues.

4. Interestingly, committees are important enough in the House and Senate to be the subject of roughly one-third and two-thirds (respectively) of the total language in each chamber's rules.

5. On the development of legislative norms in the Senate and House, respectively, see Donald R. Matthews, *U.S. Senators and Their World* (Chapel Hill: University of North Carolina Press, 1960); and Herbert B. Asher, "The Learning of Legislative Norms," *American Political Science Review* 67 (June 1973): 499-513.

6. See Keith Krehbiel, "Spatial Models of Legislative Choice," *Legislative Studies Quarterly* 13 (August 1988): 259-319; and Steven S. Smith, *Call to Order: Floor Politics in the House and Senate* (Washington, D.C.: Brookings Institution, 1989), 168-196.

7. There is a historical irony in this. Before 1880, and especially in the very early congresses, committees were the primary originators for most legislation. But this did not give them much power since they frequently had no choice but to report—favorably or not—to the floor. Following the 1880 rule, individual members formally gained a power they had been developing for some time, that of freely introducing legislation. But upon introduction they also quickly lost control of their bills to the committee with appropriate jurisdiction. As of 1880, House committees were guaranteed a first look at legislation in the House of Representatives. And that first look has more frequently than not also been the last for most bills and resolutions. On this important development see Joseph Cooper and Cheryl D. Young, "Bill Introduction in the Nineteenth Century: A Study of Institutional Change," *Legislative Studies Quarterly* 14 (February 1989): 67-105.

8. A formal treatment of these advantages in the House is provided in Barry R. Weingast, "Floor Behavior in Congress: Committee Power Under the Open Rule" (paper prepared for the 1987 annual meeting of the American Political Science Association). Of course, second-degree amendments also may be employed by rank-and-file senators seeking to limit the options of others. If committee leaders do not anticipate such developments, they may discover that their opponents have gained a procedural edge.

9. The ex post veto, too, is an imperfect tool for committees. Its success is contingent on the willingness of the other chamber's conferees to agree to the change and of floor majorities in both chambers to support the conference report. The ex post veto also can be undermined in a number of ways. For example, the floor may reject a conference report, send the report back to conference, reconstitute the conference delegation, bypass the conference through an exchange of amendments with the other chamber, discharge the conference, or use other means to limit the discretion of conferees. And the preferences of the other chamber, its committee, and its conferees may severely restrict a chamber's conferees from repealing the decisions of its own floor. For background on the ex post veto, see Kenneth A. Shepsle and Barry R. Weingast, "The Institutional Foundations of Committee Power," *American Political Science Review* 81 (1987): 85-104; Keith Krehbiel, Kenneth A. Shepsle, and Barry R. Weingast, "Why Are Congressional Committees Powerful?" *American Political Science Review* 81 (1987): 929-945; and Steven S. Smith, "An Essay on Sequence, Position, Goals, and Committee Power," *Legislative Studies Quarterly* 13 (1988): 151-176.

10. For a formal treatment of the proposal power, see David P. Baron and John A. Ferejohn, "The Power to Propose," *Working Papers in Political Science*

P-88-3, Stanford University, Hoover Institution, March 1988.

11. For a recent discussion of the long-appreciated importance of information advantages, see David Austen-Smith and William H. Riker, "Asymmetric Information and the Coherence of Legislation," *American Political Science Review* 81 (1987): 897-918.

12. In the 100th Congress, the Senate Budget Committee's charter was under serious threat. Many senators believed the committee should be supplanted by a committee composed of the leaders of the other standing committees, and at least one candidate for majority leader supported the proposal. See David Rapp, "Budget Breaks Up in Acrimony," *Congressional Quarterly Weekly Report*, April 30, 1988, 1165-1166. For additional discussion of why changing jurisdictions may be difficult, see Melissa P. Collie and Joseph Cooper, "Multiple Referral and the 'New' Committee System in the House of Representatives," in *Congress Reconsidered*, 4th ed., ed. Lawrence C. Dodd and Bruce I. Oppenheimer (Washington, D.C.: CQ Press, 1989), 253-259.

13. The literature on these topics is very large. An excellent place to begin is James G. March and Johan P. Olsen, *Rediscovering Institutions: The Organizational Basis of Politics* (New York: Free Press, 1989). Treatments of individual interests, collective interests, and environmental change that inform the discussion in the text include Joseph Cooper, "Congress in Organizational Perspective," in *Congress Reconsidered*, 1st ed., ed. Lawrence C. Dodd and Bruce I. Oppenheimer (New York: Praeger, 1977); Joseph Cooper and Cheryl D. Young, "Bill Introduction in the Nineteenth Century: A Study of Institutional Change," *Legislative Studies Quarterly* 14 (February 1989): 67-105; Roger H. Davidson and Walter J. Oleszek, "Adaptation and Consolidation: Structural Innovation in the U.S. House of Representatives," *Legislative Studies Quarterly* 1 (February 1976): 37-65; Christopher J. Deering, "Congressional Politics: An Introduction and an Approach," in *Congressional Politics*, ed. C. J. Deering (Chicago: Dorsey Press, 1989), 1-13; Morris P. Fiorina, *Congress—Keystone of the Washington Establishment* (New Haven: Yale University Press, 1977); Gerald Gamm and Kenneth Shepsle, "Emergence of Legislative Institutions: Standing Committees in the House and Senate, 1810-1825," *Legislative Studies Quarterly* 14 (February 1989): 39-66; Burdett Loomis, *The New American Politician* (New York: Basic Books, 1988); David R. Mayhew, *Congress: The Electoral Connection* (New Haven: Yale University Press, 1974), part 2; Nelson W. Polsby, "The Institutionalization of the U.S. House of Representatives," *American Political Science Review* 62 (March 1968): 144-168; and James L. Sundquist, *The Decline and Resurgence of Congress* (Washington, D.C.: Brookings Institution, 1981).

14. See Chapter 5.

15. Richard F. Fenno, *Congressmen in Committees* (Boston: Little, Brown, 1973). See also George Goodwin, Jr., *The Little Legislatures* (Amherst: University of Massachusetts Press, 1970).

16. Fenno, *Congressmen in Committees.*

CHAPTER 2

Development of the Congressional Committee Systems

Congress has made use of committees since its first session in 1789. As central components of the congressional infrastructure, committees have played a wide variety of roles in the legislative process, roles that have changed as the character of the membership and the institution's political environment have evolved. This chapter traces the development of the House and Senate committee systems, focusing on the ebb and flow in the independence and autonomy of standing committees.

In the modern Congress, committees have considerable *independence* to conduct investigations, devise and revise legislation, and report recommended legislation to the floor. In fact, under current House and Senate rules, committees are obligated to survey policy developments and oversee the activities of executive and judicial agencies within their jurisdictions. As this chapter explains, such independence was not granted to committees at the start but rather evolved over many decades. And even after committees gained independence to act at will, policy-making *autonomy* was not guaranteed. The constitutional requirement that legislation be approved by a chamber majority binds committees to their parent chambers and parties. The degree to which chambers and parties have acted to limit the exercise of policy-making discretion on the part of committees has varied greatly during the last two centuries. Committees acquired a remarkable degree of autonomy during the middle decades of this century, but that autonomy has been challenged in recent decades.

An appreciation of committees' history is vital to placing the current committee systems in proper context. Not only does a historical review illuminate the power and complexity of the modern committee systems; it also demonstrates how malleable legislative processes are in Congress. While past organizational decisions always influence future directions, Congress has shown a remarkable capacity to alter its decision-making processes in response to changing demands from its members and environment.

To examine the development of the congressional committee systems, we have somewhat arbitrarily identified six periods that reflect changes in the number of standing committees in the two chambers. The years that make up these six periods are demarcated in Figure 2-1. Standing committees were used infrequently during the first period, that of the earliest congresses. In the second period, the five decades preceding the Civil War, the standing committee systems were established and acquired most of their essential functions. In the third period, the latter half of the nineteenth century, standing committees proliferated in both houses but eventually were brought under the control of majority party leaders—a process that limited their autonomy. Shortly after the revolt against Speaker Joseph Cannon of Illinois in 1909-1910, a process of consolidation occurred, which constitutes the fourth period. By the late 1940s and the beginning of the fifth period, the legislative process was dominated by powerful committee chairs in newly reorganized and largely autonomous committees, setting the stage for the reform movement of the late 1960s and 1970s, which marks the start of the sixth period.

THE EARLY CONGRESSES: 1789-1810

Members of the first congresses were influenced by their previous experiences with legislative institutions. Most of them had served in the Continental Congress or their colonial and state legislatures, and several of them were keen observers of the British House of Commons. These experiences led them to devise mechanisms allowing the full expression of the will of congressional majorities while maintaining the equality of all legislators—an approach that would be alien to modern legislators.[1] Members of the first congresses preferred that each chamber, as a whole, determine general policy by "majority decisions through rational discussion and mutual enlightenment" before entrusting a subgroup of the membership with the responsibility to devise detailed legislation.[2]

The House of Representatives shouldered the greatest legislative burden in the early congresses. It acted first on most matters and led the way in creating legislative procedures. One of the most important of these was a parliamentary creature called the *committee of the whole*, designed to maximize members' participation by minimizing structural constraints. A committee of the whole operates as a committee but is composed of all members of the House. Most significant policy questions, and many less significant ones, were considered first by the entire

FIGURE 2-1   Number of Congressional Standing Committees (1789-1990)

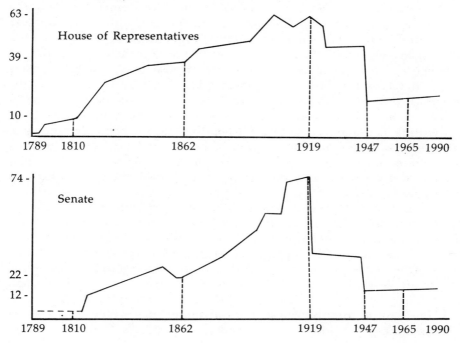

Source: The Congressional Directory; Lauros G. McConachie, Congressional Committees (New York: Thomas Y. Crowell, 1898); Annals of Congress; Register of Debates in Congress; Congressional Globe; Journal of the House; Journal of the Senate; the Congressional Record.

Note: Graph smoothed between major points of change.

House membership in the flexible procedural setting of this committee, where a relatively free exchange among members was permitted.

Because legislators feared that committees with substantial policy discretion and permanence might distort the will of the majority, House committees for the first eight or nine congresses usually took the form of special or select committees. This approach retained original debate and policy determination for the full membership, yet turned over the drafting of details to more manageable select committees. These select committees were dissolved upon the completion of their tasks. Several hundred of these small ad hoc committees were created in the House (and the Senate) during this early period.

The House, nevertheless, began to develop the foundations of a standing committee system at an early point, by establishing a few permanent committees in routine policy areas and in other recurrent, complex policy areas requiring regular investigation.[3] The House had created ten standing committees by the end of this first period. For example, the Interstate and Foreign Commerce Committee (now the Energy and Commerce Committee) and the Committee on Ways and Means were established as standing committees in 1795 and 1802 respectively. These committees had from 3 to 17 members at the time of their creation, while membership in the House grew from 64 members in the First Congress to 142 members in the Tenth. Gradually, the practice of first referral to a committee of the whole began to lose its significance, and the committees began to assume more discretion in writing legislation. As early as the Fourth Congress, parts of presidential messages to Congress routinely were sent, without directives, to committees. And even on other legislative matters, discussion of principles in a committee of the whole came to have less influence on the final legislative product.[4]

In its formative years, the Senate used select committees exclusively on legislative matters, creating only four standing committees to deal with internal housekeeping matters: the Joint Committee on Enrolled Bills, the Committee on Engrossed Bills, the Committee on the Library, and the Committee to Audit and Control the Contingent Expenses of the Senate. A smaller membership, greater flexibility in floor procedure, and a much lighter work load—with the Senate always waiting for the House to act first on legislation—permitted the Senate to use select committees in a wider variety of ways than did the House, while still maintaining full chamber control over legislation.[5] Some select committees were limited to legislative drafting; others were directed to make policy recommendations; still others were told to do both. These tasks were assigned either before or after, or both before and after, initial floor consideration. The Senate treated its select committees as convenient tools to be employed in the manner most appropriate to the matter at hand.[6]

At first, debate by the entire Senate before referral of legislation to a select committee was the standard procedure, but in 1806 the Senate adopted the practice of referring to a committee all matters relating to the subject for which the committee had been created. For example, the committees created to consider the various parts of the president's annual message to Congress continued to receive all related matters throughout the session. These "sessional" committees exhibited some continuity of jurisdiction from congress to congress, providing a rationale for creating permanent standing committees.

In the early congresses, the chamber majority created select committees composed of individuals who were in agreement with the majority's views. As Thomas Jefferson's *Manual of Parliamentary Practice* put it, "The child is not to be put to a nurse that cares not for it." [7] Beginning in 1790, each House committee was appointed by the Speaker, with the primary sponsor of a legislative proposal typically appointed as chair. The House retained the authority to make committee assignments by other means if it should decide, by majority vote, to do so—as, for example, when there was some suspicion that the Speaker could not be trusted to appoint proponents of the legislation under consideration. The Senate chose its committees by ballot, and the chair usually was given to whoever received the most votes in the balloting. Committee assignments in both houses also were made with some concern for geographical balance, knowledge, and expertise. Indeed, attempts were made to provide representation for each state on important House committees until the increasing number of states made it impractical to continue the practice. In both chambers partisanship, which often was related to policy views, quickly became the primary criterion for assignment.

Initially, committee chairs were conceived merely as agents or moderators of the committees. [8] By the beginning of the nineteenth century, however, several House and Senate committee chairs dominated their committees' activities, determining when and where the committees would meet and controlling their proceedings while in session. In fact, a committee chair's ability to delay committee action became a widely recognized problem in the second term of the Jefferson administration. Acting on behalf of Jefferson, John Randolph, chair of the House Ways and Means Committee, was responsible for delays in moving his committee to action on matters the president wanted to stall or kill. As a result of such abuses, the House adopted a rule in the Eighth Congress that permitted committees to elect their own chairs. The House adopted a further rule in the Ninth Congress that allowed any two members of a committee to call a meeting of their committee. [9]

In both the House and the Senate, then, the use of committees was dictated by the desire to maximize the participation of the full membership in decision making. Full participation, in turn, required that each chamber depend as little as possible on permanent committees and, where committees were necessary, limit procedurally their autonomy and tenure. Even in this early period, movement away from this ideal could be seen. Practical and political considerations hastened that movement in the following years.

INSTITUTIONALIZATION: 1811-1865

In the fifty-year period before the Civil War, the standing committee systems of both chambers became institutional fixtures. Both houses of

Congress shifted from using select committees to using standing committees, and regularly added to the number of standing committees while eliminating or combining only a handful of them. In the House, the number of standing committees increased from ten to twenty-eight between 1810 and 1825 and to thirty-nine by the beginning of the Civil War. The Senate established its first significant standing committees in 1816, when it created twelve. Of these twelve, Foreign Relations, Finance, and Judiciary have retained their names up to the present, although their jurisdictions have been altered several times. The Senate's standing committee system had grown to twenty-two committees by the time of the Civil War. But, in both chambers the standing committees remained small in size. House standing committees ranged from three to nine members, although three committees reached fifteen or sixteen members for short periods of time. Senate committees typically had only three members in the early 1800s but had grown to six members by 1860.[10]

Several factors played important roles in the expansion and institutionalization of the committee systems.[11] For the House, an increasing work load, dramatic growth in its own size, the greater importance of committees to individual members, more congressional interaction with executive departments, and the coincidence of a series of relatively weak presidents, combined to induce committee growth. Larger work loads required a division of labor. A larger House—which grew from 64 members in 1789 to 241 in 1833—made open-ended floor debate chaotic. And standing committees facilitated strong and mutually beneficial relationships between committee members and the growing number of executive departments and agencies.[12]

The Speaker of the House also played an important role as he began to exercise forcefully the committee appointment power, in order to gain control over committee consideration of major pieces of legislation. Henry Clay of Kentucky, who assumed the speakership in 1811 and served as Speaker for six nonconsecutive terms over the next fifteen years, transformed the role of Speaker into one of policy leadership and increased the partisan significance of committee activity.[13] Rather than allowing the full House first to determine the nature of the legislation to be written, Clay preferred to have a somewhat stable group of members supportive of his policy views write the legislation and shape a winning coalition before bringing it to the floor. Standing committees served this function very well for Clay, and he encouraged their creation during his speakership.

Two procedural changes further transformed the role of House committees. First, the practice of referring legislation to a committee of the whole before referral of legislation to a select or standing

A Selected, Chronological List of House Standing Committees

Congress has used committees for more than two hundred years. And during that time these committees have frequently been established in response to events and trends in the development of the nation itself. Thus, committees to some extent reflect national changes, as can be seen in this list of selected, but not very well-known, House committees:

Elections	1789
Revisal and Unfinished Business	1795
Revolutionary Claims	1813
Territories	1825
Invalid Pensions	1825
Railways and Canals	1831
Coinage, Weights, and Measures	1865
Pacific Railroads	1865
Levees and Improvements on the Mississippi River	1875
Alcoholic Liquor Traffic	1893
Ventilation and Acoustics	1895
Industrial Arts and Expositions	1901
Woman Suffrage	1917
World War Veterans' Legislation	1924
Un-American Activities	1945
Science and Astronautics	1958

Source: George B. Galloway (rev. by Sidney Wise), *History of the House of Representatives* (New York: Thomas Y. Crowell, 1976), 72-73.

committee was discontinued by the end of the 1820s.[14] Instead, first referral of legislation to a standing or select committee became the norm. Second, the original procedure requiring the House to grant a formal leave (or permission) before a committee could report a bill to the floor was discontinued. The practice of allowing several standing committees to report at their own discretion was codified into the rules of the House in 1822.[15] And by the late 1830s all House committees could introduce new legislation and report it to the floor at will. With these changes, House standing committees gained a critical role in proposing legislation and assumed a now routine role in the consideration of virtually all legislation.

Changes in the operation of the House committee system coincided with a fundamental and lasting shift in members' views about the proper relationship between participation and structure.[16] While policy control by the House majority continued to be a dominant principle, a division of labor through standing committees came to be seen as a necessity. Preliminary debate by the full House came to be viewed as a useless procedure, and the participation of the full membership soon was reserved for review of committee recommendations. Restricted participation in a committee setting gradually was perceived as the appropriate approach to determining both general policy principles and the details of legislation. And by contrast to the select committee practice, the House came to recognize that the minority should receive representation on standing committees. By degrees, then, the standing committees became much more than mere agents of the House. They gained great independence and assumed the legislative initiative in most policy areas.

Pressures for change in the Senate's committee system were not as great as in the House of Representatives. The Senate continued to depend largely on House-passed bills for its legislative agenda. As a result, the Senate could manage its legislative agenda in serial fashion, depending less on the simultaneous consideration of a broad range of legislation in committees. Moreover, the Senate did not grow in size as quickly as did the House. In 1835, for example, the Senate had only forty-eight members—fewer than the House had had during the First Congress. Finally, the development of party activity in the Senate had the effect of deemphasizing committee decisions, in sharp contrast to the House. There were no comparable party leaders in the Senate who could control standing committees during most of the antebellum period. Factional rivalries motivated at least a dozen changes in the method of appointing committees during this period, as senators sought to devise mechanisms to suit their political advantage. Committees and their chairs often opposed the majority party leaders' policy positions. Consequently, Senate party leaders assumed the personal responsibility of managing most of the important legislation on the floor. They often did not seek to have legislation referred to committee in the first place. Ironically, it was Henry Clay, as Senate Whig leader during the 1830s, who was particularly careful to avoid unfriendly committees.[17]

As a result, the Senate's standing committees, with one or two important exceptions, played a relatively insignificant role in the legislative process before the Civil War.[18] Committees were given the authority to report bills at their own discretion on all subjects referred to them in 1817, but they seldom made important revisions, and often their reported legislation was not considered on the floor. In fact, the debates on Senate committee reform in 1856 indicated that fifteen Senate committees simply had nothing to do.[19] Nonetheless, assignments to such committees retained political value because membership, and particularly the chair, on some of them was prestigious and allowed members ready access to executive officials. Committee chairs also could hire clerks who were commonly used as personal secretaries, and a committee usually could be maintained on the grounds that future legislative business was foreseen. Nearly all important decisions were made when the legislation was before the full Senate. This, indeed, was the heyday of great floor debate led by several of the most renowned orators in Senate history: John C. Calhoun, Henry Clay, and Daniel Webster.

The House and Senate also continued to differ in their development of committee assignment procedures. The Speaker of the House appointed committee members throughout this early period. But committee assignments were not a simple responsibility that the Speaker managed routinely. To the contrary, assignment decisions often were part of the bargaining process for the speakership itself, and, as has been noted, they were a central component of an elected Speaker's efforts to control the House on behalf of his party or faction. Prior service and the developing norm of giving minority party members some representation on committees in proportion to their representation in the full House tempered the Speaker's discretion in making assignments. Yet Speakers seldom permitted placement of minority and senior members on committees that might subvert partisan policy goals. The earlier rule giving committees the option to elect their own chairs was allowed to expire as the Speaker's control over the process increased.

By contrast, although political parties eventually gained control over committee assignments, the procedures for making those assignments never stabilized in the Senate.[20] The Senate experimented with committee appointment by ballot, by the vice president, by the president pro tempore, and by combinations of these procedures. In the mid-1840s the Senate used a procedure of suspending Senate rules and adopting committee lists drawn up by the leaders of the two major parties. The majority party allocated fewer seats on each committee to the minority party than their proportion in the chamber might dictate, but minority leaders were given the discretion to make minority assignments as they saw fit, a procedure that later would become routine. But when the Democrats assumed control of the Senate in 1849, they returned to the practice of having the president pro tempore, whom the majority party controlled, make committee appointments.

While many congressional committee chairs gained public notoriety during this period, party leaders in both chambers prevented them from becoming the dominant political powers within the spheres of their committees' jurisdictions. Speakers of the House appointed chairs, like other committee members, with an eye toward retaining control over major policy decisions. There was a tendency to reappoint chairs to their former posts, but that practice was subservient to the Speaker's political preferences.[21] Senate committee chairs showed greater stability during this period, generally changing only with turnover in membership and changes in party control of the Senate (with the exception of a brief period when chairs were rotated among committee members of the majority party). As in the House, chairs normally cooperated with party leaders; when there was conflict between the two, the leaders were able to keep legislation on the floor without referral or to have it referred to a select committee.[22] House and Senate committee chairs often assumed nearly dictatorial powers within their committees—occasionally presenting them with completely drafted legislation or bypassing them altogether—completing the majority party leaders' chain of command.[23]

By the 1860s the practice of hiring committee clerks at public expense had become routine in both the House and the Senate. Also, committees regularly were assigned rooms in the Capitol to conduct their business. Because many committees had no business to conduct, the rooms and clerks simply became perquisites of office for committee chairs. Senate committees usually could obtain approval to hire a clerk for one session or congress at a time.[24] The House kept a tighter rein on the hiring of committee clerks, adopting a rule in 1838 that required committees to receive special approval from the full House before hiring a clerk. Approval routinely was given to most committees, however.[25]

By the Civil War, standing committees had assumed a central role in the legislative process—albeit still a limited one by today's standards. Questions about the fundamental functions of congressional committees had disappeared. The House floor and especially the Senate floor continued to be critical decision-making centers, but increasingly the participation of rank-and-file members was molded by the committee systems.

EXPANSION: 1866-1918

In the half-century following the Civil War, the role of committees was strongly influenced by three factors. First, dramatic economic, geographic, and population growth placed new and greater demands on Congress, which responded with more legislation and new committees. Second, further development of American political parties and the increasing strength of congressional party leaders, especially in the late nineteenth century, led to an even greater integration of congressional parties and committee systems. Third, members of Congress, first in the Senate and then in the House, came to view service in Congress as a desirable long-term career, which in turn gave more personal significance to congressional organization, particularly the committee systems.[26]

In both the House and Senate a strong tendency existed to create new committees rather than to enlarge or reorganize old committees' jurisdictions. Quite often, leaders and other members were unwilling to entrust certain types of legislation to the senior members of old committees. Majority party leaders also found useful the flexibility of making a large number of committee assignments. And the perquisites of chairs and the political value of claiming membership on some committees continued to make it difficult to eliminate committees. By 1918 the House had acquired nearly sixty committees and the Senate, thanks to a blanket grant of standing committee status to many select committees in 1913, had seventy-four. Nearly half of these probably had no legislative or investigative business; in the early 1900s, junior members regularly complained about receiving assignments to committees that never met.[27] Further structural complexity developed in Congress's committee systems with the creation of subcommittees, a development that would come to have much greater significance later in the twentieth century. Although the historical record does not identify when subcommittees were first used or give a precise count of their number, a member of Congress reported in 1915 that about thirty-five House committees and twenty-seven Senate committees were using formal subcommittees on a regular basis. About half of those committees had permanent or standing subcommittees.[28] Even in the early 1900s, the work loads of active committees, especially those with appropriations authority, made further division of labor desirable, if only to make it easier for them to establish quorums to conduct business. The standing subcommittee structure within some committees further reduced the number of members participating in the initial development of legislation.

The most important jurisdictional changes during this period concerned money matters. The House Ways and Means and Senate Finance committees' expenditure and revenue-raising responsibilities greatly increased during the Civil War. Their increased burdens and power stimulated successful efforts in both houses to create separate appropriations committees in the mid-1860s.[29] Personal, factional, and intercommittee antagonisms later led to a further distribution of appropriations authority to several other committees of the House and the Senate. By 1900 the unified control over government financial matters originally invested in the Ways and Means and Finance committees had been distributed among nearly twenty committees.

One might think that these structural developments led automatically to a more "decentralized" Congress, particularly in the House, which in 1880 adopted a rule requiring legislation to be referred to committee. But they did not. Instead, majority party leaders of both chambers used the committee systems as tools for asserting control over decision making. In the House, the period between the Civil War and 1910 brought a series of activist Speakers—Samuel J. Randall, John G. Carlisle, Thomas B. Reed, and Joseph G. "Uncle Joe" Cannon—who substantially expanded their control over the flow of legislation.[30] These Speakers aggressively used the committee appointment power to stack important committees with friendly members and took advantage of a new bill referral power to send legislation to friendly committees. In addition, these Speakers asserted that a petition to discharge a bill from a committee was not a privileged motion; assumed the discretion, without appeal, to recognize members seeking to speak on the floor; transformed the Rules Committee into a standing committee chaired by the Speaker; and gave the Rules Committee the authority to report *special orders* that set the floor agenda for the consideration of legislation. Special orders were particularly important because they could set the length of debate and the number and type of amendments allowed. These powers gave the Speaker the ability to grant a right-of-way to certain legislation. They also allowed him to block legislation by selectively recognizing members on the floor or by clogging the floor agenda with preferred legislation. Through the appointment process and the Speaker's control over the flow of legislation on the floor, committees often served as the Speaker's extended arms.

Senate organization in the years following the Civil War was dictated by Republicans who gained majorities in that chamber for all but two congresses between 1860 and 1913. The Republicans emerged from the war with no party leader or faction capable of controlling the Senate. Relatively independent committees and committee chairs became the dominant force in Senate deliberations.[31] By the late 1890s, however, elections had made the Senate Republican party a smaller and more homogeneous group, and a coterie of like-minded Republicans had ascended to leadership positions. This group controlled the party's Committee on Committees, which made committee assignments, and the Steering Committee, which arranged the legislative schedule of the Senate.[32] These developments made all Senate committees handling important legislation the instruments of an interlocking directorate of party leaders.

Despite party leaders' control over committee assignments in the House and Senate in the late nineteenth century, their discretion became limited by the emerging custom of seniority. The *seniority principle* gave committee chairs to members with the longest continuous service on each committee and allowed members to remain on a committee as long as they wished. Seniority gained importance earlier in the Senate than in the House. This was due, at least in part, to the fact that the House had developed a regular appointment procedure at an early date, while the Senate had struggled with conflict-ridden assignments in nearly every congress up to the Civil War. Seniority provided a routine process that minimized conflict among most senators. It also was consistent with the developing careerism prevalent in the Senate, which made rank-and-file members more concerned about their long-range committee responsibilities and power and less willing to depend upon the whims of party leaders.[33] Thus, even by the 1870s, seniority had become the standard guide for making Senate committee assignments and chair selections. By the turn of the century it had become such an "iron-clad formula" that in both House and Senate party leaders' real discretion in committee assignments was limited primarily to new members.[34]

The increasing use of seniority as a guide to committee assignments in the House was reversed, albeit temporarily, in the first decade of the twentieth century. Republican Speaker Joseph Cannon from Illinois employed his appointment and recognition powers to block the legislative efforts of progressives within his own party. In 1907, for example, Cannon failed to reappoint four incumbent progressive committee chairs and passed over three other senior members in line for chairs. The removal of the incumbent chairs after a Speaker's first term—in ways unrelated to building a coalition in the speakership contest—was unprecedented.[35] It also bucked the trend toward a more routine application of the seniority principle at a time when members were seeking longer, more secure careers in the House. These dictatorial actions, combined with the ideological differences underlying them, stimulated a revolt against Cannon by Republican insurgents and opposition Democrats.

The most important lasting product of the revolt was the composition of the Rules Committee. New House rules prohibited the Speaker from membership on the committee, expanded the size of the committee, and stripped away the Speaker's power to appoint the committee's members. It was hoped that an elected Rules Committee would be more representative of House opinion in its consideration of special orders and changes in House rules.[36]

When the Democrats gained control of the House after the 1910 elections, major changes were instituted in their committee assignment procedures. The Democrats transferred assignment authority for their caucus from the Speaker to the Democratic members of the Committee on Ways and Means. Because the majority leader typically chaired Ways and Means, the power remained in the leadership's hands, although not in the hands of the Speaker. Democratic leaders also used the temporarily cohesive party caucus, the so-called "King Caucus," to bind party members to policy positions. The caucus's cohesion began to wane in 1916, reducing the effectiveness of Majority Leader Oscar Underwood's centralized control and resulting in a decline in the use of the caucus and in violations of seniority in committee assignments. House Republicans continued to allow their party leaders to make committee assignments for them until they created a separate Committee on Committees within the party in 1917.

Committee chairs rose to even greater importance during this period. Indeed, Woodrow Wilson concluded in 1885 that American government was best characterized as "government by the chairmen of the Standing Committees of Congress." [37] They often delayed, and sometimes refused to report to the floor, legislation that their committees had approved. They also managed the floor debate on all legislation that originated in their committees. As noted, though, committee chairs soon were constrained by majority party leaders. Consider the following complaint by progressive representative George Norris:

> At the very first meeting of one of the important committees of the House, to which a new member had been assigned, Norris was astounded to hear one of the older members of the committee inquire of the chairman if he had seen the Speaker in regard to a particular bill that was then under consideration. He was still more astounded when, at that meeting, a motion actually was made and passed instructing the chairman to have a conference with the Speaker and to ascertain whether he would permit the passage of the bill in question. [38]

This kind of relationship between the central party leaders and committee chairs continued until about 1916 in the House and nearly as long in the Senate.

From 1915 to 1920, majority party Democrats began to fractionalize, undercutting the power of their leaders and contributing to a greater disenchantment with the structure and operation of the congressional committee systems. That the bloated, incoherent committee systems had not resulted in chaos much earlier is testimony to the strength of previous party leaders. With declining leadership power, however, the fragmented, overlapping jurisdictional structure of the committee systems was less tolerable, and by 1918 demands for reform had become loud and frequent.

CONSOLIDATION: 1919-1946

The most striking feature of the 1919-1946 period was a decline in the number of standing committees. During this time, few new standing committees were added, and in 1920 the Republican Senate eliminated forty-one inactive standing committees, a move tolerated by senators because of the greater availability of personal staff assistance and office space. The most important jurisdictional change before the 1940s involved the reconcentration of appropriations authority in the Appropriations committees. In anticipation of an improved executive budgeting system ordered by the Budget and Accounting Act of 1921, the House restored its Appropriations Committee's jurisdiction in June 1920. The Senate followed suit in 1922. The revived Appropriations committees restructured their subcommittees so that each would have jurisdiction over one of the appropriations bills within the full committees' jurisdiction.

House Republicans attempted to retain strong party control of the House when they gained the majority after the 1918 elections,[39] but the Republican years of the 1920s resulted in a substantial weakening of the links between party leaders and committees.[40] The majority leader no longer chaired a major committee, chairs of major committees could not serve on the party's Steering Committee, and no committee chair could sit on the Rules Committee. Democrats adopted similar practices. In the House both parties earmarked certain major committees, such as Appropriations, Rules, and Ways and Means, as exclusive assignments, by preventing their members from gaining membership on other committees (although Republicans occasionally granted exemptions). Finally, both parties began to apply the seniority rule rigorously in committee appointments. These changes formally divorced the leadership from the committee system, allowing committee chairs to become independent powers within the jurisdiction of their committees. Party leadership became a somewhat more fluid group of elected leaders and selected lieutenants, who were now more dependent upon personal skills than formal powers to shape House decision making.

The House Rules Committee benefited greatly from the changes of the 1920s. The Rules Committee retained all of its vital functions in setting the floor agenda and gained even greater independence with the complete institutionalization of the seniority rule. The committee often refused to report a special order allowing important legislation to be considered on the floor and held legislation hostage until a legislative committee made certain changes. The Rules Committee chair even refused to report special orders adopted by the committee itself.[41] During most of the 1920s and 1930s, the Rules Committee cooperated with the majority party leadership, so its decisions were not as arbitrary and self-serving as they sometimes appeared. Beginning in late 1937, however, a coalition of conservative, majority party Democrats and minority Republicans used the committee to block President Franklin D. Roosevelt's programs and to pave the way for conservative legislation.

Senate committees operated relatively independently of majority party leaders in the 1920s, but their success on the floor declined because of deep cleavages within the ranks of the majority party Republicans. Progressive Republicans and Democrats had effective control of the Senate on several issues and were able to reject or simply neglect the actions of committees controlled by regular Republicans. Senate Republican insurgents and Democrats were aided by their ability to filibuster legislation they opposed.

As a result of Republicans' ability to win nonsouthern seats during the 1920s, southern Democrats made up a high proportion of all Democrats in Congress and were able in large numbers to gain seniority and access to prestigious committees. When the Democrats took control of the House in 1931 and of the Senate in 1933, southerners acquired far more than half the committee chairs, much more than their proportion of the party.[42] President Roosevelt and party leaders were able to keep these committee leaders in line during his first term, but conservative chairs, especially the southerners, began to challenge Roosevelt's program in his second term. This factional split within the Democratic party marked not only the origin of the conservative coalition in Congress, but also the beginning of a long period of strong, independent committee chairs willing to oppose a president and congressional leaders of their own party.[43]

By the 1940s a confluence of pressures for reform of the committee system had developed. The power of committee chairs, the seniority system, and the Rules Committee's power all came under attack from liberals wary of the long-term domination by conservatives then in power. Nonetheless, the increasing size and power of the executive branch during the New Deal and World War II led many members to recognize the ineffectiveness of congressional organization and operation. With the help of reports prepared by a committee of the American Political Science Association and others, attention was drawn to weaknesses in the committee systems. The large number of committees and their overlapping jurisdictions were responsible for unequal distributions of work and participation among members. They caused difficulties in coordination between the House and the Senate and made oversight of executive branch activities difficult. Numerous assignments made it difficult for members to concentrate on any one committee's work or to develop the expertise necessary for an effective review of legislative proposals and executive operations. Committees also lacked staff assistance to conduct studies of policy problems and executive branch activities.

The reform effort resulted in the Legislative Reorganization Act of 1946. Because of its members' purported inability to reach a consensus, the joint committee studying reform recommended no changes affecting the seniority system or the powers of the House Rules Committee, and none were included in the act. Even so, the act featured a series of important innovations. Sweeping changes were enacted in the number and jurisdictions of standing committees, with the number of standing committees reduced to nineteen in the House and fifteen in the Senate. This reduction in number primarily resulted from consolidating several groups of committees into single committees.[44] The standing committees in each house were made nearly equal in size, and the number of committee assignments was reduced to one for most representatives and two for most senators. The act authorized committees to hire a staff of up to four professional and six clerical workers on a nonpartisan merit basis; the House and Senate Appropriations committees were permitted to appoint as many as they deemed necessary. The staff of the Legislative Reference Service was strengthened by the act, and many of these new staffers would be detailed to committees for special projects. Finally, the act directed the standing committees to exercise "continuous watchfulness" over the implementation of laws by the executive branch. The reorganized and well-staffed committees would be in a better position to perform this function.

The Legislative Reorganization Act of 1946 had the effect of further increasing the power of chairs of standing committees. Provisions of the act dealing with regular committee meetings, proxy voting, and committee reports constrained chairs in some ways, but most of them benefited from greatly expanded jurisdictions and the new committee staff, which they would control. The act helped guarantee that committee chairs would dominate congressional policy making for the foreseeable future and that the participation of rank-and-file members, especially in the larger House of Representatives, would be centered in their assigned committees. The act had consolidated the structure of the standing committee systems, and the power of independent committee chairs as well.

COMMITTEE GOVERNMENT: 1947-1964

The central features of congressional politics remained relatively stable during the 1947-1964 period. Democrats controlled both houses in all but two congresses and during most of the period were led by two skillful Texans, Lyndon B. Johnson in the Senate and Sam Rayburn in the House. The House and Senate standing committee systems exhibited their greatest structural stability during this period, with each chamber adding only an aeronautics and space committee in 1958. House and Senate membership also was exceptionally stable. Usually more than 80 percent of the members were reelected from one congress to the next and a marked increase occurred in the number of House members serving ten or more terms.[45] Committee chairs also exhibited great stability. More than 60 percent of committee chairs serving during this period held their positions for more than five years, including approximately two dozen who served more than a decade in their positions, despite the fact that it took longer than ever before to gain a chair.

Students of Congress during this period noted the presence of a set of strong, informal norms governing individual behavior. Donald Matthews discovered in the late 1950s that the Senate had its unwritten rules of the game, its norms of conduct. Some things were just not done; others were met with widespread approval. "There is great pressure for conformity," one influential senator said. "It's just like living in a small town."[46]

Matthews noted two norms directly affecting committees. The first was specialization: a member "ought to specialize, to focus his energy on the relatively few matters that come before his committees or that directly and immediately affect his state."[47] The second norm was the expectation that new members would serve an apprenticeship period during which they listened and learned from senior members and refrained from active participation in committee or floor deliberations. These norms, which were also found to be important in the House,[48] emphasized the development of expertise in the affairs of one's own committee and deference to the assumed expertise of other committees. The collective justification for these norms was that such expertise and deference produce better legislation and promote more efficient decision making. The individual's tolerance of these constraints was based upon the belief that his or her own expertise would eventually serve as an important base of power as seniority accrued.

The powers of committee chairs during this period were succinctly summarized by George Galloway in 1953:

> Just as the standing committees control legislative action, so the chairmen are masters of their committees. . . . They arrange the agenda of the committees, appoint the subcommittees, and refer bills to them. They decide what pending measures shall be considered and when, call committee meetings, and decide whether or not to hold hearings and when. They approve lists of scheduled witnesses and authorize staff

studies, and preside at committee meetings. They handle reported bills on the floor and participate as principal managers in conference committees. They are in a position to expedite measures they favor and to retard or pigeon-hole those they dislike.[49]

The power of Senate chairs was bolstered by membership on major committees other than the ones they chaired, which placed them in an excellent bargaining position with most rank-and-file members.[50] In short, chairs were in an excellent position to enforce the norms of proper conduct and to pursue their own policy objectives.

Despite maintaining tight control over committee activities, most chairs were not tyrants within their committees. Rank-and-file members were well aware of their power, of course, but most chairs were effective because they were among the most knowledgeable and active members of their committees.[51] Typically, committee chairs held political views similar to those of their committee majorities, which often were composed of conservative Democrats and minority party Republicans. Consequently, they seldom needed to resort to strong-arm tactics.[52] The aura of great power surrounding many chairs often came as much from personal skill and flexibility in molding successful coalitions as from their formal authority.

Nevertheless, conservative chairs, particularly southerners, proved to be a major obstacle to Democratic liberals even when a clear majority of the party supported the liberal view. For example, Graham Barden (D-N.C.), chair of the House Committee on Education and Labor, and A. Willis Robertson (D-Va.), chair of the Senate Committee on Banking and Currency, used their offices' powers to thwart federal aid to education and to block challenges against conservative banking policies.[53] The disproportionate number of conservatives serving as committee chairs by virtue of their seniority was especially irritating to liberals. The seniority system had allowed members from electorally stable areas of the country to rise up through the ranks without interruption, while members from more competitive areas were less likely to remain in Congress long enough to gain committee chairs. Committee transfers among northern members also contributed to southern overrepresentation among chairs. And although southern strength declined during this period, anxious liberals perceived only bleak prospects for replacing conservative chairs in the near future.[54]

House liberals organized the Democratic Study Group in 1959 to combat the conservative power structure. Their immediate target was a conservative coalition on the Rules Committee, led by Chairman Howard Smith of Virginia, that held a stranglehold on committee actions. The liberals recommended reinstatement of the twenty-one-day rule that permitted the reporting legislative committee to demand floor consideration of legislation on which the Rules Committee had refused to act for at least twenty-one days. A similar rule, adopted in 1949, had been repealed in 1951. The liberals also sought to expand the Rules Committee to permit liberals to be appointed to it. Speaker Rayburn talked them out of pursuing their proposals after assuring them that the Rules Committee would cease its blockage of legislation. But Rayburn was unable to deliver on his promise; and after the Democrats regained control of the White House in 1961 House liberals renewed their efforts to curb the committee's obstructionism. This time, with the help of Rayburn and the new Democratic administration, they successfully expanded the Rules Committee and new, more party-oriented Democrats were added to it.

The reduction in the number of standing committees as a result of the 1946 reforms stimulated the creation of new subcommittees. An estimated ninety-seven House subcommittees and thirty-four Senate subcommittees existed before the 1946 reforms.[55] After the reorganization, the number of subcommittees initially dropped to a little more than sixty in the House but rose to about sixty in the Senate (see Figure 2-2). Most of the newly created Senate subcommittees mirrored previous standing committees' jurisdictions, which had been folded into new committees by the 1946 act. The number of subcommittees gradually grew throughout this period, reaching more than one hundred in the House and more than eighty in the Senate by 1964. A majority of the committees in both houses exhibited increases in the number of their subcommittees.[56]

The growth in the number of subcommittees had roots in the practical problems involved in managing larger and more complex work loads, in the desire of larger numbers of senior members for a "piece of the action," and in isolated efforts on individual committees to loosen the grip of chairs on committee activity.[57] Chairs of less important committees—especially in the Senate where members held at least two full committee assignments—occasionally discovered that it was necessary to give subcommittee chairs to certain members as an incentive to get them interested in the committee's work and to help shoulder the committee's work load.

Generally, however, subcommittees served as important political tools of the full committee chairs. The committee chair determined the subcommittee structure and membership. In some cases, chairs merely numbered subcommittees and gave them no standing policy jurisdiction, in order to maintain freedom to refer legislation to a subcommittee that would act on the legislation in accordance with the chair's views. By directing a subcommittee as well, the full committee chair and a small group of friendly colleagues frequently dominated the committee's

FIGURE 2-2   Number of Standing Subcommittees of House and Senate
Standing Committees (80th to 101st Congress)

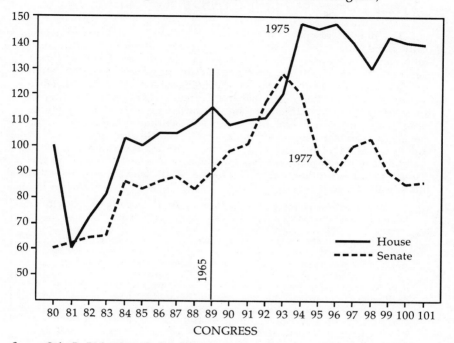

CONGRESS

Source: Sula P. Richardson and Susan Schjelderup, "Standing Committee Structure and Assignments: House and Senate" (Congressional Research Service, March 12, 1982). Updated by authors.

consideration of such legislation. A few chairs, most notably those of the House Ways and Means and Senate Finance committees, refused to establish subcommittees in order to retain personal control of all legislation at the full committee level. Effective participation often became limited to two or three people in each chamber, as structured by the committee and subcommittee systems.

Congressional committee staffs blossomed during this period, further augmenting the resources of committee chairs. Chairs took advantage of the Legislative Reorganization Act of 1946 to bolster their staffs, and they acquired additional authorizations to move well beyond the levels set by the act. The total staff of standing committees more than doubled between 1947 and 1964: from 182 to 489 in the House and from 232 to 492 in the Senate.[58] Committee staff continued to be appointed and managed by the full committee chairs, although a few committees permitted the minority party to appoint a small number of staff

"What Congress Hath Created, Let No Man . . ."

The number of subcommittees in both chambers increased dramatically during the 1950s and 1960s, and they became nearly as difficult to eliminate as committees had been in the nineteenth century. When subcommittees were challenged—a rare occurrence—their defenders often devised ingenious responses to protect their positions. One such instance stands out. In 1967 Republican senator Everett M. Dirksen of Illinois, one of the few minority party members permitted to chair a subcommittee after the 1946 reorganization, sought a $7,500 authorization from the Senate for his subcommittee's only employee. He was challenged by Democrat Allen J. Ellender of Louisiana, who took the opportunity to question the need for the subcommittee itself. Senator Dirksen, who was known for his sharp wit and his deliberate, mellifluous speech, defended his subcommittee:

Mr. President, in the first place, I am against disposing of this subcommittee, and the most important reason that I can assign is that I am the chairman. I want no legislative throatcutting here. . . . I have been the chairman or a member of this subcommittee for so long that the memory of man runneth not to the contrary. You are not going to do this to me, are you, and destroy my one and only chairmanship? Why, that is discrimination. . . .

The second reason, Mr. President, is that I am a stickler for tradition. . . . I have to let the Senate in on a little secret. Once upon a time there was a distinguished member of this body by the name of William Langer, from North Dakota, and at the time he was ranking Republican member on the Committee on the Judiciary. The distinguished chairman was the Honorable Pat McCarran of Nevada. I recall the day when Senator Langer went to Senator McCarran and said: "There is no justice. There ought to be at least one Republican chairman of one subcommittee on Judiciary." And Senator McCarran, with all the grace and all the generosity in his soul, said: "You are on and you are it. You name the subcommittee that you want." And Senator Langer said: "I'll take Charters, Holidays, and Celebrations." That is how that subcommittee came into being. It was an absolute, unadulterated, unmitigated, unrefined, unconfined deal. But I did not make the deal. I am only the inheritor of the deal. And I do not want my inheritance destroyed since I came by it very honestly. So you see, this is in the great tradition.

The third reason I assign is that I think this is probably the most important subcommittee in the Senate of the United States. Just think of the question of charters that we have to pass on . . . in due course there may be organizations like the Sons of Rest or the Association of Indigent Senators, or what have you, and maybe they want a Federal charter, and if they do, they march up to my subcommittee door and they get good attention. So, you see, this is an important subcommittee, because it involves a lot of people. . . .

So, do not destroy this little subcommittee of two men and do not destroy this responsibility of the chairman of this little subcommittee. . . . I stand here today to protect this little subcommittee, and lay no profane hand on it because it will be a charge on your conscience.

Dirksen's position was supported by a voice vote.

Source: Congressional Record, 90th Congress, 1st sess., 3784-3785.

members. While many of these workers were highly professional, nearly all were loyal to the chair and his or her political goals. Even when a staff was highly competent, additional workers gave the chairs better access to policy and legislative drafting expertise.

Formal procedures for committee assignment did not change during the 1947-1964 period. The chair of Ways and Means, Wilbur Mills (D-Ark.), and his fellow committee Democrats developed power well beyond the scope of their substantive policy jurisdiction by continuing their role in the assignment process.[59] In the Senate, Majority Leader Lyndon Johnson instituted the so-called "Johnson rule," which gave all Democrats, even the most junior members, the opportunity for a seat on one of the major committees, which included Appropriations, Armed Services, Finance, and Foreign Relations. Johnson, as chair of his party's Steering Committee, nevertheless retained centralized control over majority party assignments. Senate Republicans later followed the Democratic lead by adopting the practice of sharing top committee slots among all party members. With the exception provided by the Johnson rule and its Republican counterpart, Senate committee assignments were made according to the seniority of senators seeking particular assignments.[60] Leadership discretion, therefore, was greatest in making assignments for new members.

Chairs of this period have been described as "barons" and "lords" ruling over fiefdoms of broad jurisdiction. More accurately, they served as the chief brokers of many competing interests in their committees' broad jurisdictions.[61] Chairs were effective brokers because of their committees' preeminence in the decision-making process and the control they exercised over the staffing and activities of their committees. For the rank-and-file member, the role of committees and their chairs meant that virtually all their participation was restricted to their assigned committees, especially in the House. Moreover, in most committees, participation was limited or structured by the chair. In many respects, House and Senate leadership resembled confederations of committee chairs, each acting as the sovereign over a committee's jurisdiction.

REFORM: 1965-1980

By the late 1960s, members of Congress had begun to make concerted demands for major congressional reform.[62] These demands were especially strong among junior members and some long-standing liberal Democrats, who found their efforts to shape public policy stymied by their more conservative senior colleagues. These members, and the outsiders whose causes they supported, were concerned about issues that were not receiving active committee consideration and did not fall easily into existing committee jurisdictions. A nascent environmental movement, opposition to the Vietnam conflict, and a continuing interest in civil rights legislation placed new challenges before congressional committees. These Democrats, with the occasional support of their party leaders and minority Republicans, sought to improve their participation in congressional decision making by wholesale restructuring of legislative structures and procedures.

Since the mid-1960s, more than a half dozen reform efforts have been made in the House and in the Senate (see Table 2-1). Five of these—two bicameral committees, two bipartisan intrachamber committees, and one party caucus committee—are worthy of more detailed examination because they produced the most important committee reforms of the period.

THE LEGISLATIVE REORGANIZATION ACT OF 1970

The first major reform effort of the 1960s was designed to emulate the endeavors that had resulted in the Legislative Reorganization Act of 1946.[63] The reformers' first strategy was to make a broad direct assault on congressional organization and procedure. On March 11, 1965, the Joint Committee on the Organization of Congress was created to take a wide-ranging look at organizational reform. Among the major topics for study were committee procedures and organization, committee staff, legislative research support, floor procedures, lobbying regulations, fiscal controls and procedures, and the role of political parties.

In its final report, based on lengthy hearings during the 1965 session, the Joint Committee made reform recommendations in every area except the role of political parties. Despite quick Senate action on the report, the Joint Committee's final recommendations took five years to be signed into law. The objections of powerful House interests to several proposed reforms were responsible for the delay. When finally enacted into law, the Legislative Reorganization Act of 1970 contained none of the provisions recommended by the Joint Committee regarding seniority, electronic voting, or lobby reform, but it did include a series of procedural reforms. Among other things, the act required committees to make public all recorded votes, limited proxy votes, allowed a majority of members to call meetings, and encouraged committees to hold open hearings and meetings. Floor procedure was affected also—primarily by permitting *recorded teller votes* (a voting procedure where members file past tellers who record their votes for or against a pending question) during the amending process and by authorizing (rather than requiring)

TABLE 2-1   Major Reform and Study Efforts, House and Senate (1965-1984)

House	Senate
Joint Committee on the Organization of Congress March 11, 1965—July 21, 1966	Joint Committee on the Organization of Congress March 11, 1965—July 21, 1966 [a]
Democratic Caucus Committee on Organization, Study, and Review (Hansen Committee) March 1970—October 8, 1974	Joint Study Committee on Budget Control October 27, 1972—April 18, 1973
Joint Study Committee on Budget Control October 27, 1972—April 18, 1973	Commission on the Operation of the Senate (Culver Commission) July 29, 1975—December 31, 1976
Select Committee on Committees (Bolling Committee) January 31, 1973—October 8, 1974	Temporary Select Committee to Study the Senate Committee System (Stevenson Committee) March 31, 1976—February 4, 1977
Commission on Administrative Review (Obey Commission) July 1, 1976—October 12, 1977	Temporary Select Committee to Study the Senate Committee System (Quayle Committee) June 6, 1984—December 14, 1984
Select Committee on Committees (Patterson Committee) March 20, 1979—April 30, 1980	

[a] Senate members of the Joint Committee continued their work as an intrachamber committee and filed an additional report on September 21, 1966.

the use of electronic voting.[64]

The Legislative Reorganization Act of 1970, despite its somewhat limited effects, remains an important milestone in legislative reformers' efforts. It marks the end of an era when powerful committee chairs and other senior members could forestall structural and procedural changes that appeared to undermine their authority. And it marked the beginning of nearly a decade of continuous change in Congress, providing the opening wedge for further committee changes.

STRUCTURAL AND PROCEDURAL CHANGES IN THE HOUSE:
THE HANSEN AND BOLLING COMMITTEES

The Legislative Reorganization Act of 1970 contained important lessons for members interested in reform. First, it demonstrated clearly that most of the reforms desired in each chamber were fundamentally different. Therefore, bicameral efforts would have to give way to intrachamber reform movements. In hindsight, it is also clear that the Senate simply was not experiencing the same level of pressure for reform that the House was. Thus, another half-decade would elapse before serious Senate reforms would be attempted.

In the House, however, pressures for reform continued to build, and reformers' strategies were altered to suit their new targets— committees and the power of committee chairs. As noted in Chapter 1, and as shown throughout this chapter, committee structures and procedures are the result of two sets of rules: the standing rules of the parent chamber and those of the two party caucuses. House standing rules focus primarily upon the jurisdictions and formal legislative authority of each panel. But these same rules are generally silent regarding the selection and powers of partisan committee leaders and members. Instead, the particulars of these requirements were written into the caucus (or conference) rules of the two parties. As a result, House reforms of this period were developed by two separate but closely linked efforts.

Within the Democratic party caucus, reform efforts were spearheaded by the Committee on Organization, Study, and Review, an eleven-member group chaired by Julia Butler Hansen of Washington (hence called the Hansen Committee). This committee was first authorized by the Democratic Caucus in March 1970 and produced substantial reform packages which passed the caucus in January 1971 and again in early 1973.[65] (See the box on pp. 50-51 for a summary of the major committee reforms.) This latter success coincided with a bipartisan leadership effort to create a House select committee to study the basic structure of the chamber's committee system. This bipartisan committee, the House Select Committee on Committees, was chaired by Richard Bolling (D-Mo.).[66] This committee's proposals ignited a firestorm of opposition because they threatened to alter fundamentally a pattern of committee jurisdictions that had developed over decades.[67] Much to the committee's dismay, these proposals were referred by the Democratic Caucus to a hastily resuscitated Hansen Committee for review. And it was the Hansen Committee's substitute reform package, stripped of all but minor jurisdictional tinkering, which passed the House in October 1974.[68] The caucus also adopted, this time without the aid of the Hansen Committee, additional substantial changes to its own rules during the party organizing caucus of December 1974. And, in a *coup de grace* in this era of reform the caucus, bolstered by seventy-five "Watergate babies" elected in 1974, deposed the senior committee chairs of the Agriculture, Armed Services, and Banking committees—W. R. Poage (D-Texas), F. Edward Hebert (D-La.), and Wright Patman (D-Texas), respectively.[69]

By 1975 the House committee system and the means by which the ruling Democrats organized and operated that system had been altered dramatically. Committee jurisdictions were altered in minor ways. Democrats on the House Ways and Means Committee lost their role as the committee on committees. Members faced strict limits on the number of committee and subcommittee chairs they could hold. Subcommittees were bolstered by the "subcommittee bill of rights." [70] And rules and procedures for selecting committee and subcommittee chairs forced these individuals to be more responsive to their colleagues.

Reform efforts did not cease, but a watershed period for reform had drawn to a close. In 1977 the House Commission on Administrative Review (the Obey Commission, named after Democrat David R. Obey of Wisconsin) produced a report recommending a wide range of procedural innovations and further investigation of the committee system. The report was rejected by the House on a procedural vote. And in 1979 a new Select Committee on Committees (the Patterson Committee, named after California Democrat Jerry Patterson) was formed and given a year to renew the study of the committee system.

The House was clearly in no mood for more reform. It rejected the Patterson Committee's proposal to consolidate energy jurisdiction into a single House committee and opted instead simply to rename the powerful Interstate and Foreign Commerce Committee the Energy and Commerce Committee. No jurisdiction was taken from other House committees that considered energy issues, but the House rules were changed to give the "new" Energy Committee a general oversight jurisdictional grant over energy problems.

Finally, it must be noted that the successive waves of reform that flowed over the House substantially increased the power of Democratic leaders. The resuscitated Steering and Policy Committee placed the Speaker, acting also as Democratic party leader, at the vortex of party politics and organization. The renewed influence in committee assignments had not been seen since that power was handed to the Democratic floor leader (then chair of the Ways and Means Committee) in 1911. Add to this the power to appoint Democratic members of the Rules Committee, to refer bills to multiple committees, to create ad hoc committees, and to appoint additional staff to the Steering and Policy Committee and, at least on paper, the leader rivaled anything seen in the House since 1910. But these were not unalloyed advantages. Substantial power had also been handed to the middle managers of the House—the subcommittee chairs. And this would prove to be a brake on leadership power and influence. Nonetheless, these powers would prove important during the next two decades as committees, parties, and chambers continued to compete with one another.

Major House Committee . . .

Committee reforms of the 1970s occurred incrementally, with some later reforms extending or amending changes adopted earlier in the period. The first two sets of changes noted here (Hansen I and II) were the product of the Hansen Committee and were changes to the Democratic Caucus rules. Hansen III was also the work of that panel but became a substitute for House rule changes proposed by the Bolling Committee. Caucus IV was, again, a set of Democratic Caucus rule changes but not a product of the Hansen Committee. Though not listed here, changes adopted by the Republican Conference mirrored (and frequently preceded) those of the Democrats.

Hansen I (1971)

- Democrats limit their members to holding one legislative subcommittee chair.
- Subcommittee chairs are allowed to select one professional staff member for their respective subcommittees.
- The system for electing full committee chairs and committee members is altered so that nominations would be presented one committee at a time.
- A request by ten or more members initiates debate, a separate vote, and, in the event of a defeat, a new nomination by the Committee on Committees for each chair nominated.

Hansen II (1973)

- Automatic votes on committee chairs are permitted, with a secret ballot to be provided on the demand of 20 percent of the caucus.
- The Democratic Committee on Committees (formerly comprising solely Democratic members of the Ways and Means Committee) is expanded to include the Speaker (who would now chair the group), the majority leader, and the caucus chair.

THE CONGRESSIONAL BUDGET AND IMPOUNDMENT CONTROL ACT OF 1974

In 1972, after nearly a decade of inter- and intrabranch wrangling over budget formulation, fiscal policy making, and executive impoundment of funds, Congress created a joint committee to study new budget mechanisms and procedures. Members of the Joint Study Committee on Budget Control were drawn almost entirely (twenty-eight of thirty-two members) from the House and Senate Appropriations committees, the House Ways and Means Committee, and the Senate Finance Commit-

... *Reforms of the 1970s*

- A twenty-three-member Steering and Policy Committee is created within the caucus.
- Procedures are adopted allowing the caucus to demand more open rules for floor deliberations.
- The "Subcommittee Bill of Rights" is adopted—reforms that include guaranteed referral of legislation, "bidding" for subcommittee seats, and fixed jurisdictions for subcommittees.

Hansen III (Bolling substitute) (1974)

- No committees are eliminated; Small Business is given standing status.
- Multiple referral and early organization are retained from the Bolling plan.
- Committees over fifteen members are to establish at least four subcommittees.
- Committee staff sizes are increased.
- One-third of House committee staffs are guaranteed to the minority.
- Proxy voting is banned in committee.

Caucus IV (1974)

- Ways and Means Democrats are stripped of role as Committee on Committees.
- The Ways and Means Committee is expanded from twenty-five to thirty-seven.
- Appropriations Committee subcommittee chairs are elected by caucus.
- Speaker nominates Democratic members of the Rules Committee.

tee.[71] Budget reform legislation was referred to the House Rules Committee and (sequentially) to the Senate Government Operations and Rules and Administration committees. These committees approved budget reform measures in late 1973 and early 1974 that subsequently were passed by both chambers. After further changes were made in the House/Senate conference, the bill was signed into law on July 12, 1974, less than two years after the first serious calls for reform.

The budget process created by the 1974 act was added to the existing committee structure, providing new mechanisms for integrating the work of appropriations, revenue, and authorization committees and producing a congressional budget for each fiscal year. House and Senate Budget committees were created, an analytical staff (the Congressional Budget Office) was established, and a timetable was fixed for constructing a budget for each fiscal year. Each year two budget resolutions, required by the act, would set spending targets in broad programmatic categories, set total revenues, and stipulate the deficit (or surplus) and total federal debt. The first resolution, to be adopted in May, was intended to provide guidelines for money committees during the summer months. The second resolution, to be adopted in September, would be binding. A *reconciliation* process was created to settle any differences between the fiscal decisions of the summer months and the second budget resolution before the start of the fiscal year on October 1. In addition, the reform included a procedure for congressional review and a veto of presidential *deferrals* (delays) or *rescissions* (cancellations) of appropriated funds—making presidential impoundments of funds more difficult.

By virtually all accounts, the Budget Act was found to be one of the most important congressional initiatives of the post-World War II period. Not the least of its effects has been on the relations among the budget, authorizations, revenue, and appropriations committees. The appropriations committees' decade-long shift from "guardians" of the federal purse to "claimants" of the purse had been cemented. Budget constraints and the new time limits had partially reoriented authorizing committees toward greater oversight. And economic conditions and changes in the budget process had forced the revenue committees into a much more active role in tax policy. Such changes often have strained relations among committees. Properly managed, the new budget process held out the possibility of much more coherent and centralized fiscal policy making. But this would be achieved only through significant alterations in committee relationships.

STRUCTURAL AND PROCEDURAL CHANGES IN THE SENATE: THE STEVENSON COMMITTEE

For most of this period, the Senate committee structure had remained remarkably unchanged, although pressures for reform had continued to build. By 1976 the Senate was ready to create its own reform committee. The Senate's major committee reform effort originated within a bipartisan group of relatively junior members. Their concerns, which were similar to those of House reformers, stimulated several changes during the first half of the 1970s: open markup sessions, some committee staff assistance for junior members, and secret-ballot elections for committee chair nominees. Nonetheless, most members still saw the need for improvement. As in the House, these early reforms failed to deal with overlapping jurisdictions, poor committee scheduling, multiple committee and subcommittee assignments, and unequal committee work loads.

These problems were especially acute in the Senate because of the greater number of committee assignments held by senators (about seventeen committees and subcommittees per senator) and the added burdens senators held by being national figures. Indeed, the Commission on the Operation of the Senate (Culver Commission) recommended in 1976 that the Senate adopt designated days for floor and committee business and computerized committee scheduling to ameliorate these very problems.

Following several unsuccessful attempts to stir members' interest, a resolution was adopted on March 31, 1976, creating a twelve-member, bipartisan Temporary Select Committee to Study the Senate Committee System.[72] The committee, chaired by Adlai Stevenson (D-Ill.), and cochaired by William Brock (R-Tenn.), was given just eleven months to make its recommendations. The Stevenson panel sketched three alternative committee plans: a minimal-change plan, a twelve-committee plan organized along functional lines, and a five-committee scheme containing sixty standing subcommittees. These proposals drew the attention of chamber colleagues and outsiders. Realizing the Senate was not yet ready for a radical restructuring of its committees, the Stevenson Committee quickly settled on the twelve-committee plan and reported its recommendations to the Senate.[73]

Stevenson introduced a resolution (S. Res. 586) embodying those recommendations on October 15, 1976. In the November 1976 elections, the chairs of three standing committees designated to be abolished were defeated.[74] And in December, Stevenson and Oregon's Bob Packwood (the new cochair replacing Brock, who had been defeated in his bid for reelection) won an agreement from key members of the Rules and Administration Committee facilitating prompt consideration of the reform resolution. The parties delayed making new committee assignments until deliberation on the resolution was completed. Stevenson reintroduced the reform resolution (now S. Res. 4) at the beginning of the next congress, and it was referred to the Rules and Administration Committee. S. Res. 4 was approved unanimously by the committee and passed the Senate on a vote of 89-1. Only Quentin Burdick (D-N.D.), who was in line to chair the abolished Post Office Committee, voted against the resolution.

By the time the Senate had finished its work, the committee reorganization plan had evolved from an innovative restructuring to a moderate, yet significant, realignment of the old committee system. Nearly all of the Senate's select and special committees had been abolished, along with the Post Office Committee and District of Columbia Committee. Wholesale jurisdictional changes involving energy, the environment, science and technology, human resources, and government affairs had been achieved. Limits were placed on the number of assignments (three committees and eight subcommittees) and the number of chairs (four committees and subcommittees in the 95th Congress and three in the 96th Congress) that senators could hold. The reforms also expanded minority staffing and computerized committee scheduling in a further effort to help relieve overburdened senators.

At each successive phase, plans of the Stevenson Committee had been weakened by members fearful of losing jurisdiction. Despite this, a substantial alteration remained, which in structural terms far exceeded the House's achievements. The reverse was true where procedural matters were involved. On these matters, the House Democratic Caucus had made more substantial progress. The question on most people's minds was what effects these reforms would have on Congress and its two committee systems.

CONCLUSION

The role of Congress's political environment in shaping its internal structure and operations is illustrated by the remarkably similar development of the House and Senate committee systems. In both chambers, a large number of committees and subcommittees had been created by the mid-1960s, and members' primary contributions to congressional decision making were made within their separate committees. The end product of two hundred years of development was a more decentralized decision-making process, with the larger House more fragmented than the Senate.

In general, the Senate has allowed greater participation of rank-and-file members in floor deliberation by making it easier for them to be recognized, to amend legislation, or even to filibuster. And it has had relatively simple, flexible rules for discharging legislation from committees. As a result of its individualist orientation, the Senate has been embroiled less frequently in controversy over the formal structure of its committee system and has felt less pressure than the House to reform its formal rules.[75] The House's decision-making processes have changed more in accordance with the centralization/decentralization continuum, from the centralized process of the late 1800s to the decentralized process of the 1950s and 1960s. There, structure and procedure have played a more important role in shaping the level and mode of rank-

and-file participation than in the Senate. At bottom, therefore, the House developed to a point where its committees seemed both independent and autonomous. By comparison, however, Senate committees were fairly independent but less autonomous.

In several respects, the House reforms of the 1970s made the chamber more similar to the Senate by reducing the structural and procedural constraints on rank-and-file participation in decision making. Democratizing majority party operations within committees and electing full committee chairs put the finishing touches on the elimination of the practice of apprenticeship. The creation of more subcommittees and the broader distribution of subcommittee chairs and staff gave more members the resources to pursue their own interests and to bargain with other members. Changes in the rules of the House Democratic Caucus, which made it easier to demand opportunities to amend legislation on the floor, considerably weakened the protective shields that closed rules had provided some committees, especially Ways and Means.

Yet reform efforts in the House and Senate reflected long-standing differences between the chambers. The House, which had been more decentralized than the Senate before the 1970s, increased the independence and autonomy of its structural units as a result of the reforms. Indeed, House reformers' focus on distributing formal authority among party leaders and committee members—in contrast to the Senate's lack of attention to procedural changes—reflected the House's characteristic attention to organization and procedure. The Senate, despite its larger percentage of junior members when reforms were adopted, rejected proposals that would have guaranteed junior members more access to subcommittee chairs and staff. Even after the House's democratizing reforms, representatives remained far more dependent than senators on their committee assignments to determine policy areas in which they would actively participate in chamber decision making.

For individual committees, externally imposed procedural or structural reforms could dramatically affect their internal politics. But reforms were not the only, nor always the most important, source of change. Shifting agendas, even with stable formal jurisdictions, and changes in membership and members' motivations could enhance or reduce the effects of reform. Regardless, the general thrust of reforms was to spread power more evenly throughout the two chambers—a move that prompted some observers to label the new arrangements "subcommittee government."

The history of the committee systems did not end in the 1970s, however. The 1980s proved to be a decade of considerable change in the membership and environments of congressional committees. Indeed, the autonomy that committees had come to take for granted during the middle decades of the century was called into question. That is the subject of Chapter 5.

Before moving to the end of our story about change in the committee systems, we consider in Chapters 3 and 4 the important ways in which individual committee memberships, environments, and internal decision-making processes differ.

NOTES

1. Joseph Cooper, *The Origins of the Standing Committees and the Development of the Modern House* (Houston: Rice University Studies, 1970), 8-17. For additional detail on this first period, see Thomas W. Skladony, "The House Goes to Work: Select and Standing Committees in the U.S. House of Representatives, 1789-1828," *Congress & the Presidency* 12 (Autumn 1985): 165-187; on the subject of bill introduction, consideration, and reporting, Joseph Cooper and Cheryl D. Young, "Bill Introduction in the Nineteenth Century: A Study of Institutional Change," *Legislative Studies Quarterly* 14 (February 1989): 67-105.
2. Cooper, *Origins*, 17-22.
3. Ibid., 11.
4. Ibid., 14.
5. Walter Kravitz, "Evolution of the Senate's Committee System," *Annals of the American Academy of Political and Social Science* 411 (January 1974): 28; George L. Robinson, "The Development of the Senate Committee System," (Ph.D. diss., New York University, 1954), 20-21.
6. Kravitz, "Evolution," 28-29.
7. Thomas Jefferson, *Manual of Parliamentary Practice*, House Doc. 95-403, 95th Cong., 2d Sess., 1979, Sect. XXVI.
8. Cooper, *Origins*, 26.
9. An important function delegated to committees from the earliest congresses, particularly in the more active House, was investigation of executive branch activity. Cooper, *Origins*, 29-40. These investigations focused primarily on the use of funds and on misconduct in office. The scope of the investigations was carefully limited by the parent body to ensure that investigations did not impinge upon the president's authority to administer the law and to supervise executive officials. Nonetheless, committees frequently delegated authority to send for persons and papers necessary for obtaining pertinent information. Investigations were nearly always delegated to select committees, and only committee chairs were allowed to question witnesses.
10. Lauros G. McConachie, *Congressional Committees: A Study of the Origins and Development of Our National and Local Legislative Methods* (New York: Thomas Y. Crowell, 1898), 349-355; Robinson, "The Development of the Senate Committee System," 149. And, on careers and committees during the 1860s, see Allan G. Bogue, *The Congressman's Civil War* (New York: Cambridge University Press, 1989).
11. Cooper, *Origins*, 41-50. Gerald Gamm and Kenneth Shepsle place these causes

in the context of the individualist versus contextualist debate in "Emergence of Legislative Institutions: Standing Committees in the House and Senate, 1810-1825," *Legislative Studies Quarterly* 14 (February 1989): 39-66.

12. See Ralph V. Harlow, *The History of Legislative Methods in the Period Before 1825* (New Haven: Yale University Press, 1917), 238; and Cooper, *Origins*, 45.

13. Cooper, *Origins*, 56; Harlow, *The History of Legislative Methods*, 216-219; and Gamm and Shepsle, "Emergence of Legislative Institutions," 48-63.

14. Cooper, *Origins*, 50.

15. Cooper, *Origins*, 56; Harlow, *The History of Legislative Methods*, 226; George B. Galloway, *The History of the House of Representatives*, 2d ed. (New York: Thomas Y. Crowell, 1976), 86; and Cooper and Young, "Bill Introduction," 71-72.

16. Harlow, *The History of Legislative Methods*, 227; Cooper, *Origins*, 58, 70.

17. Robinson, "The Development of the Senate Committee System," 74-75. On Henry Clay, and also Daniel Webster and John C. Calhoun, see Merrill D. Peterson, *The Great Triumverate: Webster, Clay, and Calhoun* (New York: Oxford University Press, 1987).

18. Ibid., chaps. 3 and 4.

19. Ibid., 151-154.

20. Ibid., 121-140.

21. Cooper, *Origins*, 67-68.

22. Robinson, "The Development of the Senate Committee System," 195-196.

23. Ibid., 72.

24. Ibid., 151-153.

25. Cooper, *Origins*, 61; Galloway, *History*, 79. It should also be noted that committee oversight activity became more vigorous during this period. The previous House practice of limiting the scope of investigations gave way to broad investigations as early as the 1820s. The Senate did not actively pursue investigations until the early 1830s. Up until the 1850s, Senate committees regularly sought to inform themselves about administrative matters—even in cases where no particular legislative response was contemplated. See Cooper, *Origins*, 78; and Robinson, "The Development of the Senate Committee System," 88, 232.

26. On the more immediate post-Civil War era, see Margaret Susan Thompson, *The "Spider Web": Congress and Lobbying in the Age of Grant* (Ithaca, N.Y.: Cornell University Press, 1985).

27. Chang-Wei Chiu, *The Speaker of the House of Representatives Since 1896* (New York: Columbia University Press, 1928), 311; Robinson, "The Development of the Senate Committee System," 302-305.

28. Burton K. French, "Subcommittees of Congress," *American Political Science Review* 9 (February 1915): 68-92.

29. DeAlva Stanwood Alexander, *History and Procedure of the House of Representatives* (Boston: Houghton Mifflin, 1916), 235; Robinson, "The Development of the Senate Committee System," 369.

30. See Mary P. Follett, *The Speaker of the House of Representatives* (New York: Burt Franklin, 1974).

31. David J. Rothman, *Politics and Power: The United States Senate 1869-1901* (New York: Atheneum, 1969), chap. 1.

32. Ibid., chap. 2.

33. Randall B. Ripley, *Congress: Process and Policy*, 2d ed. (New York: W. W. Norton, 1978), 73-74.

34. Rothman, *Politics and Power*, 51.
35. See Nelson W. Polsby, Miriam Gallaher, and Barry Spencer Rundquist, "The Growth of the Seniority System in the U.S. House of Representatives," *American Political Science Review* 63 (1969): 787-807.
36. Two other products of the revolt were Calendar Wednesday and the committee discharge procedure. Calendar Wednesday permitted committees to call legislation off a House calendar, bypassing the Rules Committee. It soon fell into disuse because majority party leaders could still block legislation by having friendly committee chairs call up their legislation, preventing other legislation from being considered. The discharge procedure was designed to make it easier for members to bring to the floor legislation that was bottled up in obstructionist committees. The requirement that a constitutional majority support a discharge motion and obstructionists' ability to clog the discharge machinery with bogus motions made the rule unworkable.
37. Woodrow Wilson, *Congressional Government* (Boston: Houghton Mifflin, 1885), 102.
38. Quoted in Chiu, *The Speaker of the House of Representatives*, 90.
39. Ibid., 331.
40. Paul D. Hasbrouck, *Party Government in the House of Representatives* (New York: Macmillan, 1927), 92.
41. See Chiu, *The Speaker of the House of Representatives*, 146-151; Joseph Cooper, "Congress and Its Committees" (Ph.D. diss., Harvard University, 1960), 161-162.
42. Barbara Hinckley, *The Seniority System in Congress* (Bloomington: Indiana University Press, 1971), 75.
43. Roger H. Davidson and Walter J. Oleszek, *Congress Against Itself* (Bloomington: Indiana University Press, 1977), 37-43.
44. George B. Galloway, *The Legislative Process in Congress* (New York: Thomas Y. Crowell, 1953), 276-278.
45. Charles S. Bullock III, "House Careerists: Changing Patterns of Longevity and Attrition," *American Political Science Review* 66 (1972): 1295-1305.
46. Donald R. Matthews, *U.S. Senators and Their World* (New York: Vintage Books, 1960), 92.
47. Ibid., 95.
48. Herbert B. Asher, "The Learning of Legislative Norms," *American Political Science Review* 67 (1973): 499-513.
49. Galloway, *The Legislative Process in Congress*, 289.
50. Matthews, *U.S. Senators and Their World*, 151.
51. Ibid., 160-161; John F. Manley, "Wilbur D. Mills: A Study in Congressional Leadership," *American Political Science Review* 63 (1969): 442-464.
52. Lewis A. Froman, *The Congressional Process: Strategies, Rules and Procedures* (Boston: Little, Brown, 1967), 180-181; Hinckley, *The Seniority System*, 86-88.
53. John F. Bibby, "The Senate Committee on Banking and Currency," in *On Capitol Hill*, ed. John F. Bibby and Roger H. Davidson (New York: Holt, Rinehart & Winston, 1967); Richard F. Fenno, Jr., "The House of Representatives and Federal Aid to Education," in *New Perspectives on the House of Representatives*, 2d ed., ed. Robert E. Peabody and Nelson W. Polsby (Chicago: Rand McNally, 1963), 283-323.
54. Hinckley, *The Seniority System*, 36-43.
55. Galloway, *The Legislative Process in Congress*, 594.

56. Sula P. Richardson and Susan Schjelderup, "Standing Committee Structure and Assignments: House and Senate," Congressional Research Service, March 12, 1982.
57. Lawrence C. Dodd and Bruce I. Oppenheimer, "The House in Transition," in Congress Reconsidered, ed. Lawrence C. Dodd and Bruce I. Oppenheimer (New York: Praeger, 1977), 33-34.
58. "The Senate Committee System," First Staff Report to the Temporary Select Committee to Study the Senate Committee System (Washington, D.C.: U.S. Government Printing Office, 1976), 198-201.
59. John F. Manley, The Politics of Finance: The House Committee on Ways and Means (Boston: Little, Brown, 1970), 77-78, 244-245.
60. Matthews, U.S. Senators and Their World, 127-128.
61. Lawrence C. Dodd and Bruce I. Oppenheimer, "The House in Transition: Change and Consolidation," in Congress Reconsidered, 2d ed., ed. Lawrence C. Dodd and Bruce I. Oppenheimer (Washington, D.C.: CQ Press, 1981), 40.
62. On the general nature of reform in Congress during this modern era, see Leroy N. Rieselbach, Congressional Reform (Washington, D.C.: CQ Press, 1986).
63. While the Legislative Reorganization Act of 1970 was the first major set of reforms, the earlier expansion of the Rules Committee in the 1960s was perhaps the first notable reform during this period. It also should be noted that in early 1965, after Republican Gerald R. Ford of Michigan had been elected minority leader, a series of reforms was implemented within the Republican Conference.
64. "Legislative Reorganization Act: First Year's Record," Congressional Quarterly Weekly Report, March 4, 1972, 485-491.
65. "House Reform: Easy to Advocate, Hard to Define," Congressional Quarterly Weekly Report, January 20, 1973, 69-72.
66. An in-depth history of the Bolling Committee is provided by Davidson and Oleszek, Congress Against Itself.
67. See "Jurisdiction Overhaul Recommended for House," Congressional Quarterly Weekly Report, December 22, 1973, 3358-3366; and U.S. Congress, House, Select Committee on Committees, "Committee Reform Amendments of 1974," 93d Congress, 2d sess., March 1973, House Rept. 916.
68. Davidson and Oleszek, Congress Against Itself, 250.
69. On the role of the "Class of '74," see Burdett Loomis, The New American Politician (New York: Basic Books, 1988), 31-36.
70. For a summary of subcommittee reforms during this period, see Christopher J. Deering and Steven S. Smith, "Majority Party Leadership and the New House Subcommittee System," in Understanding Congressional Leadership, ed. Frank H. Mackaman (Washington, D.C.: CQ Press, 1981), 264.
71. Allen Schick, Congress and Money: Budgeting, Spending and Taxing (Washington, D.C.: Urban Institute, 1980), 53-71.
72. This account of the Stevenson Committee is drawn from Judith H. Parris, "The Senate Reorganizes Its Committees, 1977," Political Science Quarterly 95 (Summer 1979): 319-337; and Roger H. Davidson, "Two Avenues of Change: House and Senate Committee Reorganization," in Congress Reconsidered, ed. Dodd and Oppenheimer, 120-128.
73. The Select Committee had no legislative authority, so it could not report legislation to the floor. Therefore, upon completion of a report, a bill or resolution embracing suggestions of the committee had to be formally

introduced.
74. The members were Frank Moss of Utah, Vance Hartke of Indiana, and Gale McGee of Wyoming.
75. On Senate individualism see Randall B. Ripley, *Power in the Senate* (New York: St. Martin's Press, 1969), 3-19.

CHAPTER 3

Committee Assignments: Agendas, Environments, and Members' Goals

"You have to decide whether you want to be on a powerhouse committee where you can raise funds or go to a committee that handles the issues that motivated you to take an interest in public office in the first place. I did the latter." As this comment from a newly elected member of the House suggests, committees present members of Congress with different opportunities and attractions. Decisions about which committee assignments to pursue are personal, and they vary from member to member. Perceptions about what advantages particular committees offer also vary. But almost all members of Congress agree with Rep. Charles E. Schumer (D-N.Y.): "It's the most important decision you can make. If you're on a good committee, you'll enjoy legislating and accomplish something. If you're on a bad committee, you won't enjoy it here."[1]

In this chapter we begin to consider the ways in which congressional committees differ. Because committee assignments are so important to individual members, and because they shape the composition and policy decisions of committees, they are the logical first step in understanding the contemporary committee systems. We then turn to considerations that influence, and are influenced by, committee assignments: variation in committee jurisdictions, environments, and agendas; and variation in the personal political goals that members seek to achieve with their committee assignments.

THE COMMITTEE ASSIGNMENT PROCESS

Committee assignments are important both to the members who receive them and to the leaders who make them. They are the most important decisions newly elected members make, particularly in the House, where members are assigned to only one or two standing committees.

For party leaders, the allocation of committee assignments is an opportunity to influence the composition of committees and reward or punish certain members. Like other members, party leaders are motivated by a mix of political goals. But in their capacity of party leaders, they assume additional responsibilities that originate in the expectations of rank-and-file members.[2] These responsibilities, translated into operational goals, are policy victories and party harmony.

In each new congress, party leaders' involvement in the committee assignment process creates their first opportunity to pursue the goals of policy victories and party harmony. Their involvement occurs in two stages. First, size and party balance on each committee must be set to reflect demand for committee positions and any shift in the number of Democrats and Republicans resulting from the last election. Second, once the number of vacancies created by retirements, defeat, or committee transfers has been determined for each committee, individuals must be assigned to fill those open positions. In practice, some committee sizes are adjusted while assignment decisions made.

COMMITTEE SIZES AND PARTY RATIOS

Committee sizes and party ratios vary between and within the two chambers. Generally, House committees are larger than Senate committees, and committees with broad jurisdictions are larger than committees with narrow ones. The size of each Senate committee is established in the standing rules of the chamber (the same rules that establish committee jurisdictions), and therefore these rules require at least minor changes at the beginning of each new congress. House committee sizes, along with party ratios in both chambers, are not stipulated in standing rules; they are, instead, the product of informal decisions among party leaders.

Because of its numerical strength, the majority party in each chamber could set the size of the various committees and their party ratios at any level it chose. In practice, the sizes and party ratios usually are set only after consultation between majority and minority party leaders. An aide to former Speaker Thomas P. "Tip" O'Neill explains that majority party leaders "generally try to accommodate the minority's requests for seats when there's no apparent cost to us. After all, they can score political points against us if we cheat them out of too much." The minority, especially in the Senate, can be irritatingly obstructionist if it believes it has been slighted by the majority.[3] Early in 1989, for example, Republicans in the Senate became concerned about Democratic attempts to increase their majorities on several key panels. The result was a protracted set of negotiations which delayed formal adoption of the committee rosters.[4] Thus party ratios on most committees are close to the chamberwide party ratio. The important exceptions are in the House, where Democrats have reserved extraordinary majorities on Appropriations, Rules, and Ways and Means in order to ensure party control of committee decisions.

In principle, there is nothing to prevent committees from being either very large or very small. For example, membership on committees could simply be left open to any interested member—a practice that would greatly enlarge some panels. At the other extreme, committees could be kept so small that only a minority of the total membership would even be allowed to serve on one. At present, neither of these extremes is acceptable to the legislators, since open committee membership would render many committees ineffective and severely restricted membership would undermine participation and careerism. Nonetheless, these two extremes help place in perspective the choices facing leaders. Should they expand the size of committees and reduce the value of assignments as a leadership resource? If they did so, they might also undercut the efficiency of some committees. Or should they keep committee sizes small so that chairs could more easily manage them and so they would serve as precious rewards for the leadership to bestow on friendly colleagues? If they did so, membership resentment might grow, their own reelection to leadership posts might be put at risk, and members might retaliate by being uncooperative on policy matters. Faced with these alternatives, it is not surprising that recent leaders have expanded the number of committee seats far more often than they have reduced them.

Indeed, the most notable characteristic of decisions regarding committee size in recent decades has been the tendency of the leadership to increase the number of seats available. Although the number of standing committees remained quite stable between 1947 and 1989 (with a net gain of four House committees and two Senate committees), the total number of standing committee seats grew from 482 to 812 in the House and from 201 to 311 in the Senate. This expansion has not been wholly without controversy. Before the beginning of the 100th Congress, for example, House leaders were hard pressed to hold the line on a retrenchment that had occurred during the 99th Congress. At that time, total slots on the so-called "major" committees had been cut back from 231 to 214.[5] Decisions about Senate committee sizes are constrained by a 1977 limit on the number of assignments senators may hold on committees of various types. But Senate leaders have proven quite willing to seek exemptions to the rule in order to grant senators' requests for additional committee assignments. In the 101st Congress, for example, thirty senators served on three or more of the twelve major committees for which a two-assignment limit had been set, and numerous others served on more than one minor committee, contrary to the 1977 rule.[6] And at the outset of the 101st Congress at least two senators far exceeded the formal limits: Christopher J. Dodd (D-Conn.) (three major and two minor) and Larry Pressler (R-S.D.) (four major and two minor).

In addition to the demands from the minority party for more committee seats, party colleagues put pressure on majority leaders to expand committees.[7] One set of pressures comes from members seeking assignments. If the number of members requesting assignment to certain committees outnumbers the vacancies created by retirement, electoral defeat, or transfers to other committees, members must compete with each other, which sometimes causes intense conflict within the party and produces dissatisfied losers. Members also may become discontented if they must be bumped from a committee to reflect a loss of party seats in the chamber following an election. Leaders can minimize these threats to party harmony by increasing the number of seats available on affected committees.

Another set of expansionist pressures is related to the goal of policy victories. Committee chairs, state delegations, and various factions often express concern about their ability to shape certain committees' decisions. In fact, party and committee leaders frequently take an active interest in the policy views of prospective members of some committees. At times, ensuring control of a committee may require increasing the number of seats to create slots for allies. And leaders may believe that they can encourage or acquire some members' support by assigning them to coveted committees. But to gain leverage with members leaders must have a supply, perhaps an increasing supply, of committee seats.[8]

Counterexpansionist forces also exist. For example, adding seats to some committees might harm the policy interests of leaders and committee chairs if adding majority members also causes the number of minority positions to increase. Moreover, leaders may wish to hoard their assignment resources so that assignments they do grant will retain special significance to recipients. Westefield argues that House leaders are most likely to take this attitude when considering the size of the most important committees, where loyalty is of great political significance to them.[9]

Counterexpansionist pressures also may affect the leadership's goal of maintaining party harmony. Leaders occasionally hear pleas from committee chairs who do not want larger, less manageable committees. Other members may not want to share the influence of their committees with a large number of new members. One scholar argues that such complaints are most likely to occur concerning the most prestigious or attractive House committees, where members are likely to be the most protective of their monopoly over important policy decisions.[10] Nonetheless, leaders also recognize that unlimited expansion would make committees too large to function effectively and would produce chaos for members trying to manage a large number of committee duties. Or, as an assistant to former Senate majority leader Howard Baker pointed out, "We do have a sense of what's good for senators, even if they [the senators] don't."

While these sorts of demands are greatest at the outset of each congress, they are by no means restricted to those periods. For example, leaders of both parties were cross-pressured in late 1989 when new and existing members of their parties demanded positions on committees deemed important to their election and reelection. On the Democratic side, party leaders had promised Gene Taylor a seat on the Armed Services Committee if he won a special election to fill a vacant House seat in Mississippi. This placed them in a bind because another Democrat, Glen Browder from neighboring Alabama, had been told to wait for a seat on the same committee because party and committee leaders did not wish to expand the panel further. In order to make good on their promise to Taylor and simultaneously avoid angering Browder they were forced to expand the size of the committee. Robert Smith (R-N.H.) also benefited because he filled the added Republican seat on the committee.[11]

Meanwhile, Republican leaders faced conflicting pressures of their own when Arthur Ravenel, Jr., of South Carolina threatened to switch parties and become a Democrat if his party leaders could not make room for him on the Merchant Marine and Fisheries Committee. His access to the committee apparently had been blocked by Don Young, a senior Republican committee member from Alaska, because Ravenel was perceived to be supportive of restrictions on oil exploration in Alaska. Young, of course, held a contrary view. Faced with the prospect of losing a seat to the Democrats, Republican leaders felt compelled to add Ravenel to the committee. Young relented. And so the committee was expanded by two seats. Coincidentally, the Democratic seat went to Gene Taylor of Mississippi.[12]

In practice, majority party leaders place far greater emphasis on party harmony than on policy victory when making decisions about committee size. Indeed, strong evidence exists that member demand is the primary cause of committee expansions made by recent House Democratic leaders. The first column in Table 3-1 indicates that members' expectations have risen dramatically during the past twenty-five years. In recent congresses, freshmen seeking only one assignment have been a very small minority, with many of them seeking assignment to an exclusive committee. The second column shows the percentage of

Democrats actually receiving two assignments among those who were eligible for two (those assigned to exclusive committees are not eligible for two assignments). In the 1950s only about one-third of all House Democrats had two assignments, but that number rose gradually in the 1960s under Speaker John McCormack's and then shot upward in the early 1970s under Speaker Carl Albert. These changes also are reflected in the number of seats per member, listed in the third column. With Albert's help, reformers successfully pushed for caucus rules guaranteeing all Democrats two assignments, except for members of the three exclusive committees. Nearly all Democrats now take advantage of that right. The final column in Table 3-1 demonstrates that majority party leaders adjust the number of their own party's committee seats to electoral gains and losses. The large Democratic electoral gains in the 89th and 94th Congresses, for example, were accompanied by increases in the party's committee seat allocation, while losses in the 90th and 97th Congresses were accompanied by decreases in committee seats.

Two scholars have estimated the independent effects of change in party ratio, level of demand, and countervailing pressure from prestigious committees on changes, in committee sizes.[13] Their research demonstrates that pressure from intraparty competition played an insignificant role in the committee size decisions of Speakers Rayburn, during the 1950s, and McCormack, during the 1960s. Their decisions primarily reflected changes in the chamber's party ratio. In fact, according to a top assistant to McCormack and Albert, Rayburn and McCormack depended greatly on the Parliamentarian of the House, Lewis Deschler, to work out changes in committee sizes and party ratios at the beginning of each congress. Deschler's recommendations represented a "fairly automatic process" of conforming committee ratios to the new chamber party ratio. Only for Rayburn did the counterexpansionist pressure associated with committee prestige have a significant effect.

In stark contrast to its significance for Rayburn and McCormack, competition for seats had a substantial effect on Albert's decisions about committee size in the early 1970s, even once change in party ratio was controlled. According to McCormack's and Albert's aide, Albert deliberately and personally sought to accommodate the demands of new activist Democrats elected in the early 1970s. Under Speaker O'Neill during the late 1970s and early 1980s, neither the level of competition nor changes in party ratios had as strong an effect on seat adjustments. O'Neill paid much less personal attention to decisions of committee size than did Albert, and he placed most of the responsibility in the hands of a staff assistant. Speaker Jim Wright, however, took personal charge of the committee size decisions, although he too increased the size of several committees in response to rank-and-file demand.

TABLE 3-1 Committee Requests and Seats for House Democrats (1959-1989)

Congress	Percent of freshmen requesting 2 assignments [a]	Percent of Democrats with 2 assignments [b]	Committee seats per Democratic member	Total Democratic committee seats
86th	38%	32%	1.28	364
87th	58	37	1.34	352
88th	56	43	1.36	352
89th	56	43	1.38	407
90th	54	50	1.44	355
91st	n.a.	55	1.49	361
92d	69	63	1.57	398
93d	89	93	1.72	412
94th	60	83	1.73	503
95th	58	93	1.78	520
96th	88	95	1.78	490
97th	83	96	1.78	432
98th	n.a.	n.a.	1.70	454
99th	n.a.	n.a.	1.73	436
100th	n.a.	n.a.	1.76	455

[a] Calculated from written requests to Democratic leaders. The authors would like to thank Kenneth Shepsle for request data for the 86th to 93d Congresses (91st Congress data were not available). Request data for the 94th to 97th Congresses were collected by one of the authors. Information on requests for more recent congresses is not available.

[b] Among the members eligible for two assignments.

Senate committee expansion has not been as great as it has been in the House. The difference appears to be a product of less frequent demands and less vigorous pressure to increase the number of committee seats in the Senate. After the implementation of the Legislative Reorganization Act of 1946, most senators held two standing committee assignments, compared with just one in the House, a difference of one committee seat per member that remained in the 1980s. Moreover, as further discussed below, senators generally are less intently concerned about their assignments. When expansionist pressure exists in the Senate, it is likely to involve the desire of an individual senator (and his or her supporters) to gain a seat on a particular committee, usually over and above the standard quota, rather than a more general demand for popular committees that is common in the House. Thus Senate pressure is less frequently complicated by the potential of conflict among requesters. Nevertheless, the number of seats on standing committees in the Senate increased by 110 between 1947 and 1989, even though there had been an increase of only four senators and one standing committee during the same period.

COMMITTEE ASSIGNMENTS

Once committee sizes and party ratios have been set, party leaders must make decisions about which members should fill open committee seats. Committee assignments are the responsibility of each party in each chamber, and each has a *committee on committees* to perform this function (see the box on p. 69). In each case, the party caucus and the full chamber must approve the committee lists prepared by the committee on committees. The two House committees are chaired by their chief party leaders. Senate Democrats followed the same practice until 1988 when the newly elected majority leader, George J. Mitchell of Maine, named Daniel K. Inouye (D-Hawaii), one of Mitchell's opponents in the leadership race, to the post. The chair of the Senate Republican Conference names both the members and the chair of that party's committee. House Democrats made the Speaker the chair of their committee on committees in 1973 and strengthened that role in 1974 when the function was stripped from Ways and Means Democrats and given to the Steering and Policy Committee. In both parties in both chambers, other party leaders also now serve on the committees on committees, providing them with opportunities to influence committee assignments directly.

Party leaders also may indirectly influence committee assignment decisions by their role in appointing members to the committees on committees. This is especially true in the Senate, where the Democratic leader has the authority to appoint all of the members of the Steering Committee, which makes Democratic appointments, and the Republican leader influences the choices of the party's caucus chair, who has the authority to name the committee on committees for Senate Republicans. Less control over members of the committee on committees is available to House leaders. For House Democrats, the Speaker appoints only eight of the thirty-one members of the Steering and Policy Committee; twelve of the members are elected by members from their region, and the remainder are other party leaders and major committee chairs. The House Republican leader is in the weakest position in this regard because, with the exception of the Republican whip, all of the committee's members are elected by constituent groups within the party conference.[14]

Although there are opportunities to do so, current party leaders do not attempt to exercise special influence on the vast majority of assignment decisions.[15] In most circumstances, the committees on com-

Committees on Committees

The Senate Democratic Steering Committee and its chair are appointed by the Democratic floor leader. The committee has twenty-five members (101st Congress), as determined by the Democratic Conference.

The Senate Republican Committee on Committees is appointed by the conference chair, except for top party leaders who sit as ex officio members, and has about fifteen members.

The House Democratic Steering and Policy Committee is composed of twelve regionally elected members, eight members appointed by the Speaker, and eleven top party and committee leaders who sit as ex officio members.

The House Republican Committee on Committees is composed of twenty-one members: the floor leader, the whip, one representative from each state with at least five Republican members, one representative from multistate groups formed by states with four or fewer members, and one representative each from the two most recently elected Republican classes. With the exception of the leader and whip, each is elected by his or her constituent group. The Republican floor leader chairs the committee.

mittees attempt to grant the requests of members seeking assignments under the constraint of the number of vacancies. Except in the most unusual circumstances (substantial changes in party ratios, for example), both parties in both chambers allow members to retain their assignments as long as they desire—the so-called *property right* norm.[16] In addition, the parties have adopted formal and informal rules to help ensure that all members are given reasonably good assignments. House Democrats spread choice seats widely by limiting the members of Appropriations, Rules, and Ways and Means to only one assignment (except Budget members) and by limiting other members to one major committee. House Republicans have essentially the same rules. As noted earlier, Senate rules formally limit members to no more than two major and one minor committee assignment but then also provide for numerous exceptions. To prevent hoarding, however, the Senate's parties guarantee each of their members a seat on one of the top committees before any member receives a second top assignment, a rule known as the *Johnson Rule* for Democrats.[17] Moreover, both chambers require membership rotation on a handful of committees: the Select Intelligence committees and the House Budget Committee, for example.

Currently, the dominant emphasis is on party harmony and accommodation of requests rather than on manipulation of assignments for political advantage. Political scientist Charles Jones concludes:

> Such measures as the Johnson Rule, while laudable on other grounds, have made it even more difficult in recent years to employ the committee assignment process for party policy purposes. All Senators are guaranteed major committee assignments regardless of their policy stands.[18]

Nevertheless, party leaders do occasionally make a special effort to place one of their members on a committee, and they usually succeed. Party leaders do not make such an effort more than a few times in any congress; they recognize that frequent demands on other party members of the committee on committees "would wear thin quickly," as one aide put it.

In many of these cases, leaders are not acting in a leadership capacity, but rather serving as advocates for home state members or close friends. Sometimes they regret such actions. For example, in early 1981 then House majority leader Jim Wright went out of his way to support fellow Texan Phil Gramm, who was campaigning for a Budget Committee assignment. Wright wrote in his diary that Gramm is

> after all, one of "our own." He wants to be friendly and doesn't really understand how his playing to the gallery on proposed budget cuts, etc., can undermine my position. He is energetic, indefatigable, resourceful. He is genuinely interested in the budget process and deserves a chance to work at it. We certainly need people on the committee, particularly this year, who will work. There's one other possible consolation in Phil's being on the committee; as a party to its deliberations, he'll be less likely to undermine the final product of its deliberations on the House floor.[19]

Despite objections from liberals, Speaker O'Neill deferred to Wright, and Gramm was placed on the Budget Committee. History proved Wright's assertions incorrect; Gramm used the assignment to conspire with Republicans against Democratic leaders. And subsequently, in an unusual move, the Steering and Policy Committee did not reappoint Gramm to Budget at the beginning of the next congress. Gramm, a conservative, took the opportunity to switch to the Republican party, won reelection to his seat, and was promptly reappointed to the committee.[20]

FACTORS SHAPING ASSIGNMENT DECISIONS

The most obvious and important factor affecting a requester's chances of success is the level of competition for assignment to a particular committee. Statistically, the effect of no other measurable factor compares with the significance of the impersonal competitive situation in explaining assignment outcomes.[21] In large part, then, it is a matter of luck: the number of vacancies and competitors varies both from committee to committee and over time. Other personal and political factors come into play when there is competition, as there always is for the most important committees. In these situations, leaders and other members of the committee on committees must discriminate among requesters who actively campaign for their support (see the box on pp. 72-73). Many requesters write lengthy memos to convince party leaders of their personal qualifications or political need for certain assignments. The requesters also seek support from their state delegations, key interest group figures, and committee chairs. Party leaders and members of the committee on committees often serve as arbitrators between members from the same state, region, or faction, who risk dividing their support on the committee on committees. These campaign activities can be the decisive factor in assignment contests.

The range of factors taken into account by members of the committee on committees has changed little during the past twenty-five years. A tally of the comments made by House Democratic Steering and Policy members in nominating requesters for assignments at the beginning of the 97th Congress is reported in Table 3-2. Paralleling findings for the House in the late 1950s, the electoral needs of nominees were the most common argument made on their behalf, followed by claims that a particular state or region "deserved" a seat because it was underrepresented on the committee.[22] A nominee's willingness to support the party and its leadership, and his or her policy views, seniority, and other personal characteristics also were mentioned. Interviews with House Republican and Senate Democratic members and leadership aides indicate that similar criteria are important in their parties' decisions.

Senate Republicans, however, apply seniority more strictly as a means for resolving competing demands. This helps reduce direct personal conflict among Republican senators, but it also reduces the number of opportunities Republican leaders have to influence assignments. Personal factors normally come into play only when senators of equal seniority are competing for the same seat. In 1984, for instance, Sen. Jesse Helms (R-N.C.) wished to take advantage of his seniority by claiming the chair of the Senate Foreign Relations Committee; he had been chairing the Agriculture Committee. His claim would have the effect of bumping Sen. Richard Lugar (R-Ind.) from that position, which he had held since the Republicans gained control of the Senate in 1980. Personal factors were sufficiently important in this case to allow Lugar to bring the matter to a vote in the Republican Conference, but Helms's seniority claim prevailed largely because even senators who preferred Lugar personally did not wish to undercut this tradition. Summing up

Kennedy Muscle No Match . . .

The clout of the Kennedys went head to head with the House seniority system, as Democrats geared up for the 101st Congress.

Seniority won.

At issue was one of the juiciest plums in the House—a seat on the Appropriations Committee.

By the time Democratic leaders made committee-assignment selections Dec. 7, it was a foregone conclusion that a vacant Appropriations seat would go to Chester G. Atkins, a third-term Massachusetts Democrat.

The real battle had been fought the day before, in a closed meeting of New England Democrats that capped a months-long tussle between Atkins and Joseph P. Kennedy II, a second-term Democrat and scion of the Kennedy dynasty who also wanted the Appropriations slot. . . .

It was a classic illustration of how bitter the competition for good committee assignments can be. . . .

The regional delegation went through a divisive battle shot through with political intrigue. It involved a rare intervention in House internal politics by a senator—Edward M. Kennedy of Massachusetts, Joseph's uncle. It tapped into personal and political obligations a generation old. And the outcome was determined by a last-minute secret-ballot betrayal. . . .

Members from around the country wanted Boland's seat. But House Speaker Jim Wright of Texas, who wields great power over the committee-assignment process, made it clear from the outset that the opening would go to someone from the New England region. He left it to the region's own members to decide who.

In addition to Kennedy and Atkins, Connecticut's Bruce A. Morrison also was in the running. But Morrison never really had a chance at getting the region's backing because Connecticut's three-person delegation of Democrats is vastly outnumbered by the 10-man Massachusetts crowd. . . .

New England Democrats had an interest in resolving their internal dispute before Steering and Policy met. If they didn't unite behind one candidate, the fear was they would lose the seat to another region.

A key factor working in Atkins' favor was that he seemed more likely to

Helms's victory, assistant minority leader Alan K. Simpson of Wyoming said, "It was simply the seniority system. You're either for it or you're agin it."[23]

For the other three parties, seniority is usually "only weighed in the balance," as a Senate Democratic leadership aide explained. When seniority differences are a factor, it is often one member's previous effort to get an assignment, rather than seniority per se, that is critical.

... for House Seniority System

stay in the House and rise in seniority on the committee than Kennedy, who colleagues suspect may some day run for office outside the House.

Atkins' supporters said he should get the regional caucus' nod because of seniority: He'd served a term longer than Kennedy. Kennedy insisted there was no ironclad rule on such matters.

Enter Uncle Ted.

Senator Kennedy called some of the New England House members on his nephew's behalf, tapping the deep roots of obligation that only a political dynasty like the Kennedys could have.

Among those he called was Barbara B. Kennelly of Connecticut, who owed a longstanding personal debt of gratitude to the Kennedy family. Twenty-eight years ago, President John F. Kennedy named her father, John Bailey, to be chairman of the Democratic National Committee.

"His family gave my family the greatest honor it ever had," said Kennelly. She was bound to support her Connecticut colleague Morrison but agreed to vote for Kennedy if it came to a two-man fight with Atkins.

Others were irritated by the senator's intervention. "Some felt the pressure was pretty heavy and they didn't like it," said one Democratic leadership aide.

Massachusetts was not helped out of its jam by the fact that a second Appropriations seat unexpectedly opened up after Election Day, with the defeat of Bill Chappell Jr. of Florida. Wright made it clear that seat would go to fellow Texan Jim Chapman.

Neither Atkins nor Kennedy would back down, so the question of who would get the region's endorsement was put to a secret ballot of the 17 Democratic members of the New England regional caucus Dec. 6.

The lineup after the first ballot: Kennedy, 8; Atkins, 6; Morrison, 3.

Morrison's name was then dropped from the ballot, clearing the way for a face-off. Atkins triumphed when his vote count jumped to 9 in the second ballot and Kennedy came up with 8 again.

Source: Janet Hook, "Kennedy Muscle No Match for House Seniority," *Congressional Quarterly Weekly Report*, December 10, 1988, 3477.

The desire to accommodate as many members as possible does not apply equally to all committees. This is especially true in the House, where the number of members assigned to the top committees is more limited. During the 95th to 97th Congresses, for example, fewer than half of the House Democratic nominees for prestige committees (including Budget) obtained the assignment, compared with more than 60 percent of policy committee nominees and three-quarters of constitu-

TABLE 3-2 Criteria Mentioned by House Democratic Steering and Policy Members Making Nominations to Standing Committees (97th Congress)

Criterion	Number of times mentioned
Electoral needs of member	19
State committee slot	13
Region committee slot (southern)	2
Team player (supports party or leadership)	7
Policy views	6
Seniority	6
Failure to receive another request	6
Responsible legislator	3
Policy expertise	3
General ability and maturity	3
Personal experiences	2
Ideology	2
Endorsements	2
Previous political experience	1
Personal interest	1
Acceptable to committee chairs	1
Served on committee as temporary assignee	1

Note: This count does not include Steering and Policy consideration of Appropriations and Ways and Means nominees.

ency committee nominees. Speaker O'Neill provided "leadership support scores" to members of the Steering and Policy Committee for nonfreshmen seeking to transfer from one committee to another, nearly 60 percent of whom were seeking an assignment to Appropriations, Budget, or Ways and Means, in the 95th to 97th Congresses.[24] It is nearly impossible to determine how seriously Steering and Policy members take these scores, but in several cases where the scores were not mentioned by the Speaker, Steering and Policy members asked for them.

Former majority leader and Speaker, Jim Wright, made clear the significance of leadership support in September 1981 when he announced to the Democratic Caucus that members of the Appropriations, Budget, Rules, and Ways and Means committees would be held to a higher standard of support than other members.[25] Wright's announcement, which helped to prevent immediate disciplinary action against Gramm and other conservative supporters of the Reagan administration's budget and tax cuts of 1981, merely made explicit what generally had been the leadership's attitude about the top committees. Indeed, Ray and Smith have demonstrated that party support was an especially important factor for Democratic assignments to the prestige committees during the 95th to 97th Congresses.[26]

In the Senate, an additional factor is often significant for a Democratic requester: personal membership on the committee on committees. This is seldom a factor in the House, where the committee on committees is a small proportion of all party members. In contrast, the twenty-five-member Democratic Steering Committee (101st Congress) is composed of nearly half of all Senate Democrats. Steering Committee members tend to be fairly senior senators who are not seeking new assignments, so there are fewer situations where there is a conflict of interest than there might be. But several participants mentioned instances in which membership on the committee on committees was decisive. In one reported case, a freshman senator had "done all the right things" and had gained the endorsement of a majority of the Steering Committee members. Later, a Steering Committee member decided he wanted an additional assignment—the one the freshman was seeking—and he won it "handily" when assignments to that committee came up.

Once the committees have completed their work, the new "line ups" are presented to and ratified by the respective party caucuses and subsequently endorsed by a vote of each chamber. These final steps are rarely subject to much debate and almost never result in any changes. Thus, committee membership is in fact the responsibility of the committees on committees, although their decision is not formally the final step.

JURISDICTIONS, AGENDAS, AND ENVIRONMENTS

"They deal with different issues and face different pressures," retorted a senator to a question about the differences between two committees. Members of Congress often refer to the variety of policy jurisdictions, active political agendas, and political environments they face when explaining how their committees differ. And rightly so. Members of Congress also have disagreed vehemently at times about the best division of labor in their committee systems, but most have agreed that related policy areas should be placed under the same committee's jurisdiction.[27] Such coherent jurisdictions permit an efficient development and application of legislative expertise and encourage simultaneous consideration of interrelated issues.

Unfortunately, coherent but distinct jurisdictions are difficult to create, even in principle. Jurisdictional lines inevitably are somewhat overlapping and arbitrary because of the interdependence of governmental policies affecting economic, political, and social life. Even if mutually exclusive and coherent jurisdictions could be devised, events outside Congress's control would gradually undermine the alignment's rationale. For individual committees, such events may create new relationships among subjects under their jurisdictions, perhaps increasing or decreasing the fragmentation of their political environments and producing new jurisdictional conflicts with other committees.

Issues and outsiders create both opportunities and constraints for committee members. Popular causes, for example, provide opportunities for strategically placed committee members to gain publicity back home or even across the nation. The attention of interest groups, constituents, and others gives committee members an opportunity to serve them and gain political credits for doing so. But the same outsiders also can constrain committee members. For example, they can help define political issues to be considered and limit the range of politically acceptable options available to a committee or to individual members. These opportunities and constraints play an important role in defining the attractiveness of committees to members and shaping the internal decision-making processes of committees.[28]

COMPONENTS OF COMMITTEE ENVIRONMENTS AND AGENDAS

Committee environments can be divided into three components, which vary in character and significance for each panel. First, most committees deal with an *interbranch environment* that includes some part or parts of the federal establishment: the administration, bureaucracy, and the courts. For example, one group of committees—those concerned with tax, budget, and foreign policy matters—interacts primarily with executive officials representing the viewpoints of the particular administration in power. Another set interacts with relatively large numbers of officials from many agencies, generally focusing on agency activities rather than activities directed by the White House. The Appropriations committees are the best examples of this type but commerce, science, banking, and public works also fall into such a group. Committees in still another set normally deal only with officials from a narrow range of agencies; these include armed services, post office, merchant marine, agriculture, and interior. Finally some committees have rather little cause for contact with the executive branch. These include the two Rules committees, the ethics committees, and the House Administration Committee.

Second, all committees function within an *institutional environment*.

Party leaders, chamber colleagues, and the other chamber make up this immediate environment. Noncommittee colleagues may shape a committee's actions as claimants on committee decisions and as judges of decisions once they reach the floor. An average member's interest in a committee is likely to stem from the relevance of the committee's decisions to the member's own political circumstances. For example, many House and Senate committees regularly receive demands from noncommittee members who are seeking benefits for their constituents. The agriculture, appropriations, armed services, commerce, interior, post office, public works, tax, and veterans' affairs committees of both chambers are in this group. Also, highly salient national issues affect members collectively by shaping public attitudes about the party to which they belong. Not surprisingly, then, party leaders are a central component of the environments of those committees with jurisdiction over salient issues dividing the Democratic and Republican parties. The tax, budget, commerce, energy, judiciary, and labor committees also regularly deal with salient issues dividing the parties. Finally, a handful of committees have environments almost entirely dominated by chamber colleagues: the House and Senate Rules committees, the ethics committees, and the House Administration Committee.

Third, each committee operates within a *public environment* comprising the general public and representatives of organized interests. While it is not possible to detail each committee's environment here, it is important to recognize the variety in committee environments and to spot extreme cases for each of these properties. Data are most complete for the public environment. Fortunately, the interbranch and institutional environments, where less systematic data are available, run closely parallel to the public environment.

Together, the interbranch, institutional, and public environments create a large and complex audience for the activities of most standing committees. But committee environments differ in important ways. Three properties of committee environments are especially useful for understanding the differences among and changes within committees: fragmentation, salience, and environmental conflict. *Fragmentation* concerns the degree to which a committee attracts the attention of outsiders who perceive their interests as unrelated to each other. Fragmentation in a committee's political environment is rooted in the committee's jurisdiction: the larger the number of topics falling under its jurisdiction, the more fragmented its political environment is likely to be. Major changes in environmental fragmentation are stimulated by changes in a committee's formal jurisdiction. But because all possible topics are not always on a committee's active agenda, most changes in environmental fragmentation reflect the number of separate issues under active consideration.

Jurisdictional and environmental fragmentation, as will be seen in the next chapter, help to structure committees' decision-making processes by defining the political problems presented to them.

Each distinguishable agenda item can vary in salience and environmental conflict.[29] *Salience* can be judged in the public at large, as it usually is,[30] within the Congress,[31] or even within particular constituencies. An issue's salience stems, at least in part, from inherent policy characteristics, such as the pattern of costs and benefits involved in policy alternatives being considered. The greater the number of people affected by a potential policy decision, the greater the issue's salience is likely to be. Not surprisingly, members of Congress are sensitive to the number of people who care about an issue.

Conflict refers to the degree to which interested outsiders see their interests as competing or compatible with each other. This distinction has been called the level of controversy, zero-sum versus positive-sum, and competitive versus noncompetitive.[32] Conflict also is grounded in a policy decision's perceived distribution of costs and benefits. Conflict among interested outsiders often forces members to pick and choose among competing interests, favoring some and perhaps alienating others. Thus the level of conflict in a committee's environment helps to shape the incentives and disincentives for members to participate in various committee activities. We will now turn to a more detailed consideration of each of these properties of committee environments.

FRAGMENTATION

Jurisdictional fragmentation varies widely among committees. In Table 3-3 House and Senate committees are grouped according to their average rank on two indicators of jurisdictional fragmentation: (1) the number of separate executive departments and independent agencies that fall under each committee's jurisdiction, and (2) the number of subjects listed in each committee's jurisdiction under its chamber's rules. While it cannot be assumed that each department or subject is politically independent of others that fall within a committee's jurisdiction, the resulting rankings yield a fairly accurate view of the spectrum of jurisdictional fragmentation.

House committees are ranked similarly to their Senate counterparts. In both chambers, the appropriations, commerce, labor, and foreign policy committees have large, highly fragmented jurisdictions.[33] The House Interior and Insular Affairs Committee and its closest Senate counterpart, Energy and Natural Resources, are important exceptions. The jurisdictional fragmentation of these committees is similar in absolute terms, but the broader, more fragmented jurisdictions of several

Senate committees result in a relatively lower standing for Energy and Natural Resources. The House rankings reflect modest increases in five House committees' fragmentation that resulted from the 1975 Bolling-Hansen reforms. The clear loser in these jurisdictional shifts was Ways and Means, which lost jurisdiction over general revenue sharing, nontax aspects of health policy, and other areas. The Senate rankings also reflect that chamber's 1977 jurisdictional realignment.

For most committees, jurisdictional fragmentation is closely related to the fragmentation of their public environments. That is, committees with highly fragmented jurisdictions also have many separate sets of groups and individuals making unrelated demands on committee members. In both chambers, the Appropriations committees attract dozens of groups' attention each year as they consider funding bills for federal programs. These committees have by far the most fragmented public environments. At the other extreme, the House and Senate Veterans' Affairs committees regularly face a handful of national veterans groups with overlapping concerns. Both Veterans' Affairs committees have established routine interaction with veterans groups by holding separate hearings on the groups' legislative recommendations each year. No other committee interacts with outside groups in this way.

Jurisdictional fragmentation is a misleading indicator of fragmentation in the public environments of two sets of committees. First, the House Government Operations and Senate Governmental Affairs committees have broad oversight jurisdictions that make their public environments highly variable from year to year. The environments of Government Operations and Governmental Affairs are more dependent on members' temporary policy interests than are those of other committees, and they are difficult to characterize in any straightforward manner.[34] Second, the two tax committees, House Ways and Means and Senate Finance, have jurisdictions that appear relatively less fragmented when judged by the committees' focus on one topic (taxation) and one agency (Treasury). While claims for favorable tax treatment all affect the government's revenues, the involved groups usually make independent appeals to the committees. These appeals are related only in that the committees usually deal with them in the same large piece of legislation.

SALIENCE

High fragmentation in jurisdictions or environments does not translate directly into high public salience. Ideally, this proposition could be demonstrated by using survey data on the scope of interest in issues falling under each committee's jurisdiction. Unfortunately, no such survey data are available. Examining the content of television network

TABLE 3-3 Fragmentation Among Congressional Committees

Jurisdictional fragmentation	House	Senate
High	Appropriations Energy and Commerce Interior Education & Labor Public Works Foreign Affairs Judiciary	Appropriations Labor Commerce Foreign Relations Governmental Affairs Judiciary Environment & Public Works
Medium	Agriculture Science & Technology Government Operations Merchant Marine Banking Armed Services	Banking Energy & Natural Resources Agriculture Finance Armed Services
Low	Ways and Means House Administration Small Business District of Columbia Veterans' Affairs Select Intelligence Rules Standards of Official Conduct	Rules and Administration Veterans' Affairs Small Business Select Intelligence

Source: Fragmentation rankings are a composite measure, which combines the number of departments and agencies under each committee's jurisdiction and the number of areas of legislative jurisdiction in the chamber rules. Departments/agencies calculated in part from Judy Schneider, "House of Representatives Committee Jurisdiction over Executive Branch Agencies," Congressional Research Service, September 28, 1979. Updated by the authors.

Note: Committees listed in rank order. Budget committees are excluded.

news broadcasts is a convenient alternative. Given the preeminent status of network television as an information source for the American public, it is reasonable to assume that the amount of time devoted to a topic in network news broadcasts is indicative of public interest in that topic.[35] For each committee, the amount of television time devoted to topics falling within its legislative jurisdiction was determined from a systematic sample of "CBS Evening News" broadcasts during the 1969-1980 period.[36] The results, a summation of the first and second halves of the period, are presented in Table 3-4.[37] Table

3-4 shows how consistently topics under the jurisdictions of the foreign policy, judiciary, and commerce committees dominate national attention.

The difference between the first and second periods for the foreign policy committees is due to the absence of Vietnam-related stories in the tallies, but it does reflect the shift in national attention from Vietnam to the Mideast. Crime and, on a less regular basis, civil rights are the dominating subjects for the judiciary committees, although including the coverage of Watergate and the House Judiciary impeachment proceedings would add a substantial amount of time to the tally for that committee. The commerce committees' salience is drawn from more than a half-dozen subjects, reflecting the committees' great jurisdictional fragmentation. The House Commerce Committee has a somewhat more salient jurisdiction than its Senate counterpart because of its jurisdiction over health and air pollution issues. The difference would be even greater, especially for the 1975-1980 period, if energy stories were added to the House committee's total. Health and air pollution fall under the Senate's Labor and Environment committees' jurisdictions, respectively. Because of these differences, both committees' jurisdictions are more salient than those of their House counterparts.

Equally important to note is that eight or nine House committees and four or five Senate committees have jurisdictions of consistently low national salience. Except for the government operations committees, these have narrow, relatively unfragmented jurisdictions. They include three committees—House Rules, House Administration, and Senate Rules and Administration—that deal primarily with the chambers' internal matters. Thus agendas change constantly—and sometimes rapidly—altering the salience of otherwise static committee jurisdictions.

The news broadcast tallies also suggest why, in addition to their smaller numbers and larger constituencies, senators typically are more visible than representatives. Senate committee jurisdictions are more salient, on the average, than are those of the House, reflecting the distribution of Senate jurisdictions among fewer committees. A more even distribution of highly salient jurisdictions also exists among the top six or seven Senate committees.

Thus senators, with their larger number of committee assignments, are more likely to belong to a committee with very salient jurisdiction: 77 percent of senators were assigned to at least one of the six most highly ranked committees in the 97th Congress, while only 47 percent of House members sat on one or more of that chamber's six most highly ranked committees.

TABLE 3-4 Minutes of "CBS Evening News" Devoted to Topics Falling Within Committee Jurisdictions (from a 50% Sample of Newscasts, Ranked by the 1975-1980 Standing)

House	1969-1974	1975-1980	Senate	1969-1974	1975-1980
Foreign Affairs	2,109	4,879	Foreign Relations	2,109	4,879
Judiciary a	1,216	1,299	Judiciary	1,518	1,299
Commerce	823	882	Commerce	698	835
Armed Services	467	524	Labor	569	808
Education & Labor	333	462	Energy (Int.)	243	772
Ways & Means	268	347	Armed Services	467	623
Public Works	180	339	Envir. (Public Works)	335	399
Interior	249	275	Finance	268	347
Merchant Marine	200	216	Banking	280	166
Science & Technology	423	211	Agriculture	101	156
Agriculture	97	155	Governmental Affairs	22	90
Banking	280	153	Veterans' Affairs	42	44
Government Operations	22	52	Rules & Administration	75	35
Post Office	52	48	Small Business	—	10
Veterans' Affairs	42	44			
House Administration	54	35	Commmittees abolished in 1977:		
Small Business	5	10	Aeronautics	387	55
District of Columbia	1	6	Post Office	52	14
Rules	10	5	District of Columbia	1	0

Cross-cutting issues excluded from the above tallies (1969-1974, 1975-1980): Vietnam/Indochina 2,606 608; Economy 733 748; Energy 343 614

Source: *Television News Index and Abstracts* (Nashville, Tenn.: Joint Universities Libraries, 1969-1980).

Note: The Appropriations committees are excluded because of duplicate jurisdiction. The Select Intelligence committees had no legislative jurisdiction when this count was made.

a Excludes Watergate-related stories, which totaled nearly 1,300 minutes in 1973-1974.

CONFLICT

Salience is closely related to conflict in committee environments.[38] The presence of conflict means that an issue is salient to *someone*. Intense conflict, moreover, may stimulate media and public interest in an issue. But committees with jurisdiction over equally salient subjects often experience quite different levels of conflict in their environments. Members and staff recognize these differences, and they are sensitive to changes in the level of conflict within their committees' environments. The same senator who was quoted at the beginning of this section spoke about "pressure": "I don't just mean pressure to do something, I mean pressure to choose between two very polarized sides to an issue—that's pressure." Based on the comments of committee members and staff, we have placed committees into three categories of conflict. The results are shown in Table 3-5, where the relative salience of each committee's environment is also indicated.

Clearly, conflict in the public environment is positively related to salience; thus the parallel between House and Senate committees' salience is present for conflict as well. Major differences between House and Senate committees occur in the commerce and interior committees. The energy and health jurisdiction of House Energy and Commerce gives it sources of environmental conflict that are not present for Senate Commerce. Democrat John Dingell of Michigan, chair of the House committee, quipped, "Controversy follows the committee around like the Earth follows the Sun." [39] The Senate counterpart also has been a hotbed of political controversy, but as consumer issues under its jurisdiction faded in significance during the 1970s, so did conflict in the committee's environment. The interior committees—House Interior and Insular Affairs and Senate Energy and Natural Resources—are more similar. Energy and Natural Resources' energy jurisdiction is substantially broader, though, bringing to it conflicts that take place before Commerce in the House. Other smaller differences exist between the chambers, but none that suggest that the committees should be placed in separate categories. For example, Senate Environment and Public Works has experienced more intense conflict in air pollution and other environmental policy battles than has its House counterpart. The declining significance of environmental disputes has made these committees more similar in recent years.

Committees that have experienced substantial increases or decreases in the level of conflict of their public environments since the late 1960s are also indicated in Table 3-5. Other sets of committees also deserve attention. The Judiciary committees' environments have been relatively high in conflict throughout this period, but the rise of abortion, school prayer, balanced budgets, and other issues involving proposed constitutional amendments has intensified conflict even more. An aide to former Speaker O'Neill declared that House Judiciary members now face "razor-sharp issues" because they confront diametrically opposed groups with passionately held beliefs. The conflict in the public environments of the Appropriations and especially the Budget committees increased as federal deficits and spending became a more salient issue in the late 1970s and throughout the 1980s. Rep. Richard J. Durbin

TABLE 3-5 Perceived Conflict and Salience of Committees' Public
Environments (Direction of Change in Conflict During the
1980s in Parentheses)

Perceived conflict	Salience		
	High	Moderate	Low
High	Budget (+) H. Commerce (+) Judiciary (+) Labor	S. Energy & Nat. Res. S. Finance H. Ways & Means (+)	
Moderate	S. Commerce Foreign Policy	Appropriations (+) Armed Services Banking (-) Public Works (-) H. Interior (-)	

Low			Agriculture
			Govt. Operations
			H. Science
			H. Merchant
			  Marine (-)
			H. Post Office
			H. District of
			  Columbia
			Veterans'
			Small Business

Source: For "conflict," authors' interviews with participants; for "salience," Table 3-4.

Note: References are to both the House and Senate committees unless otherwise indicated. Excludes House Rules, House Administration, and Senate Rules and Administration, for which the public environment is not significant. The Appropriations and Budget committees have been classified on salience based on their role in spending and economic policy.

(D-Ill.) noted that life on the Budget Committee could be hazardous: "It's not an easy assignment or a pleasant one because you're forced to vote repeatedly on matters that make people unhappy."[40] The Appropriations committees' environmental conflict was exacerbated by the increasing use of riders on appropriations bills. *Riders,* which are amendments designed to limit spending for some otherwise authorized purpose (for abortions, for example), have attracted the attention of many groups that previously had paid little attention to spending bills.

It hardly needs to be said that members of Congress do not consciously approach their decisions about which committee or committees to request by mulling over the relative fragmentation, salience, and conflict of various panels. Some feel compelled to join certain commit-tees regardless of their own predilections—like the House member who said that he hadn't chosen his committee assignment on Agriculture, he was "sentenced to it." At least a few others, albeit a diminishing handful, reach Washington without serious thought about committee assignments. Most do think seriously about their assignments, however, and when they do they ponder how such assignments mesh with their own personal political goals. And, as we will see, these goals animate their activities once they have joined their committees.

MEMBERS' GOALS

The significance of personal political goals for understanding committee differences was established by Richard Fenno in *Congressmen in Commit-tees*.[41] Through interviews with members of twelve congressional com-mittees during the late 1950s and 1960s, Fenno identified three goals that motivate members' committee activity: reelection, good public policy, and influence within the chamber. Fenno found that committees did indeed attract members differentially according to members' per-sonal goals, a finding that later was corroborated by Charles Bullock's interviews with House freshmen of the 92d Congress (1971-1973),[42] and our own interviews for the 97th (1982-1983) and the 100th/101st (1987-1990) Congresses.

Our House and Senate figures for the 97th and the 100th/101st Congresses were calculated from the responses of junior members or their knowledgeable staff to the questions: "What committees did you want to serve on (after you were first elected to your chamber)? Why?"[43] These responses include committees that members may not have re-quested formally, but which they viewed as attractive nevertheless. Unfortunately, there are no directly comparable data available for the Senate in an earlier congress. The 1948-1971 Senate figures that we use here were collected by Bullock from the archived papers of two former members of the Senate Democratic Committee on Committees.[44]

Since Fenno's seminal work, scholars have disagreed about which of the three goals motivates most members most of the time, but the finding that some mix of the three goals motivates most committee activity remained valid throughout the 1980s. We use *constituency* to replace the *reelection* label because members mention a richer set of constituency-oriented motivations than *reelection* suggests. Even so, the vast majority of constituency-oriented motivations are defined in terms of electoral needs.[45] Overall, such motivations are the most frequently mentioned reasons for preferring particular committees. Policy interests are a close second and influence or prestige a distant third, especially in the Senate.[46] And while mixed motives are characteristic of members of both chambers—appearing in 62 percent of our House interviews and 75 percent of our Senate interviews for the 100th/101st Congresses—multiple motives are infrequently expressed for the same committee. Usually only one goal is emphasized for each committee of interest, and several committees are mentioned for different reasons. Of the separate committee mentions in the 100th/101st Congress interviews, 86 percent were associated with only one goal in the House and 79 percent were associated with only one goal in the Senate (up from 77.4 percent and 73.4 percent, respectively, in the 97th Congress). Thus, these findings continue to corroborate Fenno's assumptions about members' calculations when considering their options for committee assignments.

Whether a member seeks a committee berth for purposes of serving constituency interests, good public policy, or chamber influence, his or her interest is grounded in the committee's substantive jurisdiction. The relevance of a committee's activities to any member's personal goals therefore may increase or decrease as a function of formal jurisdictional changes. And the perceived opportunity to pursue certain goals can change as political events outside members' control affect a committee's informal agenda.

MEMBERS' GOALS IN THE HOUSE

The committee-specific motivations reported in Table 3-6 indicate that, in making the important decision about which committee assignments to pursue, House freshmen distinguish among committees based on personal aspirations and goals. Interestingly, the survey of motivations for committee preference also indicates that only a handful of committees attract members who share nearly identical motivations.

INFLUENCE AND PRESTIGE COMMITTEES

The Rules, Appropriations, and Ways and Means committees remain distinctively prestigious in House members' eyes. When describing these committees, House members use terms such as "important," "powerful," "*the* committee," "where the action is," and "the mover-and-shaker committee"—descriptions similar to those Fenno heard for Appropriations and Ways and Means in the 1960s. A fourth committee, Budget, has almost reached a position comparable to the traditional troika. Driven largely by the importance of budget deficits on the national agenda and augmented by several centralizing trends in

TABLE 3-6 Committee Preference Motivations for New House Members (92d, 97th, and 100th/101st Congresses)

Committee	Constituency 92d	Constituency 97th	Constituency 100th/101st	Policy 92d	Policy 97th	Policy 100th/101st	Prestige 92d	Prestige 97th	Prestige 100th/101st
Prestige Committees									
Appropriations	5	5	7	3	6	4	7	11	4
Budget	—	0	0	—	4	2	—	5	2
Rules	1	0	0	0	1	0	0	3	1
Ways and Means	1	0	2	0	6	8	5	7	4
Policy Committees									
Banking	1	14	4	9	17	10	1	1	0
Education and Labor	5	3	2	7	2	6	0	0	0
Energy and Commerce	3	9	6	16	13	3	1	0	0
Foreign Affairs	1	2	0	4	8	8	0	0	0
Judiciary	0	0	1	7	3	3	0	0	0
Government Operations	0	0	1	0	9	2	0	0	0
Constituency Committees									
Agriculture	10	15	8	3	7	1	0	0	0
Armed Services	5	11	9	3	7	3	1	0	0
Interior	7	12	2	4	2	1	0	0	0
Merchant Marine	3	5	7	0	0	0	0	0	0
Public Works	7	4	6	1	2	1	0	0	0
Science, Space, & Technology	0	9	8	1	5	3	1	0	0
Small Business	—	13	3	—	4	0	—	0	0
Veterans' Affairs	5	2	8	0	1	0	0	0	0
Unrequested Committees									
District of Columbia	0	1	0	0	1	0	0	1	0
House Administration	0	0	0	0	0	0	0	0	0
Post Office and Civil Service	1	1	1	0	0	0	0	0	0
Standards of Official Conduct	—	0	0	—	1	0	—	0	0
Select Intelligence	—	—	0	—	—	1	—	—	0

Source: See discussion and citations in text.

national policy making, Budget must now be ranked among the most powerful House standing committees.

As noted earlier, these committees have salience for every member of the House. Their importance is reflected by their formal designation, since 1946, as the only "exclusive" committees of the House. In general, their members may not sit on other standing committees (with the exception of Budget, as explained below). Other motivations for seeking these committees are common, but what makes them unique is their attractiveness to House members beyond their value for serving constituents or pursuing personal policy interests. The importance of these committees in House politics dictates that attention be given to each of them in turn.

THE RULES COMMITTEE. The prestige and influence of the House Committee on Rules reside in its power to propose *special orders* or rules for the consideration of legislation on the floor.[47] Unlike the smaller Senate, which tolerates flexible floor procedures, the House more carefully structures its floor activity. Without special orders, House floor debate would be sheer chaos. Because rules are required to bring nearly all important legislation to the floor, to limit debate, and often to limit amendments, Rules members are in a position to block or expedite legislation important to individual members of the House. The committee's reach, then, is as broad as that of any committee in Congress, despite its limited jurisdiction. And its decisions are salient and often controversial within the chamber. Thus the Rules Committee is ideally suited to the member seeking influence and prestige within the House. With its small size (only thirteen members in the 101st Congress), the Rules Committee is truly elite.[48]

As noted in Chapter 2, a conservative coalition of southern Democrats and Republicans controlled Rules after the mid-1930s and, often contrary to the wishes of most majority party Democrats, blocked floor consideration of many liberal bills. In the 1960s the committee's expansion, the addition of moderate and liberal Democrats, and the electoral defeat of conservative chairman Howard "Judge" Smith changed the committee's political balance to one more supportive of the Democratic leadership's policy positions. And yet some key Democratic legislation continued to face effective conservative obstructionism on Rules.

Most liberals hoped that a new era had arrived in 1973 when a fellow liberal, Ray J. Madden (D-Ind.), became chair and three new Democrats, each a leadership supporter, were appointed to the committee. Instead, Rules members, accustomed to independence, endured an uncomfortable transition period, and important changes in the Democratic caucus rules cemented a closer relationship to their party leaders. Two changes made the Rules Committee a genuine arm of the Speaker. First, as was mentioned in Chapter 2, the reformist Democratic Caucus of the 94th Congress gave the Speaker the authority to name all Democratic Rules members, subject to caucus approval. Political independence was a criterion not to be applied in choosing Democratic Rules members. In fact, Democrats appointed to Rules in recent congresses have been recruited by party leaders or the committee chair. Second, Richard Bolling (D-Mo.) became chair of Rules in 1979. It was Bolling who made the motion to give the Speaker the power to nominate Democratic Rules members before the start of the 94th Congress. Bolling strongly believed that his committee should regain some of its historical status as the "Speaker's committee," helping to schedule and structure floor consideration of legislation as the majority party leadership desired.

Despite some temporary concern that the importance and prestige of the Rules Committee would decline with the loss of independence from party leaders, the committee remains attractive to House members seeking chamber influence and prestige. Indeed, the rarity of open seats on Rules makes them even more desirable. Thus, in recent years, open seats created by Bolling's retirement, and the deaths of his successor (the highly esteemed Claude Pepper of Florida) and of Sala Burton from California, were keenly, albeit discreetly in the latter two cases, contested. Few members of the committee ever become household names, but they covet the assignment nonetheless. As David Bonior (D-Mich.) put it: "I never want to get off Rules. You get to dabble . . . you're always doing favors for people."[49]

Nevertheless, the source of influence and prestige for the Rules Committee, as articulated by its members, has changed in important ways. Bruce Oppenheimer has noted, for example, that many Rules members began to view themselves as "field commanders" for party leaders in the mid-1970s, a role perception that has been strengthened since that time.[50] In this role, Rules members serve as additional sets of eyes and ears for their party leadership. Rules members often spot legislation that poses political problems for the party and draw the attention of elected party leaders to it. Majority party leaders consult with Rules Democrats on nearly all major pieces of legislation—not only to inform Rules members of leadership preferences for a rule, but also to seek information and advice about legislative strategy. As a result, Rules members' influence and prestige are closely tied to that of the party leadership, especially in the case of majority party Democrats.

Finally, the Rules Committee of the 1980s fashioned a creative role for itself by structuring new types of rules. These "innovative" rules, begun during Bolling's tenure and further exploited under his successor Claude Pepper, have placed members of the committee in an even stronger position to set legislative strategy in the House.[51] In fact, Pepper's style may have contributed to this latter trend by allowing individual members greater leeway than they believed they had under Bolling. Butler Derrick (D-S.C.) noted, "Members have more latitude, more opportunity, to participate in the decision making process. Dick [Bolling] played it very close to the vest." [52] And Pepper explained: "It's not my way of running things. I try to get the benefit of every member on the committee." [53]

THE APPROPRIATIONS COMMITTEE.   "Appropriations is the key spot. Members need you and come to you for help. If you're not on Appropriations, you are really at the mercy of other people," said Mickey Edwards (R-Okla.).[54] The committee's jurisdiction over spending bills makes it attractive to those members seeking dollars for district programs and projects and to members interested in federal fiscal policy. But more important, the committee's significance in national fiscal policy making and its importance to noncommittee members seeking district funding also make membership valuable to those members seeking influence and prestige within the chamber.[55] As Appropriations member Norman Dicks (D-Wash.) asserted, "It's where the money is. And money is where the clout is." [56]

Reforms and agenda changes since the mid-1970s have affected the relative significance of the three goals for Appropriations members. First, Democratic rule changes have reduced the power of the full committee chair and encouraged members to be more constituency oriented. Members now select ("bid for") their own subcommittees, and Appropriations Democrats now openly choose subcommittee assignments they believe are valuable to them at home.[57] David R. Obey (D-Wis.) explained, "Now the pro-defense people go to [the] Defense [subcommittee], public works people go to Energy and Water, pro-health and education people go to Labor-HHS." [58]

Formally, Appropriations subcommittee chairs are now elected by the Democratic Caucus. In practice, they continue to be selected according to subcommittee seniority, as they were in the 1960s, but the subcommittee chairs are well aware that the new procedure makes them accountable to the caucus. Consequently, many participants note, subcommittee chairs are more responsive to the demands of noncommittee members than they were in the 1960s.

Members also point out that the Appropriations Committee's hearings and meetings were closed to uninvited outsiders until the 1970s. Opening hearings and meetings to the public made members less willing to set aside the demands of colleagues, constituents, and important clientele groups. In short, opportunities to pursue district-oriented interests have improved, and pressures to do so have increased for Appropriations members.

Second, the erosion of the Appropriations Committee's control over expenditures, which was well under way in the late 1960s, was exacerbated in the 1970s, undermining the committee's source of influence and prestige in the House. Even more important, the loss of spending control was a partial cause of, and was compounded by, the creation of the budget process and Budget committees. Since the late 1970s, budget resolutions have placed constraints on the Appropriations Committee's decisions. An aide to Speaker O'Neill explained one effect of the change: "It's amazing, really, we seldom consult Appropriations members like we used to on spending politics; the ball game is now played in the Budget Committee." Appropriations members recognize the difference, and one member of both Appropriations and Budget commented: "Appropriations is still a strong committee, but it's nothing like it used to be. Everybody in the Congress is becoming an expert on spending, and they are less likely to defer to us.... Appropriations isn't top dog anymore." [59] The ranking Appropriations Republican, Silvio Conte from Massachusetts, adds: "We're not eunuchs yet, but we've lost a lot." [60] Appropriations still attracts members because of its influence and prestige, but in absolute terms these qualities have declined in importance as its monopoly over spending decisions has eroded.

Finally, despite the encroachment of the budget process into the committee's traditional role, an upsurge of policy-related interest in Appropriations occurred as federal spending became a more salient national issue in the late 1970s. This is especially true for conservative Republicans who, even in the 1960s, occasionally sought the Appropriations Committee for policy reasons.[61] All six freshmen of the 97th Congress who mentioned a policy-oriented motivation for interest in Appropriations consistently supported President Reagan's budget and tax proposals throughout the 97th Congress.

On balance, then, House Appropriations has become somewhat less attractive for reasons of prestige and influence (although these still dominate), decidedly more attractive to constituency-oriented members, and at least temporarily of more interest to conservative, policy-oriented members.

THE WAYS AND MEANS COMMITTEE. The House Ways and Means Committee long has been considered one of the most—if not *the* most—powerful and prestigious committee of Congress.[62] Throughout the 1960s and early 1970s, Ways and Means' small size (twenty-five members), its nationally salient jurisdiction (taxation, trade, Social Security, health insurance, public assistance, and unemployment compensation), and, for Democrats, its function as the Committee on Committees combined to make it especially attractive to the influence- and prestige-oriented member. Much of the committee's legislation, and nearly all of its tax legislation, was considered on the House floor under closed rules on the theory that tax bills were too complex and important for uninformed outsiders to tamper with. The Ways and Means chair for two decades, Wilbur D. Mills of Arkansas, was described as the most powerful member of Congress. Mills, a renowned expert on tax policy, operated the committee with a strong hand, closed markups, appointed no subcommittees, and was committed to the apprenticeship-seniority norm.[63]

Not surprisingly, Ways and Means became a chief target for reform in the 93d and 94th Congresses. Along with other House committees, Ways and Means was forced to open its hearings and meetings to the public. The Democratic Caucus established a procedure to make it easier to have an amendment to a Ways and Means bill considered on the floor—though closed rules are still the standard practice for this committee. And the caucus initiated a change in chamber rules requiring committees with more than twenty members to establish subcommittees. Only the Rules Committee fell below this level at that time, and only Ways and Means was without subcommittees. Hence, the committee was forced to create five subcommittees, its first since Mills's second term as chair. Finally, Ways and Means Democrats were stripped of their committee assignment authority and the committee was expanded to thirty-seven members. (Ways and Means escaped major changes in its jurisdiction, despite repeated attempts by House reformers.) In several ways, these reforms have affected the opportunities of Ways and Means members and potential members to pursue their personal goals.

First, the committee was among those most strongly affected by the reforms because of the saliency of tax and social welfare issues. Second, reforms imposed on Ways and Means also have made the committee more valuable to members with strong policy motivations, although policy goals long have been important to at least a few Ways and Means members.[64] The creation of subcommittees and the availability of subcommittee staff to more members gave them the tools to pursue their own policy interests. Third, Ways and Means members have lost some of their influence and prestige. In part, this has been a result of the damage done to the committee's reputation of expertise and moderation in tax legislation, a reputation carefully cultivated by Mills and his colleagues during the 1960s. Ways and Means members, particularly majority party Democrats, generally are less willing to suppress their personal policy preferences. Finally, Ways and Means members' loss of chamber influence and prestige was compounded by the loss of the committee on committees function by the committee's Democrats.

Catherine Rudder discovered in interviews with Ways and Means Democrats soon after the reforms that veteran members believed the loss of assignment responsibilities did not affect the committee's ability to get its bills passed on the floor.[65] In their view, the only loss was in the committee's prestige. Junior Democrats saw things differently: one junior Democrat told Rudder that the reform "constitutes a substantial diminution in power for the committee." A senior Republican concurred by noting that the assignment power had provided committee Democrats "an element of respect and gave House members second thoughts about crossing them on the floor." [66] While some current members agree with these latter views, the committee is now far removed from that set of reforms.

The Ways and Means Committee remains quite attractive for its policy, influence, and prestige. Along with Appropriations, Ways and Means is most frequently mentioned by new members as a truly plum assignment, but one that is unattainable. Its special influence now is more dependent on the committee's ability to satisfy noncommittee members' requests for special considerations when writing legislation and for its ability to generate contributions to political action committees (PACs).[67]

Changes in the balance of goals were boosted by the exceptionally large turnover in Ways and Means' membership in the 1970s. Only two House committees exhibited less continuity in overall membership; only four Ways and Means members in 1971 served through the 97th Congress (1981-1983). The committee's expansion in 1975, along with normal retirements in the previous year, meant that nineteen of the thirty-seven committee members were new in that year alone. Many of the new Democrats were strong liberals with well-defined policy goals. In sum, the Ways and Means Committee's previous attraction—primarily influence and prestige and secondarily policy—has changed to a more equal balance of influence and policy. But the committee remains one of the most attractive for House members seeking chamber influence and prestige. It continues to have little attractiveness for constituency-related reasons.

BUDGET COMMITTEE.   The House Budget Committee resembles Ways and Means in member motivation, as indicated in Table 3-6. Members seek assignments due to its recognized power and broad policy impact: "I've been very fortunate in my career, getting on Ways and Means in my first term," noted Frank J. Guarini (D-N.J.). "But I've never been on any other committee. The Budget Committee affords a huge panorama for all our nation's problems." [68] Unlike Appropriations, Rules, and Ways and Means, however, Budget has not traditionally been regarded as a prestige committee.

A major contributing factor to Budget's odd combination of power and limited prestige is the restricted tenure of its members.[69] The Congressional Budget and Impoundment Control Act of 1974 provided that the committee be composed of five members from Appropriations, five from Ways and Means, and fifteen (later seventeen) members of other House committees. Each member's service was limited to four years out of any ten-year period, a limit that was extended to six years in 1979. Consequently, Budget members do not have the opportunity to develop long-term chamber influence by virtue of membership on the committee or the prestige that might come with that influence.

The Budget Committee also suffers from its nonexclusive jurisdiction.[70] The committee's main function, writing budget resolutions, entails making judgments about expenditures and revenues that fall under other House committees' jurisdictions. As a result, Budget exercises independent discretion only by directly challenging the decision-making autonomy of other House committees. Until 1981 the Budget Committee minimized direct conflict with other committees by setting spending targets at levels that permitted most of them to act freely, without violating the ceilings.[71] In 1981, faced with President Reagan's budget-cutting program, the committee produced resolutions forcing most House committees to find programmatic ways to reduce projected spending sharply, a move that stimulated efforts to revamp the budget process in the 98th Congress.[72] To the extent that Budget is successful in influencing policy, it appears to create more enemies than admirers in the House.

These limitations led to a somewhat different definition of goals, at least for Budget's majority party Democrats. Lance LeLoup discovered in interviews with Budget members between 1975 and 1978 that Budget Democrats saw their major goal as ensuring that the new budget process worked.[73] While Budget Republicans were motivated strongly by their policy goal of reducing federal spending and deficits, Democratic members acted to establish a firm institutional footing for the new budget process and the new committee. Keeping the process alive meant avoiding direct conflicts with other powerful House committees whenever possible. LeLoup concluded that Budget Democrats in the mid-1970s should be classified as process-oriented rather than as policy- or influence-oriented. In fact, two or three Democrats had developed an excellent reputation for their expertise in understanding the details of budgeting and the budget process. He found, as we have, that members do not mention motivations related to reelection chances as a reason for their interest in Budget.[74]

During the 1980s the committee became even more central to House politics as the budget process moved to center stage. The committee is now the first congressional step in the budget process after receipt of the president's annual budget. Indeed, by the late 1980s pressure again mounted to delimit the committee's power as Appropriations Committee members saw encroachments on their traditional authority and as budget resolutions became ever more detailed. In fact, the whole budget process raises important questions about the change in the level of committee autonomy. These are treated in more detail in Chapter 5.

The common thread underlying changes in members' goals in the Rules, Appropriations, Ways and Means, and Budget committees is procedural reform. The first three committees were directly affected by the democratizing reforms of the 1970s. Rules became more closely tied to an elected party leader, the Appropriations chairs lost the ability to dictate subcommittee memberships, the Ways and Means chairs lost the stranglehold over committee deliberations, and the entire committee lost vital sources of influence to the Democratic Caucus. Few jurisdictional changes directly affected these committees, and informal agenda changes were not major factors. In each case, the net effect was a recognition on the part of committee members that their influence within the House was reduced as their decision-making autonomy was weakened. Nevertheless, each continues to control enough decisions vital to many, if not all, House members to retain great attractiveness and to hold a special status in the eyes of the rest of the House.

POLICY COMMITTEES

Members motivated by an interest in particular policy areas, or perhaps merely an interest in becoming involved in important issues, see things somewhat differently than their prestige- or power-oriented colleagues. Salient national issues are attractive because the policy-oriented member seeks to contribute to the shape of important policies. If they are conflict-ridden issues, so be it. Conflict, after all, probably reflects the importance and complexity of the issues. Thus policy decisions with concentrated perceived costs, but only diffuse benefits, do not keep the policy-oriented member away from a committee facing such decisions. And the broader the committee's jurisdiction, the better it is for a member attracted to challenging issues.[75]

In contrast to the importance of reforms for influence-oriented committees, agenda change has driven most of the major shifts in members' attitudes about service on House committees that are viewed as policy-oriented (Table 3-6). Two policy-oriented committees—Education and Labor, and Judiciary—already had experienced internal democratizing reforms when the House and the Democratic Caucus imposed reforms on other committees during the 1970s. For most policy-oriented committees, however, the reforms allowed their members to pursue more vigorously policy interests already motivating their committee activity. This was the case for Banking, Commerce, Foreign Affairs, and Government Operations. Some members perceived externally imposed reforms as the only way to achieve their personal policy goals. Only in the Banking Committee did the reforms of the 1970s provide an opportunity for members to pursue a substantially different mix of goals in their committee activity. In each policy-oriented committee, though, the rise and fall of issues on the national agenda have affected the committee's attractiveness.

Except for the recently popular Government Operations Committee, the policy-oriented committees of the House are considered "semi-exclusive" or "major" by the two parties. Such a designation reflects the view that these committees are important enough to require that no member be allowed to sit on more than one of them, but not so important as to prevent members of major committees from holding a seat on other committees designated as "nonmajor." [76] Consequently, except for members of the exclusive Appropriations, Rules, and Ways and Means committees, Democratic and Republican party rules limit members to two committee assignments on either (1) one major and one nonmajor committee or (2) two nonmajor committees. Unlike the rather prosaic designations used by Democrats, House Republicans have designated their committee categories as "red," "white," and "blue." The only difference between the two parties, however, is that the popular Energy and Commerce is on the "red," or exclusive, list.

With few exceptions, the list of committees attracting policy-oriented members remains remarkably stable. From the 1960s to the 1970s changes in the national agenda burnished the reputation and attractiveness of the Energy and Commerce Committee to the point where vacancies on the panel were nearly as hotly contested as the prestige committee slots. That situation may have reversed somewhat in the late 1980s as the committee receded from public view and its agenda came to be viewed in more distributive terms. For example, at the outset of the 100th Congress the three new Democratic members all came from coal-producing districts that would be adversely affected by acid rain legislation within the committee's jurisdiction. [77] Thus, by 1989, our interviews show a decidedly more constituent bent to recent requesters than occurred a decade earlier.

Three other important differences between the 1960s and the 1970s and 1980s should be noted. First, Government Operations has been among the top choices of members requesting policy committees only since the early 1970s. Continuing budget crises and repeated procurement scandals also helped to buoy member interest in slots on the Government Operations Committee—an interest enhanced by its categorization as a nonmajor (or blue) committee by the two parties. Second, by the late 1970s and early 1980s Education and Labor requesters became less likely to mention their policy interests than in the 1960s (a pattern that fit Judiciary as well). In fact, members had to be recruited to fill vacant committee positions. By the late 1980s this situation seems to have been reversed, and our recent interviews show Education and Labor once more decisively in the policy category.[78] And third, the Interior Committee has moved into or up list of policy-oriented committees, which is a clue to the presence of more policy-oriented Interior members during the 1970s and 1980s.

CONSTITUENCY COMMITTEES

Members motivated by constituency-oriented concerns seek committees with jurisdictions salient to their constituents. But, as Morris Fiorina has indicated, the single-minded pursuit of reelection also leads to an avoidance of issues that alienate elements of one's constituency and to an emphasis on activities that alienate no one. Acquiring federal dollars for local projects and serving constituents who have problems with the federal government would be two examples of this.[79] Avoiding controversial issues often means avoiding salient national issues and the committees that consider them. Successful efforts to bring federal dollars to a state or district often require that one avoid drawing national and broad congressional attention to the purposes for which the dollars are to be spent.[80]

A committee with jurisdiction over programs that have concentrated benefits (for one's constituents) but widely dispersed costs (taxes, consumer prices) is well suited to these needs. Such a committee is typically one with a narrow jurisdiction over programs of interest to a limited number of members and constituencies. Thus a committee with low national salience, high local salience, low conflict, and a narrow jurisdiction is especially attractive to constituency-oriented members. These committees are the classic pork-barrel committees of the House. The committees' products are readily identifiable by their names (further elaborated in most cases by their subcommittee arrangements). And they have a clear set of constituent consumers for these products.

This approach is summed up nicely in a comment made by Douglas H. Bosco (D-Calif.): "As far as I can see, there is really only one basic reason to be on the Public Works committee . . . certainly not for intellectual stimulation. Most of all, I want to be able to bring home projects to my district."[81]

Eight House committees attract members primarily for constituency-oriented reasons. An additional committee, Post Office and Civil Service, also is district-oriented but is nevertheless desired by so few members that it is listed in the "unrequested" category in Table 3-6. The most striking characteristic of member goals in the constituency committees is their stability. Only one of these committees, Science and Technology, has changed markedly in attractiveness during the past twenty years. The others have retained moderate attractiveness for the same balance of reasons observers noted fifteen or twenty years ago. It is not surprising then that several of these committees also feature quite distinctive patterns of regional representation (see Table 3-7).

Except for Science and Technology and Interior, neither agenda changes nor procedural reforms have had a major effect on the goal orientation of constituency committees. Most new issues retain a district orientation for members concerned about them. The constituency orientation is not surprising for committees whose jurisdictions involve clear benefits for limited constituencies. Of course, dramatic shifts in agendas are not likely to occur on constituency committees with very narrow jurisdictions, and when shifts do occur, they are likely to be short-lived. Procedural reforms alone do not make these committees any more attractive to members without relevant constituency interests or to members seeking committees for reasons of policy or chamber influence. In the absence of significant national issues, policy- and influence-oriented members will continue to see membership on other committees as more useful. Science and Technology, the only constituency committee that acquired substantial new formal jurisdiction, also increased in attractiveness to members for policy reasons.

UNREQUESTED COMMITTEES

In addition to Post Office and Civil Service, three House standing committees consistently attract few members. The first, Standards of Official Conduct, is a special case because of its unique jurisdiction over ethics violations by House members. As one party leader described it, "anyone who wants a seat on Standards doesn't deserve a seat on Standards." This comment reflects the discomfort felt (or that ought to be felt) by members sitting as judges of colleagues' behavior. The second committee, District of Columbia, attracts members of three types, as a committee member explained: (1) members from districts bordering the District who have constituency-related reasons for

TABLE 3-7 Regional Representation on Selected House Committees: 89th/90th, 96th/97th, and 99th/100th Congresses (Percent from Each Region)

Region	House seats per region			Agriculture			Interior			Merchant Marine		
	89/ 90	96/ 97	99/ 100	89/ 90	96/ 97	99/ 100	89/ 90	96/ 97	99/ 100	89/ 90	96/ 97	99/ 100
East	25%	24%	22%	11%	5%	2%	24%	14%	11%	33%	31%	31%
South	24	25	27	36	27	33	12	12	12	21	23	31
Border	6	6	6	4	4	7	9	8	7	7	10	10
Midwest	29	30	26	34	39	35	24	18	16	19	13	8
West	16	15	20	15	25	23	32	48	54	19	23	20

Note: Regions: East: Conn., Del., Maine, Mass., N.H., N.J., N.Y., Pa., R.I., Vt.; South: Ala., Ark., Fla., Ga., La., Miss., N.C., S.C., Tenn., Texas, Va.; Border: Ky., Md., Okla., W.Va.; Midwest: Ill., Ind., Iowa, Kan., Mich., Minn., Mo., Neb., N.D., Ohio, S.D., Wis.; West: Alaska, Ariz., Calif., Colo., Hawaii, Idaho, Mont., Nev., N.M., Ore., Utah, Wash., Wyo.

membership, (2) urban and black members who have a personal interest in District problems, and (3) members who serve as a favor to the chair, ranking minority member, or party leaders. The pool of potential interest is small, and the actual interest is even smaller. The committee's previous attractiveness came from its ability to influence personnel decisions, police activity, and other aspects of District of Columbia government (for personal benefit or the benefit of colleagues) and was eliminated after the Home Rule Charter was enacted in the early 1970s. The committee now is in the hands of a small number of members who look out for the District's interests on Capitol Hill.

Finally, House Administration's previous control of office accounts and supplies, which gave it special chamber influence when Wayne L. Hays was chair, was substantially reduced after Hays resigned in the midst of the Elizabeth Ray sex scandal and after the House reformed its accounting and personnel procedures in 1976. The committee retains a certain amount of cachet among relatively senior members. This, combined with a smaller than average size, also works to allow a handful of members to gain a second subcommittee chair in spite of rules limiting members to one such position. The committee's jurisdiction over election laws and campaign finance regulation is its only substantial policy attraction, but that alone is not enough to attract many younger members to the panel.

MEMBERS' GOALS IN THE SENATE

Members' goals are less easily characterized in the Senate than in the House. There are several reasons for this. First, mentions of chamber influence or prestige are less common in the Senate; for no Senate committee was this objective the most frequently mentioned motivation (Table 3-8). Second, reelection and other constituency-oriented motivations were mentioned by a higher proportion of Senate respondents than House respondents despite the fact that senators are up for reelection only once every six years. As a result, a number of Senate committees whose House counterparts are clearly policy-oriented are also constituency-oriented to a substantial extent. And the desire to be reelected appears to lead to a greater emphasis on publicity in the Senate than in the House, perhaps as a consequence of senators' larger and more diverse constituencies and their greater dependence on the electronic media for communicating with their constituents. For many senators, the publicity emphasis makes it more difficult to differentiate personal policy interest from reelection interest because both goals often entail attracting public attention to an issue.

Above all else, distinguishing committee types in the Senate is difficult because senators simply have a lower level of certainty and intensity about their motivations for preferring particular committees than do representatives.[82] The lack of intensity sensed among the Senate respondents in the 97th and 101st Congresses also reflects the larger number of opportunities the Senate committee system offers its members to pursue their goals. First, as mentioned earlier, nearly all senators receive a seat on one of four top committees. (Traditionally these have been Appropriations, Armed Services, Finance, and Foreign Relations, with Foreign Relations lagging in recent years.) Senators of both parties are permitted only one assignment on these committees. Second, senators' larger number of committee assignments permits them to pursue more easily both state and personal policy goals. By 1989, for example, the average senator had three standing committee assignments as compared to slightly more than two in 1955.[83] Third, several Senate committees have larger jurisdictions than their House cousins. This allows senators to pursue a wider range of personal political objectives on those committees. Finally, it is easier for Senate noncommittee members to influence a committee's decisions. This greater permeability is reinforced by the Senate's more open and flexible floor procedures, which make it easier for noncommittee members to amend bills after they are reported to the floor, to filibuster, or to place a *hold* on a bill. (In recent years, senators have been able to ask the majority leader to delay action on a bill, and as a matter of courtesy the majority leader has felt

TABLE 3-8 Committee Preference Motivations for New Senators (Pre-92d, 97th, and 101st Congresses)

Committee	Constituency			Policy			Prestige		
	Pre-92d	97th	101st	Pre-92d	97th	101st	Pre-92d	97th	101st
Policy Committees									
Budget	—	1	1	—	4	6		0	0
Foreign Relations	3	1	0	19	5	2	2	0	0
Governmental Affairs		1	0		3	0		0	0
Judiciary		2	0	9	7	2		0	0
Labor	2	3	0	4	4	1		0	0
Mixed Policy/ *Constituency Committees*									
Armed Services	4	4	4	4	6	4		0	0
Banking		2	1		3	6		0	0
Finance	4	8	1	13	9	2		4	1
Small Business	—	4	1	—	4	0		0	0
Constituency Committees									
Agriculture	4	13	8		2	2		0	0
Appropriations	31	6	3	15	3	3	2	2	3
Commerce	13	5	5	5	2	3		0	0
Energy	4	6	3	2	3	2		0	0
Environment	5	5	2	4	1	2		0	0
Unrequested Committees									
Rules and Administration		0	0		0	0		0	0
Veterans' Affairs		2	2	3	0	0		0	0

Source: See discussion and citations in text.

Note: Bullock does not report N's for cells with fewer than 2 cases; these have been left blank in this table.

bound by their requests.)[84] And senators, who have memberships on more committees and subcommittees and the ability to filibuster on the floor, often are in a better bargaining position than are their colleagues in the House.

POLICY COMMITTEES

Five Senate committees contain a majority of members who are policy-oriented in their approach to committee activity. Of the five, Foreign Relations is the most exclusively policy-oriented. Members of Foreign Relations mention such things as "personal interest," "my previous job

sent me to Central America often," "I wanted to broaden my experience," and "no real political reason" when commenting on why they
sought the committee. For at least a couple of decades now, Foreign
Relations members have not considered the committee especially
powerful or prestigious within the Senate. (For example, see the box on
p. 103.) As one Foreign Relations member said,

> Well, you know, it is fun to hobnob with foreign leaders and discuss
> world affairs, but it doesn't get me any place with my Senate col-
> leagues. . . . Foreign Relations doesn't have much legislative jurisdiction
> that's important to other senators—it's nothing like Finance or Appro-
> priations.

Senate Budget members also listed policy goals for their committee
activity particularly because budget issues figured prominently on the
national agenda. "Where the action is" was a phrase used by three junior
committee members during the 97th Congress. By the 100th Congress,
the centrality of budget deficits continued to attract members. "The issue
that has the single greatest bearing on our trade deficit is the budget
deficit," said Timothy Wirth (D-Colo.), a new Budget member. "It's also
the area over which Congress has the most control." [85] Some senators do
believe that Budget membership allows them to protect programs
important to their states.[86] As with the House Budget Committee, Senate
Budget's lack of direct substantive jurisdiction over programs and the
congressional budget process's high level of aggregation do not permit
its members to take much positive action on behalf of constituents or
colleagues.

Senate Governmental Affairs is much like House Government
Operations in its members' policy motivations. Although Governmental
Affairs in 1977 gained jurisdiction over areas that have a constituency
orientation in the House (civil service, postal service, District of Columbia), the committee's main attractions are its broad oversight authority
and a few issues such as government regulation and intergovernmental
relations. Committee leaders of both parties take pride in the committee's moderate political composition and have sought to maintain it
during recent congresses. No chamber influence or prestige is gained by
membership on Governmental Affairs, but some members perceive
electoral value accruing to them from publicity they receive in oversight
hearings.

Senate Labor and Human Resources and Senate Judiciary also are
similar to their House counterparts in their policy orientation. Both
attract members of ideological extremes who push their personal policy
views on divisive issues. Senate Labor differs from House Education and
Labor in that it has additional jurisdiction over health issues, which

Another Day, No Quorum

Sen. Claiborne Pell, D-R.I., chairman of the Foreign Relations Committee, has spent several hours in recent weeks sitting in a nearly empty meeting room waiting for his colleagues. Pell waited patiently for 47 minutes on June 2 before deciding that his committee was not going to get the necessary quorum for a meeting on a routine bill (S 928) authorizing $4.5 billion annually in fiscal 1990-91 for the State Department and related agencies.

Pell bemoaned the "profound lack of interest" in the bill as he gaveled the sparsely attended meeting to order. Three senators besides Pell had shown up for the meeting—Jesse Helms, R-N.C., Paul Simon, D-Ill., and Terry Sanford, D-N.C. A fourth, Paul S. Sarbanes, D-Md., walked in just as Pell closed the meeting. Seven members are needed under committee rules for a "working" quorum, and the 19-member committee needs 10 members present to report legislation.

Pell set another business meeting for June 6. The panel has been working on the bill intermittently since May 16, with progress delayed at several points by the lack of a quorum. Pell said he is anxious to complete work on the bill because Majority Leader George J. Mitchell, D-Maine, has offered floor time for it during the week of June 12.

Source: "Another Day, No Quorum," *Congressional Quarterly Weekly Report*, June 3, 1989, 1338.

senators see as a constituency-oriented, low-conflict policy area. Labor lost a strong constituency-oriented area, veterans' affairs, when the Veterans' Affairs Committee was created in the early 1970s. Senate Judiciary, like House Judiciary, is a difficult assignment for some members because of the salient social issues under its jurisdiction. At least four members attempted to leave Judiciary in the early 1980s for that reason. Not surprisingly, Senate party and committee leaders have had difficulty attracting members, especially of certain types, to these two committees over the last few years. In both cases, ideological factionalism within the parties has been a stumbling block to finding "acceptable" members and placing them on the committee involved.

MIXED POLICY/CONSTITUENCY COMMITTEES

Senators seeking assignment to the Finance, Armed Services, and Small Business committees express an even mix of policy- and constituency-related goals. A fourth committee, Banking and Urban Affairs, appears much more policy-oriented based upon our recent interviews than was the case in the 97th Congress. In the case of Finance, no change has occurred in the blend of members' motivations since the 1960s, when Fenno concluded that its members "emphasize about equally the pursuit of policy and reelection goals." Senators find the committee's jurisdiction over tax, trade, and Social Security matters both personally interesting and electorally useful. In contrast to Fenno's findings, however, a few members of the 97th Congress, both within the committee and outside it, viewed Finance as an influential and prestigious Senate committee. These senators clearly perceived Finance's tax jurisdiction as salient to the entire chamber, and several of them mentioned Finance members' ability to do favors for noncommittee members in writing tax legislation, applying terms such as "powerful," "influential," and "prestigious." Many senators identify Finance as the most powerful and prestigious Senate committee.

Armed Services and Small Business also are seen as useful for both policy and constituency reasons. The Senate Armed Services Committee is comparable to House Armed Services in that the significance to individual states of military installations, personnel, and defense contractors attracts many members. Similarly, on the policy side, a large number of Senate Armed Services members have strong and usually conservative policy views that coincide with their constituencies' interests. Nevertheless, the Senate committee attracts a larger contingent of members with insignificant state connections to the defense establishment who also have a personal policy interest in the committee's activities.

Our 1982 interviews showed Senate Banking to be more constituency-oriented than its House counterpart. According to one Senate Banking member at that time, the committee had lost some of its appeal to liberal activists when issues such as urban decay and redevelopment slipped from the national agenda during the 1970s. Though relatively few mentions appeared, our more recent interviews suggest that some change may have occurred. Urban and housing issues still attract members for state-oriented reasons, but personal interest in the committee's issues appears more pronounced, with the committee's jurisdiction being described as "interesting," "intellectually stimulating," and "educational." Small Business has had legislative jurisdiction only since 1977. While interest in Small Business is very low, it does attract members who are looking for another state-oriented committee and who have a small business background—members with a personal interest in the committee's jurisdiction.

CONSTITUENCY COMMITTEES

Six Senate committees attract senators primarily for constituency-related reasons. (So few senators desire Veterans' Affairs that it has been placed in the "undesired" category.) All six have exhibited little change in member goals during the past twenty years.

Senate Agriculture is the chamber's most purely constituency-oriented committee (see the box on p. 106). Like its House counterpart, Senate Agriculture's membership is disproportionately southern and midwestern, with the midwestern bias having grown during the 1970s and been maintained in the 1980s (Table 3-9). The Energy and Natural Resources Committee (Interior before the 1977 reforms) has retained primarily state-related interest for senators and, like House Interior, has retained a distinct western bias in its composition. But world events and the regrouping of energy jurisdiction in 1977 have changed the geographic composition of Energy and Natural Resources. A handful of senators from energy-poor states have been attracted to Energy and Natural Resources to protect their states' interests in the face of energy shortages and rising energy prices. Also, the addition of domestic atomic energy production, coal, and other energy matters to the committee's jurisdiction has attracted senators seeking to serve state interests. Energy issues have enticed to the committee several senators with personal policy interests in energy, but for the most part jurisdictional changes have reinforced its constituency orientation.

Throughout the 1960s, senators' primary objective on Appropriations was to provide funding for programs in their states, with chamber influence and good public policy of secondary interest. No evidence exists to indicate that this has changed in any important way. Appropriations still provides an opportunity for members seeking money for programs in their states to do favors for colleagues, and it thus provides some extra influence and prestige in the Senate. But when more than half of the states are represented on the committee, opportunities to serve noncommittee members are not nearly so numerous as they might be. If a change has occurred during the last decade or so, it has been toward a lighter emphasis on chamber influence or prestige. Personal policy goals seldom have been significant to most Appropriations members, although Republicans appointed to the committee since the late 1970s express some personal concern about holding down federal spending. The strength of their state orientation is indicated by the fact that the same Republicans were unhappy about spending cuts imposed on them by the budget resolutions of the 97th and 98th Congresses. This change in the budgeting environment has shifted their role away from one of merely serving as an appeals court for agencies and affected

The Senate Agriculture Committee: All Things to All Senators

It was a case of traditional farm politicking on a most untraditional farm bill.

After two years of trying, Agriculture Committee Chairman Patrick J. Leahy, D-Vt., finally maneuvered his prized rural-development bill (S 1036) through the Senate Aug. 2. Leahy has been pushing the idea of some sort of economic assistance package for rural America since he took over the committee in 1987. . . .

This year, Leahy came out with a modest, $300 million bill that was artfully crafted to bring his committee along. Republicans could not stomach the idea of creating an entirely new bureaucracy within the Agriculture Department . . . so Leahy proposed to channel the aid through established agencies and organizations. . . . The bill was constructed to give virtually every lawmaker on the committee a little of what he wanted. . . . Even that was not enough, however.

Before the bill passed the Senate, Leahy agreed to accept more than 30 floor amendments in order to get the support of various farm-state senators. . . . Member after member stepped forward with parochial amendments, and in the end, member after member was accommodated.

Here is a sample of the committee and floor amendments Leahy accepted on behalf of:

- Rudy Boschwitz, R-Minn., a provision that makes all cooperatively owned rural businesses eligible for revolving funds. . . .
- Christopher S. Bond, R-Mo., and Tom Harkin, D-Iowa, a provision increasing emergency water grants in the bill by $10 million. . . .
- Jim Exon, D-Neb., a provision authorizing the transportation secretary to provide grants to improve or maintain bus service to small towns.
- Dave Durenberger, R-Minn., a provision that makes non-profit organizations specializing in applied research, such as land grant colleges, eligible [for] research grants under the bill.
- Quentin Burdick, D-N.D., a provision that authorizes the agriculture secretary to make grants to public television systems in rural areas. . . .
- Howell Heflin, D-Ala., a provision that allows the Tennessee Valley Authority (TVA) to undertake rural-development projects in such areas as export trade expansion and manufacturing.
- John D. Rockefeller IV, D-W.Va., a provision that makes non-profit entities eligible for $10 million a year for the purpose of promoting business creation in rural areas.

Source: David S. Cloud, "All Things to All Senators," Congressional Quarterly Weekly Report, August 12, 1989, 2119.

TABLE 3-9 Regional Representation on Selected Senate Committees: 89th/90th, 96th/97th, and 99th/100th Congresses (Percent from Each Region)

Region	Senate seats per region	Agriculture			Energy & Natural Resources		
		89/90	96/97	99/100	89/90	96/97	99/100
East	20%	12%	5%	6%	0%	27%	11%
South	22	47	36	29	0	18	17
Border	8	6	9	12	0	9	17
Midwest	24	23	40	41	17	5	6
West	26	12	9	12	83	40	50

Note: Regions: *East:* Conn., Del., Maine, Mass., N.H., N.J., N.Y., Pa., R.I., Vt.; *South:* Ala., Ark., Fla., Ga., La., Miss., N.C., S.C., Tenn., Texas, Va.; *Border:* Ky., Md., Okla., W.Va.; *Midwest:* Ill., Ind., Iowa, Kan., Mich., Minn., Mo., Neb., N.D., Ohio, S.D., Wis.; *West:* Alaska, Ariz., Calif., Colo., Hawaii, Idaho, Mont., Nev., N.M., Ore., Utah, Wash., Wyo.

interests that suffered cuts in House action, to one of more actively protecting established programs.

Senate Commerce's balance of goals is the opposite of the balance on House Energy and Commerce. While Senate Commerce has had a core of strongly policy-oriented members for many years, the majority of senators attracted to the committee have had state-related goals. As for House Commerce, consumer protection, some environmental protection issues, and other areas have stimulated strong policy interest, as well as state-related interest, in Senate Commerce, but its broad jurisdiction over constituency-oriented areas, such as the merchant marine, U.S. Coast Guard, space programs, transportation, and tourism, attracts most members. Space programs were added to Commerce's jurisdiction when the Aeronautics and Space Sciences Committee was abolished in 1977. That jurisdiction remains under Science and Technology in the House. Senate Commerce also lacks most of the health and energy jurisdiction that attracts policy-oriented members to House Commerce, having lost some energy jurisdiction in the 1977 reforms. The Senate committee, in the view of two former aides, has become somewhat more constituency-oriented as a result of these agenda changes.

Finally, Senate Environment and Public Works has become even more constituency-oriented since the early 1970s. In the late 1960s and early 1970s, major legislation for control of air and water pollution was written in the committee, which in turn attracted senators with personal policy interests in the field. "Since then," one senior aide explained, "the committee has not been as much fun as it was. Those big issues are gone and we don't attract the same kind of member that we once did." In original proposals for jurisdictional reform, Public Works was slated to pick up additional jurisdiction over pesticides, ocean policy, coastal management, and other environmental areas that eventually were left under other committees' jurisdictions. Such a change might have boosted the interest of policy-oriented senators in the committee. Instead, the committee remains attractive to senators primarily for its jurisdiction over rivers and harbors, water projects, highways, and other constituency concerns.

UNREQUESTED COMMITTEES

Many members of both Rules and Administration and Veterans' Affairs indicate that they did not seek assignment to these committees. Rules and Administration primarily is concerned with Senate housekeeping matters, although it does have jurisdiction over election and campaign practices. But no special influence or reelection benefits are gained by membership on this committee. Veterans' Affairs members mention their association with veterans' programs and veterans' groups as electorally useful, but most members discount its value.

CONCLUSION

Despite the similarity of congressional environments in corresponding House and Senate committees, a marked difference continues to exist between chambers in the relative significance of the rank-and-file members and the party leadership. Chamber colleagues tend to be more important in the Senate than in the House. One thoughtful senator, a former House member, explains:

> When I wanted to influence a committee's decision in the House, all I could do is testify, talk to a few friends on the committee, and then, if I didn't like their bill, cast a lonely vote on the floor against it. But as soon as I walked into the Senate it became clear to me ... that my options are better here. Even after just four years, I tend to know more of the fellows on the committee better than I often did in the House, and everyone seems to respect the fact that you can go to the floor if you're not happy about what went on in committee.

This senator describes what Richard Fenno has termed the "permeability."[87] He also indicates two underlying causes of differences between the two chambers in this respect: the stronger personal relationships among senators and the greater importance of floor deliberations in Senate decision making. Fenno points out that the Senate's smaller size and greater overlap in committee memberships, the product of a larger number of assignments per member, permit strong relationships to develop among a higher proportion of senators.[88] As a result, noncommittee members in the Senate generally have greater access to committee members and thus have more opportunities to influence committee decisions. The House has opened some additional access to its committees as a result of the 1970s reforms, but the underlying causes for the differences remain.[89]

In contrast, House party leaders play a more significant role in committee environments than do Senate party leaders. House leaders have firmer control of resources important to committee members. Moreover, as we have seen, House leaders more firmly control committee assignments. In the larger House, the party whip systems, which can be used to gather information about support and opposition to committee bills, are often an important tool for committee members; they operate under party leaders' supervision. And House majority party leaders face fewer effective challengers to their control of floor scheduling than do Senate leaders, who must worry about filibusters destroying their plans. As a result, House committee members concerned about the fate of a controversial bill on the floor are more likely to seek out party leaders for assistance. In part, the role of House leaders reflects the Democratic reforms of the 1970s, but, as we saw in Chapter 1, it also represents long-term differences between the chambers.

Committees vary widely in the character of their jurisdictions and environments. They also differ greatly in the degree to which issues under their jurisdiction attract attention and engender conflict among interested outsiders. Some committees, such as the budget, commerce, judiciary, labor, and tax committees, regularly consider highly salient and controversial issues. Others, such as agriculture, veterans' affairs, and small business committees, have legislative jurisdictions that attract little attention and conflict. Jurisdictional reform and evolving national issues also affect committees' agendas and the character of their environments. Thus, in addition to opportunities and constraints associated with change in formal structures and procedures, shifting agendas and environments alter opportunities and constraints perceived by members.

Even though students of Congress have disagreed about what motivates members to seek one assignment rather than another, most of them agree that the committee systems play a central role in members' goal attainment. One observer notes that "if a group of planners sat down and tried to design a pair of American national assemblies with the goal of serving members' electoral needs year in and year out, they would be hard pressed to improve on what exists."[90] In contrast, others claim that "understanding the drive for internal power and status explodes the misconception that the activities of Capitol Hill are geared to reelection." [91] They argue that the fragmented committee systems are designed to fill members' insatiable hunger for bases of personal power.[92] In fact, Congress's committee systems are remarkably well suited to these and other member goals. Jurisdictional fragmentation certainly helps. Members representing similar constituencies can join together to determine policy affecting those constituencies with minimal interference from disinterested members; influence-oriented members thrive on their committees' exclusive jurisdictions; and members with particular policy interests are given an opportunity to focus on and have a major influence over policy decisions in those areas. Just as important, legislative jurisdiction, in terms of its salience and conflict potential, is not evenly distributed among congressional committees. As a consequence, members with different main goals can seek out committees suited to their needs and separately pursue those goals enthusiastically in their committee activities. This is truer in the House than the Senate, where fewer committees with more evenly divided jurisdictions make committee distinctions more difficult for members. But in both chambers the uneven distribution of jurisdiction, agendas, and environments facilitates the achievement of members' multiple goals.

NOTES

1. Jonathan Fuerbringer, "Desperately Seeking the Right Committees," *New York Times*, November 11, 1986.
2. Barbara Sinclair, *Majority Leadership in the U.S. House* (Baltimore: Johns Hopkins University Press, 1983), chap. 1.
3. Kenneth A. Shepsle, *The Giant Jigsaw Puzzle* (Chicago: University of Chicago Press, 1978), 111.
4. *National Journal*, February 4, 1989, 269.
5. *Congressional Quarterly Weekly Report*, November 22, 1986, 2935.
6. See Judy Schneider, "Senate Rules and Practices on Committee, Subcommittee, and Chairmanship Assignment Limitations, as of April 20, 1982," Congressional Research Service, May 18, 1982.
7. This discussion is adapted from Shepsle, *The Giant Jigsaw Puzzle*, chap. 6.
8. Louis P. Westefield, "Majority Party Leadership and the Committee System in the House of Representatives," *American Political Science Review* 69 (December 1974): 1593-1605.
9. Ibid., 1599.
10. Shepsle, *The Giant Jigsaw Puzzle*, 117-118.
11. Craig Winneker, "Seven Dems Get New Panel Seats," *Roll Call*, November 6, 1989, 18.
12. Richard E. Cohen, "Short-Circuiting a Republican Switch," *National Journal*,

November 18, 1989, 2842.
13. Bruce A. Ray and Steven S. Smith, "Leverage, Reward, Accommodation, and Administration: Four Theories on the Growth of Congressional Committee Seats" (paper presented at the annual meeting of the Southern Political Science Association, Atlanta, Georgia, October 27-30, 1982).
14. In 1989, the Republicans did attempt to strengthen the leaders' position somewhat by raising the number of votes cast by the floor leader from one to twelve and by the whip from one to six. Nonetheless, this amounts to only 18 votes out of a total of 195 possible in the committee's weighted voting scheme. Background on the dispute that led to this change may be found in Janet Hook, "Bitterness Lingers from GOP Assignments," *Congressional Quarterly Weekly Report*, May 16, 1987, 961.
15. On the House, see Sidney Waldman, "Majority Leadership in the House of Representatives," *Political Science Quarterly* 95 (Fall 1980): 373-393. On the Senate, see Robert L. Peabody, *Leadership in Congress* (Boston: Little, Brown, 1976), 349-350. During his brief tenure as Speaker, Jim Wright used committee assignments more aggressively than most recent occupants of that office. For examples, see John M. Barry, *The Ambition and the Power* (New York: Viking, 1989), 82-83, 467, 542, 568.
16. On the House, see Shepsle, *The Giant Jigsaw Puzzle*, 29. On the Senate tradition, see Donald R. Matthews, *U.S. Senators and Their World* (New York: Vintage Books, 1960), 127.
17. Robert L. Peabody, "Senate Party Leadership: From the 1950s to the 1980s," in *Understanding Congressional Leadership*, ed. Frank H. Mackaman (Washington, D.C.: CQ Press, 1981), 82.
18. Charles O. Jones, "Senate Party Leadership in Public Policy," in U.S., Senate, Commission on the Operation of the Senate, *Policymaking Role of Leadership in the Senate*, 94th Cong., 2d sess., 26.
19. Steven S. Smith, "The Budget Battles of 1981: The Role of the Majority Party Leadership," in *American Politics and Public Policy*, ed. Allan P. Sindler (Washington, D.C.: CQ Press, 1982), 43-78, esp. 49-50.
20. Gramm's switch was not entirely without cost. Not only did he join the House's minority party; he also lost a coveted seat on the Energy and Commerce Committee. As a Republican, he was limited to a single committee seat. Gramm subsequently resigned his House seat for a successful bid to become Texas's junior senator.
21. Shepsle, *The Giant Jigsaw Puzzle*, chap. 9; Steven S. Smith and Bruce A. Ray, "The Impact of Congressional Reform: House Democratic Committee Assignments," *Congress & the Presidency* 10 (Autumn 1983): 219-240.
22. On this issue, see Charles S. Bullock III and David England, "Prescriptive Committee Seats in Congress," unpublished manuscript, March 17, 1989, 1-42.
23. John Felton, "In Victory for Seniority System, Helms Wrests Post from Lugar," *Congressional Quarterly Weekly Report*, January 24, 1987, 143-144.
24. See Table 8-5 in Steven S. Smith and Christopher J. Deering, *Committees in Congress*, 1st ed. (Washington, D.C.: CQ Press, 1984), 243.
25. Smith and Ray, "The Impact of Congressional Reform."
26. Ray and Smith, "Theories on the Growth of Congressional Committee Seats."
27. For discussions of the problems of jurisdictional alignments, see U.S. Congress, Senate, Temporary Select Committee to Study the Senate Commit-

tee System, *The Senate Committee System*, 94th Cong., 2d sess., 151-187; U.S. Congress, Senate, The Commission on the Operation of the Senate, *Policy Analysis on Major Issues*, 94th Cong., 2d sess., 4-24; U.S. Congress, House, Select Committee on Committees, Monographs on the Committees of the House of Representatives, 93d Cong., 2d sess.

28. The claim that agendas and interested outsiders differ in important ways among committees would not be disputed by any observer of Congress, and yet identifying a useful set of properties to characterize committees' agendas and environments is a difficult task. One possible approach is to focus on the subject matter or policy decision per se, that is, to identify properties inherent to the policy issue itself. Properties such as the pattern of costs and benefits, complexity, divisibility, volume, and novelty have been noted. See, for example, John Ferejohn, *Pork Barrel Politics* (Stanford, Calif.: Stanford University Press, 1974), 5; James Q. Wilson, *Political Organizations* (New York: Basic Books, 1973), 330; Theodore J. Lowi, "American Business, Public Policy, Case Studies and Political Theory," *World Politics* 16 (July 1964): 677-715; John F. Manley, *The Politics of Finance* (Boston: Little, Brown, 1970), 92-95. Committees' agendas may differ on each of these properties and may become more or less alike over time.

   Policy properties, unfortunately, have proven difficult to use for empirical research. Consequently, most scholars attempt to establish the empirical import of their concepts only by example or else shift away from direct measures and rely instead on decision-makers' perceptions of issues they face. The latter approach usually is justified further on the grounds that it is the participants' perceptions that are significant anyway, although it is often implied that perceptions are closely related to the objective characteristics of issues. Unfortunately, when dealing with the multifaceted jurisdictions of congressional committees, even perceptual measures are difficult to employ rigorously.

   Policy properties, in turn, usually are assumed to have a strong causal connection to the nature of committees' political environments. James Q. Wilson, for example, argues that a policy with very concentrated benefits for a small segment of society, but with widely dispersed costs, will engender less interest and opposition than a policy with concentrated benefits and costs. See Wilson, *Political Organizations,* 327-337. From committee members' point of view, it is often the political alignments stimulated by an issue, rather than the characteristics of the issue itself, that are significant.

29. David E. Price, *Policymaking in Congressional Committees* (Tucson: University of Arizona Press, 1979), 45-50; also see David E. Price, "Policy Making in Congressional Committees: The Impact of 'Environmental' Factors," *American Political Science Review* 72 (June 1978): 549, 569-571.

30. Price, *Policymaking,* 564; E. E. Schattschneider, *The Semisovereign People* (Hinsdale, Ill.: Dryden Press, 1975), chap. 2.

31. Barbara Hinckley, "Policy Content, Committee Membership, and Behavior," *American Journal of Political Science* 19 (August 1975): 543-557.

32. Hinckley, "Policy Content"; Lowi, "American Business"; and Price, *Policymaking.*

33. The Budget committees have not been included in the ranking because, strictly speaking, they do not have direct jurisdiction over specific agencies or programs, except for the area of budget policy.

34. In absolute terms, Senate Governmental Affairs has a more complex environ-

ment than does House Government Operations because of its jurisdiction's greater diversity. The Senate committee gained jurisdiction over the Postal Service, the District of Columbia, and other areas in 1977.

35. An even better measure has been constructed by Stephen Hess. Hess has exploited the files of the Senate's press gallery staff to determine the number of cameras in committee hearings and meetings (from February 1979 to June 1985) that represented national and local media outlets. He then summarizes these using our grouping of Senate committees. And the results are fairly dramatic. For that period, 61.8 percent of the national cameras appeared at the seven policy committees, 15.0 percent at the three mixed policy/constituency committees, 19.6 percent at the constituency committees, and 3.4 percent at the two housekeeping panels (Rules and Ethics). By contrast, 49.3 percent of the local crews appeared at the policy committees, 15.7 percent at the mixed panels, 31.6 at the constituency panels, and 3.2 percent at the two housekeeping committees. Thus, Hess's findings provide additional support for our findings regarding the national and local appeal of Senate committees. Regrettably, no similar data are available for the House. We are grateful to Steve for an advance look at this research and for sharing other data with us in the past. See Stephen Hess, "Washington as Seen on Local TV Newscasts" (paper prepared for delivery at the annual meeting of the American Political Science Association, San Francisco, California, August 30-September 2, 1990, pp. 51-52). See also Stephen Hess, *The Ultimate Insiders: U.S. Senators in the National Media* (Washington, D.C.: Brookings Institution, 1986).

36. These data were collected from Vanderbilt Television News Archive, *Television News Index and Abstracts* (Nashville, Tenn.: Joint Universities Libraries, 1969-1980). This source provides a synopsis of each story and a running time count of each broadcast. Every other weekday news broadcast was used. Stories involving events that fell under no committee's jurisdiction, such as those on presidential election campaigns or World Series results, were excluded, as were features such as the daily stock market report. CBS stories were used because the CBS evening news program consistently had more viewers than ABC's or NBC's during the period examined.

   Three sets of news stories present special coding difficulties because they fall within the legislative jurisdictions of two or more committees. These sets are listed at the bottom of Table 3-4. The tallies for the affected committees do not include the time allocated to these stories and thus understate the media's attention to matters falling under their jurisdictions. In the case of the war in Indochina, the foreign policy and armed services committees shared common interests. No standing committee has explicit jurisdiction over the state of the economy, although committees with jurisdiction over fiscal and monetary policy, especially the appropriations, tax, and banking committees, have directly related jurisdictions. Finally, as noted in Chapter 2, several committees with jurisdiction over energy, especially the House Commerce Committee, have higher relative standing than their ranking indicates. Beginning in 1977, energy stories were placed under the Energy and Natural Resources Committee, reflecting the Senate's jurisdictional reforms.

37. This approach has two limitations. First, it provides a measure of national salience only. We have no comparable measure for salience within particular constituencies. Second, restricting the study to each committee's legislative jurisdiction means that topics a committee explores as a part of its wider

oversight jurisdiction are neglected. This restriction, which is necessary for reducing coding ambiguities, should not affect the relative standing of committees, with the exception of the House Government Operations and Senate Governmental Affairs committees.

38. Price, *Policymaking*, 46.

39. Andy Plattner, "Scrappy House Energy Panel Provides High Pressure Arena for Wrangling over Regulation," *Congressional Quarterly Weekly Report*, March 12, 1983, 502.

40. Stephen Gettinger, "Newest Budget Panel Members Confront Jargon, Turf Battles and a Looming Deficit," *Congressional Quarterly Weekly Report*, January 31, 1987, 189.

41. Richard F. Fenno, *Congressmen in Committees* (Boston: Little, Brown, 1973). The implication of Fenno's work and our earlier work, of course, is that members of committees from noncommittee members not only in their motivation for membership on congressional committees but also in terms of their policy preferences. We do not suggest that legislative outcomes or even committee outputs reflect these differences in every case. Anticipated responses by committee members, lack of positive power, and sheer indifference at the floor stage may mute those differences—at least as measured by committee and floor voting. Also, some committees are arguably "representative" of chamber majorities. Nonetheless, we do feel that differences go to substance as well as to motivation and indeed, that the two are closely linked. For a somewhat different view, at least regarding preference outliers, see Keith Krehbiel, "Are Committees Composed of Preference Outliers?" *American Political Science Review* 84 (March 1990): 149-163.

42. Charles S. Bullock III, "Motivations for U.S. Congressional Committee Preferences: Freshmen of the 92d Congress," *Legislative Studies Quarterly* 1 (May 1976): 201-212.

43. Bullock used this question in his study of the 92d Congress House freshmen. We used the same question during interviews with freshmen of the 97th Congress. See Steven S. Smith and Christopher J. Deering, "Changing Motives for Committee Preferences of New Members of the U.S. House," *Legislative Studies Quarterly* 8 (May 1983): 271-281.

44. This written record is not quite so useful because it often represents a senator's attempt to sell himself or herself to party leaders as a candidate for a particular committee assignment, instead of reflecting his or her genuine personal motivation for interest in a committee. The correspondence also excludes committee preferences expressed orally to party leaders and preferences that did not lead to a formal request for assignment. Charles S. Bullock III, "U.S. Senate Committee Preferences and Motivations" (paper prepared for the 1982 meeting of the American Political Science Association, Denver, Colorado, September 2-5, 1982).

45. Two additional motivations—predecessor cues and a delegate-model philosophy—were mentioned by members. Nine House freshmen in the 97th Congress indicated that they listed a committee because their predecessor was on the committee. In some cases, the predecessor's cue was tied directly to the reelection goal because freshmen saw the predecessor's assignments as an indicator of which committees would be useful at home. In most instances, though, the predecessor's assignments served merely to direct a member to certain committees, or else state delegation colleagues had

explicit expectations that someone from that state or district should fill the vacancy. Delegate philosophy motivations were expressed by many House and Senate members who believed that someone from their district or state ought to serve on a certain committee to represent its constituency properly. These members made no mention of reelection needs.

These variations in constituency-oriented motivations may stem from the focus of these data on preference motivations rather than on goals pursued after assignment. The predecessor version can lead merely to assignment to a certain committee (dictating no particular behavior once on the committee) and thus would be difficult to detect when focusing on participation in committee activities after appointment. The delegate motivation is more similar to the reelection motivation in that it usually requires further pursuit of district interests after appointment to the committee. Indeed, it is difficult to distinguish delegate-motivated from reelection-motivated behavior in committee activities, despite the fact that the two goals are clearly separable in members' responses about committee preferences. This interpretation is similar to the discovery by Herbert Weisberg and his colleagues that Ohio state legislators often distinguish between service to their constituents and reelection as goals for their activity. See Herbert S. Weisberg, Thomas Boyd, Marshall Goodman, and Debra Gross, "Reelection and Constituency Service as State Legislator Goals: It's Just Part of the Job" (paper prepared for the American Political Science Association's 1982 meeting, Denver, Colorado, September 2-5, 1982).

46. Eighty-five percent of our House respondents mentioned constituency concerns in interviews for the 100th/101st Congresses—down from 87 percent in the 97th. The Senate figures for constituency mentions are 85 percent (101st) and 100 percent (97th). Policy mentions: for the House, 74 percent (101st) down from 80 percent (97th); and for the Senate, 85 percent (101st) down from 89 percent (97th). Power/prestige mentions: for the House, 17 percent (101st) down from 34 percent (97th); and for the Senate, 15 percent (101st and 97th). These changes reflect a higher proportion of respondents mentioning only a single motivation during interviews.

47. Rules reported from the Rules Committee are in the form of simple resolutions that are passed by a majority vote on the House floor before a bill's consideration in the Committee of the Whole. The resolution stipulates in detail the conditions for debate on a piece of legislation.

48. Few Democrats actively consider Rules because the Speaker has virtual control over appointments; also, few freshmen mention it as a committee preference.

49. Janet Hook, "Influential Committees: Money and Issues," *Congressional Quarterly Weekly Report*, January 3, 1987, 23.

50. Bruce I. Oppenheimer, "The Rules Committee: New Arm of Leadership in a Decentralized House," in *Congress Reconsidered*, 1st ed., ed. Lawrence C. Dodd and Bruce I. Oppenheimer (New York: Praeger, 1977), 103-105.

51. On the development of these innovative rules, see Stanley Bach and Steven S. Smith, *Managing Uncertainty in the House of Representatives: Adaptation and Innovation in Special Rules* (Washington, D.C.: Brookings Institution, 1988). See also Walter J. Oleszek, "Legislative Procedures and Congressional Policymaking: A Bicameral Perspective," in *Congressional Politics*, ed. Christopher J. Deering (Chicago: Dorsey Press, 1989), 176-196.

52. Andy Plattner, "Rules Under Chairman Pepper Looks Out for the Demo crats," *Congressional Quarterly Weekly Report*, August 24, 1985, 1672.
53. Plattner, "Rules Under Chairman Pepper," 1672.
54. Hook, "The Influential Committees," 22.
55. See Fenno, *Congressmen*, 3-4.
56. Quoted in Diane Granat, "House Appropriations Panel Doles Out Cold Federal Cash, Chafes at Budget Procedures," *Congressional Quarterly Weekly Report*, June 18, 1983, 1209.
57. Fenno, *Congressmen*, 97; also see Richard F. Fenno, *The Power of the Purse* (Boston: Little, Brown, 1966), 141.
58. Granat, "House Appropriations," 1210.
59. Lance T. LeLoup, *The Fiscal Congress* (Westport, Conn.: Greenwood Press, 1980), 123.
60. Granat, "House Appropriations," 1215.
61. Fenno, *Congressmen*, 4.
62. See Malcolm E. Jewell and Chu Chi-Hung, "Membership Movement and Committee Attractiveness in the U.S. House of Representatives, 1963-1971," *American Journal of Political Science* 18 (May 1974), 433-441.
63. See John F. Manley, *The Politics of Finance* (Boston: Little, Brown, 1970), chap. 4.
64. Fenno, *Congressmen*, 4-5.
65. Catherine E. Rudder, "Committee Reform and the Revenue Process," in *Congress Reconsidered*, 1st ed., ed. Dodd and Oppenheimer, 128-130.
66. Ibid., 129.
67. On PAC contributions see Steven Pressman, "PAC Money, Honoraria Flow to Tax Writers," *Congressional Quarterly Weekly Report*, September 14, 1985, 1806.
68. Gettinger, "Newest Budget Panel Members," 188-189.
69. Allen Schick, *Congress and Money: Budgeting, Spending and Taxing* (Washington, D.C.: Urban Institute Press, 1980), 100.
70. Ibid., 110.
71. The House Budget Committee rejected strong reconciliation orders to other House committees in 1980, in contrast to its Senate counterpart.
72. Schick, *Congress and Money*, chap. 8.
73. LeLoup, *Fiscal Congress*, 53-61. Also see John W. Ellwood and James A. Thurber, "The Politics of the Congressional Budget Process Re-examined," in *Congress Reconsidered*, 2d ed., ed. Dodd and Oppenheimer, 254.
74. Schick, *Congress and Money*, 118, 129.
75. Controversy is not entirely without electoral benefits. Members of the Energy and Commerce Committee, for example, enjoyed a welcome rise in donations from PACs interested in the fate of the Clean Air Act in 1990. See Chuck Alston, "As Clean-Air Bill Took Off, So Did PAC Donations," *Congressional Quarterly Weekly Report*, March 17, 1990, 811-817.
76. Rules of the House Democratic Caucus distinguish committees as follows: exclusive—Appropriations, Rules, Ways and Means; major—Agriculture, Armed Services, Banking, Commerce, Education & Labor, Judiciary, Public Works; nonmajor—Budget, District of Columbia, Government Operations, House Administration, Interior, Merchant Marine, Post Office, Science & Technology, Small Business, Standards of Official Conduct, Veterans' Affairs. House Republicans use the designations "red," "white," and "blue," respectively, but they are the same with the exception that Energy and

Commerce is a "red" or exclusive committee.

77. Janet Hook, "House Leaders Make Committee Assignments," *Congressional Quarterly Weekly Report*, January 10, 1987, 86.
78. Careful readers may note that we have dropped Education and Labor's (ambiguous) double listing that appeared in the first edition of this book. There is some consensus that the committee had become fairly dormant, at least as far as labor was concerned. It also frequently lost its legislative battles on the floor. For more see Richard E. Cohen, "Labor Comes Alive," *National Journal*, July 16, 1988.
79. Morris P. Fiorina, *Congress—Keystone of the Washington Establishment*, 1st ed. (New Haven: Yale University Press, 1977), 41-46.
80. Randall Ripley and Grace A. Franklin, *Congress, the Bureaucracy, and Public Policy* (Homewood, Ill.: Dorsey Press, 1980), 92-110.
81. Alan Fram, "A Member's Menu for Airport Pork," *Washington Post*, May 14, 1987.
82. This observation is consistent with Fenno's findings, of course. See Fenno, *Congressmen*, 148.
83. Norman J. Ornstein et al., *Vital Statistics on Congress, 1989-90* (Washington, D.C.: CQ Press, 1990), 120. See also on this point Barbara Sinclair, "The Distribution of Committee Positions in the U.S. Senate: Explaining Institutional Change," *American Journal of Political Science* 32 (May 1988): 277-301.
84. In mid-1983, Republican Senate majority leader Howard Baker of Tennessee announced that he would no longer feel compelled to honor "holds" on legislation. Holds had become so commonplace that Baker found it very difficult to set the schedule for the floor. Nonetheless, his attempts, and those of his successors, failed. See Oleszek, "Legislative Procedures," 186-188.
85. Gettinger, "Newest Budget Members," 188.
86. Schick, *Congress and Money*, 95, 99.
87. Fenno, *Congressmen*, 148.
88. Ibid., 145-148. This is not a universally accepted point of view. Some recently elected senators have argued that while they knew a smaller portion of the much larger House, they knew those members better. In the Senate, by contrast, larger staffs, more work, and generally pressing schedules generate broader familiarity but fewer close friendships.
89. For a somewhat different view, see Norman J. Ornstein, "The House and the Senate in a New Congress," in *The New Congress*, ed. Thomas E. Mann and Norman J. Ornstein (Washington, D.C.: American Enterprise Institute for Public Policy Research, 1981), 367-369.
90. David Mayhew, *Congress: The Electoral Connection* (New Haven: Yale University Press, 1974), 81-82.
91. Rochelle Jones and Peter Woll, *The Private World of Congress* (New York: Free Press, 1979), 235.
92. Ibid., chaps. 3 and 6; see also Lawrence C. Dodd, "Congress and the Quest for Power," in *Congress Reconsidered*, 1st ed., ed. Dodd and Oppenheimer, 270-272.

CHAPTER 4

Committee Leaders, Subcommittees, and Staff

Each congressional committee has an internal world of its own. Most members serve on their committees for many years, often decades, gaining long-standing friendships, and sometimes making enemies, while waiting their turns for leadership posts. Each committee seems to have its own clown, bully, curmudgeon, and compromiser, and each develops its own traditions and standard operating procedures. Rapid turnover in membership occasionally transforms the character of a committee, but in most cases the mix of policy problems, political demands, and personal goals present on the committee yields substantial continuity in how it conducts its internal affairs.

The central place of committees in writing legislation means that control over committee decisions often is critical to eventual policy choices by Congress. This chapter assesses the role of committee chairs, subcommittees, and committee staff. Three themes emerge. First, the power of full committee chairs has declined in recent decades but remains remarkably strong in most committees. Second, subcommittees have become far more important to policy decisions in the House, but not in the Senate. And third, the internal decision-making practices of House and Senate committees vary greatly, each reflecting the character of its jurisdiction and political environment, as well as the mix of political goals pursued by its members.

COMMITTEE LEADERSHIP

Each party designates its formal leader for each committee and subcommittee.[1] The majority party names the chairs of all committees and subcommittees, and the minority party appoints a "ranking minority member" for every committee and subcommittee. By tradition, the parties select their committee leaders on the basis of seniority, subject to

119

certain restrictions on the number and type of such positions any one member may hold. The member of each party with the longest continuous service on a committee serves as the chair or ranking minority member, and subcommittee chairs and ranking minority posts are allocated by choice in order of committee seniority. Accruing seniority toward leadership posts is one reason members are reluctant to transfer to other committees, where they must start at the bottom of the seniority ladder.

The ironclad rule of seniority was broken in both the House and Senate chambers by the mid-1970s with adoption of new party rules that require the secret-ballot election of full committee chairs and ranking minority members. House Democrats led the way by requiring that all committee chairs and subcommittee chairs of the Appropriations Committee stand for election in the Democratic Caucus at the start of each congress. Three full committee chairs were deposed in 1975, another was defeated in 1985, and an Appropriations subcommittee chair was replaced in 1977.

Subcommittee chairs traditionally were appointed by the full committee chair of each committee, giving full committee chairs the opportunity to manipulate subcommittee activity. That procedure also was transformed into a more egalitarian one in the 1970s. House Democrats require that committee Democrats bid for subcommittee chairs in order of seniority and that their choices be ratified by a majority vote of the party members on the committee. While seniority generally is observed by this procedure, it gives to party members on the committee the right to reject a subcommittee chair and elect an alternative. This has happened more than a dozen times since the mid-1970s. House Republicans leave the appointment process to each committee's ranking minority member, but in practice Republicans select most of their subcommittee ranking members by seniority on the committee. In the Senate, both parties also allow committee members to select their subcommittee chairs or ranking positions in order of seniority.

In order to limit the power of senior members and give more members committee leadership posts, both chambers moved in the 1970s to limit the number and type of chairs any one member can hold. In the House, the rules of the Democratic Caucus limit its members to one full committee and one subcommittee chair. Full committee chairs may only chair a subcommittee on the committee they chair. Senators, in contrast, are limited to one subcommittee chair on each of the committees on which they serve (normally three), with the exception of full committee chairs, who are limited to chairing two subcommittees in most cases.

FULL COMMITTEE CHAIRS IN THE HOUSE AND SENATE

The full committee chair is the most powerful member on the vast majority of committees. The chair, who benefits from years of experience in dealing with the policy problems and constituencies of the committee, exercises considerable control over the agenda of the committee, schedules meetings and hearings of the full committee, influences the scheduling of subcommittee meetings and hearings, normally names conferees, controls the committee budget, supervises a sizable full committee staff, and often serves as a spokesperson for the committee and party on issues that fall within the committee's jurisdiction. Consequently, the support of the full committee chair can be critical to bill sponsors and opponents. That is as true today as it was thirty and forty years ago.

Generally speaking, the negative or blocking power of committee chairs is stronger than their positive power to get legislation passed. The blocking power of a chair stems primarily from the ability to delay consideration of legislation by the committee even when a majority of its members favors the legislation and a subcommittee has endorsed it. In both the House and Senate, rules provide ways for members to call committee meetings if the chair refuses to do so, but the process is cumbersome and seldom employed.

Moreover, the negative power of chairs is stronger in the House than in the Senate. In the House, the most obvious way of circumventing an obstructionist chair—offering a bill as a floor amendment to another bill—rarely is possible because of a strict rule requiring amendments to be germane to the bill on the floor. The Senate lacks a general germaneness rule for amendments, which allows senators to sponsor floor amendments that embody legislation being blocked in committee. And yet chairs can do favors for their colleagues, such as expediting the consideration of another bill or agreeing to hold a hearing on an issue, that give them something to trade for support in their efforts to block legislation. Thus, chairs have substantial advantages over rank-and-file members and can deter routine circumvention of standard committee practices, even in the Senate.

Full committee chairs vary in the manner and degree to which they exploit parliamentary procedure to influence committee decisions. To a degree, of course, this variation is a function of personality, but it also is a function of the political context in which chairs operate. Chairs who frequently find themselves in combat with committee colleagues and outsiders on highly controversial legislation cannot afford to take the same approach as chairs who normally find consensus on major legislation within their committees. Broadly speaking, chairs of prestige and policy committees are more likely to find themselves in a political struggle with committee colleagues and therefore are more likely to exploit the full range of their parliamentary tools to pursue their policy objectives.

Nevertheless, compared with their predecessors of the 1950s and 1960s, committee chairs now are more constrained and accountable and find more effective competitors for control of the policy recommendations of their committees. This is due in part to changes in the formal rules limiting chairs' discretion on a variety of procedural matters, particularly in the House, and in part to the acquisition of resources by other members who may not share the policy views of chairs.

The House and the House Democratic Caucus adopted rules in the 1970s to reduce the influence of full committee chairs on the decisions of their committees by democratizing full committee procedures and requiring more formal powers for their subcommittees. (See Chapter 2 for details.) The Senate lacks chamber rules that directly limit the role of committee chairs in organizing their committees. Like the House, however, the Senate also adopted rules in the 1970s that provide guidelines for the conduct of committee meetings, hearings, and voting, and require committees to publish additional rules governing committee procedures. But, unlike the House, Senate chamber and party rules do not specify internal committee organization in any detail and are silent on the functions of subcommittees.

Compared with the rules of House committees, most Senate committees' rules are very brief and usually do not even mention the structure, jurisdictions, or functions of subcommittees. In most cases, the full committee chair is assumed to have great discretion, although even that is left unstated. The referral of legislation to subcommittees, the discharge of legislation from subcommittees, and the distribution of power between the full committee and subcommittees remain under the formal control of nearly all the Senate's full committee chairs. Nonetheless, most committees abide by the practice of allowing senators to choose a subcommittee before anyone receives a second choice. Thus, Senate chairs are granted more discretion in designing the internal decision-making processes of their committees than House chairs, and Senate subcommittee chairs enjoy less autonomy than their House counterparts.

It is in the House, then, that the ability of full committee chairs to control committee decisions by procedural means has declined the most in recent decades. Even the ability to keep issues off the agenda was undermined by the empowerment of subcommittees. House committee chairs must be responsive to the demands of the Democratic Caucus or risk losing their positions, and they must tolerate independent subcommittees with professional staffs. Senate chairs enjoy greater freedom in the internal affairs of their committees, but they must tolerate and anticipate more frequent and successful efforts to circumvent their committees altogether. In both chambers, however, a majority of committee members may call and set the agenda for committee meetings if chairs refuse to do so on their own authority.

Resources acquired by other members also reduced the power of full committee chairs. We have noted the guarantee of staff for subcommittees and the minority party contingents. In addition, rank-and-file members of both chambers gained larger personal staffs to support their legislative activity. In the House, a limit on the number of people a member could hire for a personal staff increased from just eight employees in the 1950s to eighteen full-time and four part-time employees today. In the Senate, no limit exists on the number of persons to be hired; rather, senators are limited by a budget, which is set according to state size and has greatly increased in recent decades. The effect has been to increase the average senator's personal staff from around ten in the early 1960s to more than forty in the 1980s. Rank-and-file members benefited from other developments as well. As organized groups have proliferated in Washington, rank-and-file members have found additional sources of expertise, bill-drafting assistance, and support for building coalitions. Innovations in information technology have increased the ability of nonleaders to gather information that challenges the assertions of committee chairs. And the expansion of the congressional support agencies (Congressional Budget Office, Congressional Research Service, Office of Technology Assessment, and General Accounting Office) in the last two decades has multiplied the number of experts whom members can summon for assistance at any time.

A consequence of larger subcommittee and personal staffs and improved political resources is that more members have the capacity to participate in committee decision making in a meaningful and timely way. Committee chairs no longer monopolize access to policy and political expertise, they are less likely to win by default because potential opponents could not draft timely amendments, and they can count on their competition to appeal important decisions to the floor and to the other chamber. In short, the context of committee chairs has become substantially more complex, less predictable, and more competitive.

COMMITTEE TYPES AND CHAIRS

The role of full committee chairs is shaped in important ways by the rules and practices of each chamber. Formal rules have become more constraining in the House than in the Senate during the last two decades. Moreover, House members seem to be more insistent that their chairs carefully observe formal procedures. Senate chairs often are given substantial leeway as long as no senator's interests are affected. These patterns reflect the tendency of the House to rely on formal procedures more heavily than the Senate does.

Within the constraints set by formal rules, the role of full committee chairs is shaped by other characteristics of their committees.[2] Systematic analysis of such questions is virtually nonexistent, but a few informed observations are in order. Most obviously, the character of committees' agendas directly conditions the role of full committee chairs. In general, chairs facing highly fragmented, nationally salient, and divisive agendas confront the greatest challenges. In response, chairs on the prestige and policy committees (see Chapter 3 for details on these categories) generally attempt to build large committee staffs. But the sheer size of these committees' agendas usually requires full committee chairs to set their own priorities carefully and to become actively involved in writing legislation on only a few of the most important issues. In some cases, particularly in the House, chairs are most active in their capacity as chairs of subcommittees, where they are free to pursue issues and investigations quite independently.

Chairs on prestige and policy committees also have personal policy goals and often find themselves in conflict with committee colleagues. As a result, chairs of such committees are policy combatants who draw upon their formal and personal resources to further a cause. While they would like to develop a consensus behind their own positions, consensus positions cannot be found on many important issues. Therefore, successful chairs of prestige and policy committees are generally very assertive and known for their aggressiveness in promoting particular issues and policy positions. Dan Rostenkowski (D-Ill.) of House Ways and Means, John Dingell (D-Mich.) of House Energy and Commerce, Bob Dole (R-Kan.) of Senate Finance, and Edward Kennedy (D-Mass.) of Senate Labor and Human Resources are examples of aggressive chairs of prestige and policy committees.

Constituency committee members appear to have more clearly defined expectations about committee leadership than do policy committee members. Unlike policy committee members, whose definition of a "good" leader varies from issue to issue, constituency committee members seek a dependable, consensus-oriented leader committed to providing or preserving benefits for fairly stable, predictable, and bounded constituencies. Logrolling, comity, and specialization are stronger on constituency committees than elsewhere, and leaders are expected to reinforce these norms. Constituency committee members who want to compliment their chairs describe them as "consensus builders," "pragmatists," and "permissive" leaders, rather than as aggressive friends or foes. Maintaining a usually long-standing coalition in support of constituency benefits is normally the first priority for constituency committee chairs.

SUBCOMMITTEE CHAIRS IN THE HOUSE AND SENATE

The number of members who hold subcommittee chairs has increased dramatically in recent decades (Table 4-1). The increase was due to the growth in the number of subcommittees (see Chapter 2) and to rules adopted in both chambers during the 1970s that limit the number of such chairs held by a single member. House Democrats bar full committee chairs from heading more than one subcommittee and prohibit them from heading a subcommittee on a committee that they do not chair. More than half of the House Democrats now hold chairs, up from just over one-quarter in 1955. The Senate limits its members to chairing no more than one subcommittee on any one committee. Nearly all members of the Senate majority party chair a committee or subcommittee and, in 1989-1990, just over half of the majority party Democrats held two or three subcommittee chairs on standing committees.

The expansion in the number of House subcommittee chairs increased the speed with which majority party members could expect to obtain a formal committee leadership position. In 1979-1980, after the reforms, new subcommittee chairs had served an average of less than six years in the House, less than half of the nearly twelve-year average of a decade earlier. Typical House subcommittee chairs now are less experienced than chairs of the 1950s and 1960s and they are substantially less experienced than full committee chairs. But these changes also mean that more members, at an early stage in their congressional career, gain control over subcommittee staff and are in a position to pursue their own policy interests through subcommittee hearings and meetings.

How important is the expansion in the number of subcommittee chairs? It is possible that full committee chairs continue to manage legislation, dictate strategy, and control policy within their committees. After all, subcommittee recommendations must be approved by the full committee. Unfortunately, it is very difficult to determine, with any precision, the extent to which genuine legislative leadership responsibilities have shifted from full committee chairs to subcommittee chairs. But the evidence is clear that members consider subcommittee chairs to be important.

One indication of this importance is that several House members in

TABLE 4-1 Number of Committee or Subcommittee Chairmanships and Percent of Majority Party Holding Chairmanships, Selected Congresses (1955-1990)

Congress	Number of committee and subcommittee chairmanships [a]	Percent of majority party holding chairmanships
House		
84th (1955-1956)	102	27.2
90th (1967-1968)	153	44.9
94th (1975-1976)	173	49.1
98th (1983-1984)	152	46.4
100th (1987-1988)	162 [b]	49.6
Senate		
84th (1955-1956)	103	87.5
90th (1967-1968)	115	85.9
94th (1975-1976)	168	91.9
98th (1983-1984)	119	96.3
100th (1987-1988)	101	87.0

Source: Norman J. Ornstein, Thomas E. Mann, and Michael J. Malbin, *Vital Statistics on Congress, 1987-1988* (Washington, D.C.: Congressional Quarterly, Inc., 1987), 128-129, 131-132.

[a] Standing committee and subcommittee chairmanships only.

[b] Includes formal task forces when committee has no other subcommittees.

line for subcommittee chairs have been rejected by committee colleagues in favor of less senior competitors (see the box on p. 127). Between the mid-1970s and mid-1980s, more than a dozen subcommittee chairs and heirs apparent were challenged.[3] In 1985, for example, George E. Brown, Jr. (D-Calif.), was next in line for a subcommittee chair on the House Science and Technology Committee. After more senior members made their subcommittee choices, Brown chose the subcommittee with jurisdiction over the space program. Brown had been a critic of the space shuttle program and other activities of the National Aeronautics and Space Administration (NASA). His views were not completely in line with his Democratic colleagues on the committee, who generally supported the space shuttle and NASA. Brown was challenged successfully by Bill Nelson (D-Fla.), whose district is home to the Kennedy Space Center and related aerospace and defense industries.[4] Nelson later flew in the space shuttle.

Significantly, virtually no serious challenges to incumbent sub-

Challenging Seniority in Subcommittee Chairs

Since Rep. Bruce A. Morrison became chairman in February [1989] of the Judiciary Subcommittee on Immigration, Refugees and International Law, world events have propelled thousands of refugees and would-be immigrants toward U.S. shores.

Now, after having temporarily "cleared the decks" of refugee emergencies, the new chairman is taking on the visa-allotment system, prodded by Senate passage in July of a major revision to legal-immigration policy. . . .

Morrison has shepherded through the subcommittee legislation that would aid Soviet Jews, Chinese students, Nicaraguans and Salvadorans who are either seeking shelter here or are already in the country, some illegally. Although he insists "we should tie the [refugee] numbers to what we can pay for," Morrison basically has responded with beckoning arms to those escaping persecution.

So far, Morrison, 44, has impressed members and immigration activists with his diligence and leadership.

But some question how effective he will be, given that the powers he must ultimately bargain with—Judiciary Chairman Jack Brooks, D-Texas, veteran Senate immigration experts Edward M. Kennedy, D-Mass., and Alan K. Simpson, R-Wyo., and the administration—are generally more conservative on the question of who should be let into the country.

On Feb. 2, 1989, Judiciary Committee Democrats chose Morrison to lead the subcommittee after voting 16-5 to strip Rep. Romano L. Mazzoli, D-Ky., of the chairmanship. The ouster was masterminded by the other subcommittee Democrats, who were aided by members of the full committee equally dissatisfied with Mazzoli.

Still Mazzoli is a tough act to follow.

He had held the post for eight years and had coauthored (with Simpson) several versions of a landmark immigration bill that finally cleared in 1986. The law (PL 99-603), six years in the making, sought to clamp down on illegal immigration.

Morrison's liberal slant on immigration policy and his intensity distinguish him from Mazzoli. So does his tendency to invite in a wide cast of witnesses to hearings. Ranking Minority [m]ember Lamar Smith of Texas quipped, "I do get tired of sitting in the same chair for six or seven hours a day."

But it is that effort to hear from all sides that pleases panel members such as Smith, who has clashed with Morrison on standards for refugee status.

"Bruce is intellectually honest," Smith said. "He is interested in getting to the heart of issues. He is fair in his approach to those with differing opinions."

Source: "Chairman Morrison: Open Arms," *Congressional Quarterly Weekly Report,* September 30, 1989, 2567.

committee chairs or heirs apparent have occurred in recent years in the Senate. As we explore further below, subcommittee leadership positions are not worth fighting over on most Senate committees. On many Senate committees, subcommittees do not have a role in writing legislation, and on nearly all Senate committees the work of subcommittees on important legislation is shown little deference by the full committee.

More systematic evidence on the importance of subcommittee chairs also is being gathered. Two scholars, C. Lawrence Evans and Richard L. Hall, have attempted to measure with some care the roles of members in the internal deliberations of a few House and Senate committees. By asking informed committee staff about the influence of committee members on specific bills and tracking the level of participation in committee markups, Evans and Hall were able to rank committee members by their contributions to the legislative product of the committee. Not too surprisingly, Evans's study of four Senate committees demonstrates that the most active and influential members are the full committee and subcommittee chairs and ranking minority party members, with other members of the relevant subcommittees following in importance.[5] Senate subcommittee leaders were more active participants in shaping the content of legislation than full committee leaders, Evans found, although the tendency was more pronounced on two of the committees studied—Judiciary, and Labor and Human Resources—than on the other two—Commerce, Science, and Transportation, and Environment and Public Works. However, when it came to using procedural tools to slow or speed committee consideration of legislation, full committee chairs were somewhat more active than subcommittee chairs.[6] Similarly, Evans and Hall found House subcommittee chairs and ranking minority party members the most active participants in shaping the content of legislation on Energy and Commerce, Agriculture, and Education and Labor, followed in roughly descending order by full committee chairs, full committee ranking minority members, and other members of the reporting subcommittee.[7]

Evans's and Hall's findings support the now accepted view that subcommittee leaders are the central players in most legislative battles. Unfortunately, only a few committees have been studied with the care represented in Evans's and Hall's studies. Just as important, no committees have been studied over time with the systematic approach of Evans and Hall, which has prevented an assessment of change in patterns of influence within committees.

In the absence of detailed analysis of the sort developed by Evans and Hall for several congresses, we must rely on a less refined indicator to assess change in the role of subcommittee chairs over time. One such measure is the frequency with which subcommittee chairs manage legislation on behalf of their committees when the legislation reaches the chamber floors.[8] Each bill coming to the House or Senate floor is "managed" by a member who assumes the leading role in debate, defends the bill against unfriendly amendments, and normally controls time for the majority party when the time for general debate is restricted. Sometimes the skills of the bill manager—knowledge of parliamentary procedure, sensitivity to shifting policy preferences, and good personal relations with colleagues—are crucial to preserving committee recommendations. At other times, lack of controversy on the floor makes bill management a ministerial function. But even then, bill management can have symbolic importance because it indicates who represents the committee on that matter before the chamber.

Since 1971, the Democratic Caucus of the House has directed committee chairs to allow subcommittee chairs to manage bills whenever possible. In the following years, after the adoption of the reforms guaranteeing a meaningful role for House subcommittees, this proved to be a quite natural responsibility for subcommittee chairs. As Table 4-2 indicates, subcommittee chairs now manage most of the bills that reach the House floor. Full committee chairs still manage legislation out of proportion to their numbers, and they manage some of the most important legislation. For example, the major legislative product of the House Armed Services Committee, its annual defense authorization bill, is managed by the full committee chair with the assistance of sub-committee chairs. But the basic pattern for the House in recent congresses is for subcommittee chairs to manage the legislation that originates in their subcommittees. In some cases, particularly for the Banking, Energy and Commerce, Judiciary, and Ways and Means committees, the central role of subcommittee chairs as bill managers represents a sharp break with the practice of the pre-1970s period.[9]

There has been no need for a rule on bill management in the Senate, where bill sponsors long have managed their own legislation on the floor (Table 4-2). In many cases, it is the full committee or subcommittee chair with jurisdiction who serves as both sponsor and bill manager. In recent decades, the most important change in the Senate has been the assumption of more bill management duties by the majority leader. Since the early 1970s, majority leaders have sought ways to streamline floor consideration of minor, noncontroversial bills. By managing such bills themselves, floor leaders minimize the speechmaking by bill sponsors and often save sponsors the trouble of having to go to the floor for the consideration and passage of their bills. Both Democratic majority leader Robert Byrd (in the 96th Congress) and Republican majority leader Robert Dole (in the 99th Congress) assumed personal responsibility for shepherding bills through.[10] The reliance on

TABLE 4-2 Institutional Position of Bill Managers, Selected Congresses (1955-1986), in Percentages

Institutional position	Congress							
	86th (1955-1956)	89th (1965-1966)	91st (1969-1970)	92d (1971-1972)	93d (1973-1974)	94th (1975-1976)	95th (1977-1978)	99th (1985-1986)
House								
Full committee chair	54.1	48.3	40.0	39.4	35.7	30.8	28.2	25.2
Subcommittee chair	30.3	41.8	49.0	49.4	53.1	63.3	66.9	70.6
Other	15.6	10.0	11.1	11.2	11.1	5.9	4.9	4.2
Total	100.0	100.1	100.1	100.0	99.9	100.0	100.0	100.0
Senate								
Full committee chair	15.3		14.3				13.6	12.2
Subcommittee chair	30.6		26.8				21.9	11.2
Majority leader/whip	12.7		23.2				45.2	59.0
Other	41.4		35.7				19.4	17.6
Total	100.0		100.0				100.1	100.0

Source: Congressional Record.

bill sponsors and the majority leaders to manage bills has meant that Senate committee and subcommittee chairs manage a very small proportion of bills compared with their House counterparts. As we will see, this also reflects the less significant role of Senate subcommittees generally.

PARTY SUPPORT AMONG COMMITTEE AND SUBCOMMITTEE CHAIRS

In the 1950s, 1960s, and early 1970s, the Democratic majorities in both chambers were substantially more liberal in ideological outlook than many full committee chairs. As we noted in Chapter 2, this mismatch of committee leaders and their party caucus was a by-product of the seniority system and the defeat of many northern, more liberal Democrats in the 1946 and 1952 elections when the Republicans gained majorities in both chambers. Southern conservatives continued to gain seniority on their committees and eventually gained a disproportionate share of the chairs. The reforms of the 1970s were, in part, a reaction to the power exercised by chairs whose policy views were not congruent with those of most of their fellow partisans. Conditions gradually changed. Turnover due to retirement, election defeat, and death eventually led to more liberal Democrats holding chairs during the late 1960s and 1970s. Remaining conservative chairs moderated their policy positions, particularly in the House, where they faced election by the Democratic Caucus every two years. In terms of their voting behavior on partisan issues, chairs in both chambers increased their support for positions supported by a majority of their party (Table 4-3). The trends in each chamber are worthy of note.

In the House, the trend among chairs is quite remarkable when compared with the trend in party voting among all Democrats. In 1971-1972, full committee chairs were far less supportive of party positions than the average Democrat; indeed, the average party support score for full committee chairs was nearly identical to the average score for southern Democrats. Party reforms to make chairs more accountable, along with a few retirements, yielded higher levels of party support among chairs. Since the mid-1970s, when the reforms were instituted, full committee chairs have been at least as supportive of party positions as the average Democrat, and usually have been nearly as supportive as northern Democrats. Subcommittee chairs, whose accountability runs to committee colleagues rather than to the party caucus, actually have been somewhat less supportive of party positions, on average, than the typical Democrat, although they are substantially more supportive than southerners, on the whole.[11]

In the Senate, separate scores for subcommittee chairs are not

TABLE 4-3 Percent Support for Party Positions Among Full Committee Chairs, Subcommittee Chairs, and Party Groups, Selected Congresses (1971-1986)

Group	92d (1971-1972)	93d (1973-1974)	94th (1975-1976)	95th (1977-1978)	96th (1979-1980)	97th (1981-1982)	98th (1983-1984)	99th (1985-1986)
House								
Leaders [a]	78.3	85.3	87.0	80.0	82.6	73.5	74.5	84.8
Full committee chairs	47.2	56.1	62.8	69.1	71.3	70.5	76.3	79.6
Subcommittee chairs	53.6	65.5	64.1	64.2	68.1	68.9	75.5	78.8
All Democrats	65.6	57.7	67.7	65.4	68.6	70.5	75.0	79.3
Northern Democrats	74.9	71.2	77.2	72.8	74.6	77.5	80.8	83.1
Southern Democrats	47.5	37.5	46.6	48.4	56.3	54.3	60.7	69.3
Senate								
Leaders [a]	70.0	74.0	72.0	78.5	82.5	86.5	82.1	91.3
Full committee chairs	47.6	55.1	60.7	64.7	63.0	76.3	74.3	73.2
Majority party [b]	60.0	66.0	65.0	64.5	66.0	78.5	75.5	75.8
Northern Democrats	69.5	76.0	74.0	73.5	71.5			
Southern Democrats	43.0	39.5	42.0	44.5	55.0			

Source: Congressional Quarterly party support score, appropriate congresses.

[a]House leaders include majority leader, whip, and chief deputy whip, except for the 92d, when leaders include majority leader, whip, and the two deputy whips. Senate leaders include majority leader and whip.

[b]The Senate majority was Democratic in the 92d-96th Congresses and Republican in the 97th-99th Congresses.

necessary because nearly all majority party members hold such a position. Like their House counterparts, Senate full committee chairs were substantially less supportive of their party's positions than the average majority party member in the early 1970s. They became more supportive of the party position during the 1970s, when Democrats maintained majority control of the Senate, but they remained less supportive of party positions than their House counterparts, on average. After the Republicans gained majority control in the 97th Congress (1981-1982), their full committee chairs proved more supportive of majority party positions than had their Democratic predecessors. In both chambers, then, chairs of the 1980s demonstrated greater policy congruence with their parent parties than they had in the preceding decades. With two important exceptions, there have been no serious challenges to the reelection of full committee chairs and little serious consideration has been given to further constraints on the behavior of chairs.[12] The action has been at the subcommittee level, where members in line for chairs by virtue of their seniority have been challenged by committee colleagues. These challenges sometimes have reflected important policy differences, although not always on issues of partisan concern.

The two important exceptions involved the House Armed Services Committee, a committee whose views on defense matters have been much more conservative than House Democrats and somewhat more conservative than the House as a whole. In 1985, Les Aspin (D-Wis.) successfully challenged Melvin Price (D-Ill.), the incumbent chair of the committee. Price was in poor health and had a track record of support for the Republican administration's defense policies. Aspin, then the seventh-ranking Democrat on the committee, offered more vigorous leadership and promised more active opposition to administration policies. However, two years later Aspin himself was nearly defeated for reelection as chair. Many of his party colleagues charged that on a few critical issues—new strategic missiles, procurement reform, chemical weapons, aid to the Nicaraguan contras, and defense spending generally—Aspin was less supportive of their views than they had hoped.[13] On the first vote on Aspin's reelection, Aspin was rejected, but he later won a three-way vote against committee colleagues who sought to replace him.

Aspin's experience has important lessons for the operation of the seniority system in the House. First, Aspin's 1985 challenge to Price demonstrated the willingness of House Democrats to ignore seniority under the right circumstances. Aspin's challenge represented the first time that an individual member campaigned both to unseat an incumbent chair and to be elected himself. The second instance was the effort to unseat Aspin in 1987, which was led by a mid-ranking member who sought the chair for himself.[14] Second, Aspin's close call in being reelected himself reflected the fairly high standard of conformity to party preferences expected of chairs managing legislation that House Democrats considered to be vital to their party interests. It is a message that other chairs must have received and registered. Third, Aspin's reelection indicates how difficult it is to find a satisfactory alternative to an incumbent chair. It is one thing to express displeasure with the performance of an incumbent chair, but quite another to find a majority to support an alternative candidate. Reliance on seniority, unless there is overwhelming reason to oppose the most senior member, resolves the question of choosing between the alternatives and minimizes internal party strife.

COUNTERVAILING DEVELOPMENTS

In spite of a net shift in power from full committee chairs to subcommittee chairs in the last three decades, some developments in the 1980s have modestly restrengthened the hand of full committee chairs. One such development was the move to omnibus measures to package disparate legislation, particularly for budget-related measures, such as reconciliation bills and continuing appropriations resolutions.[15] Committees found it useful in the 1980s to add miscellaneous provisions, even the text of whole bills, to necessary or priority measures in order to ensure that their legislation was considered on the floor and by the other chamber. Full committee chairs play a central role in coordinating the packaging of such measures for their committee and representing the committee before the Rules Committee, on the floor, and in conference.

The introduction of tough "reconciliation instructions" also enlarged the role of full committee chairs.[16] Beginning in 1980, Congress adopted budget resolutions that required various committees to report legislation, known as *reconciliation bills,* that saved money or enhanced revenues for the federal government. Chairs have assumed a major role in representing their committees in discussions with the budget committees and party leaders about reconciliation instructions and bills, and they normally serve as the chief negotiators in conference. The partisanship of the issues involved in budget and reconciliation measures also thrust full committee chairs to the fore as spokespersons for the majority party. Of course, other committee members, particularly subcommittee chairs, also play a major role in crafting omnibus and reconciliation measures. Full committee chairs do not perform these functions in isolation. But these developments and adaptations have increased both the importance of coherent, effective strategy for committees and the prominence of the most obvious source of such strategy, the full committee chairs.

Furthermore, budget constraints in the 1980s limited the number of new policy initiatives that could be pursued by subcommittees. Some previously active subcommittees turned to oversight hearings and investigations to fill the void; other subcommittees became dormant. And with fewer pieces of legislation flowing from subcommittee to full committee, subcommittee legislation could be afforded closer scrutiny by the full committee. The sheer volume of legislation passing through full committee no longer served to preserve the autonomy of sub-committees as it had in the 1970s. The work load and agenda changes placed full committee chairs and members in a better position to question subcommittee recommendations.

Full committee chairs have adapted in other ways as well. Many chairs have chosen to chair an important subcommittee on their commit-tee and managed to dominate policy making within its jurisdiction, often to the dismay of committee colleagues.[17] And several full commit-tee chairs have chosen to shift their attention to oversight hearings and investigations. House Energy and Commerce chair John Dingell (D-Mich.), as chair of his committee's oversight subcommittee, has stolen the political limelight from other subcommittee chairs by using his subcommittee's broad oversight jurisdiction to conduct investigations in areas falling under the legislative jurisdiction of other subcommittees. House Banking Committee chair Henry Gonzalez (D-Texas) reserved for the full committee widely publicized hearings on the supervision of the savings and loan industry during the Reagan administration—hearings that just as easily could have been held by the subcommittees for financial institutions or general oversight. In both cases, the full committee chairs' quick action and control over a substantial staff allowed them to become the central players on important issues.

Thus, while full committee chairs are not nearly as autocratic as they once were, they retain important advantages and in most cases continue to be the most powerful members of their committees.

SUBCOMMITTEES

Subcommittees, we noted in Chapter 2, became more important on many committees after the Legislative Reorganization Act of 1946 consolidated committee jurisdictions and reduced the number of stand-ing committees in both chambers. The number of subcommittees grew after World War II and continued into the 1970s as individual commit-tees responded to changes in the policy problems they faced and to demands from members for their own subcommittees. Today, of the committees with authority to report legislation, only the House's Budget and Standards of Official Conduct committees and the Senate's Budget,

Rules and Administration, and Veterans' Affairs committees lack standing subcommittees.

In the House, some full committee chairs resisted efforts to create legislative subcommittees. Their resistance was eventually overcome by the 1974 House rule that requires that "each standing committee . . . , except the Committee on the Budget, that has more than twenty members shall establish at least four subcommittees." Later, the problems associated with the growth in the number of House subcommittees—jurisdictional squabbles between subcommittees, scheduling difficulties, the burden of subcommittee hearings on executive officials—led the Democratic Caucus to limit the number of subcommittees. Hence, a 1981 caucus rule limits large committees (those of at least thirty-five members) to eight subcommittees, with the exception of Appropriations, and small committees to six subcommittees.

Neither the Senate nor the Senate parties have a formal rule on the number of subcommittees any committee may have, although limits on the number of subcommittee assignments that individual senators may hold effectively constrain the number of subcommittees that can be created. The stricter enforcement of limits on subcommittee assignments in 1985 led five committees to eliminate one or more subcommittees after a few senators were forced to give up one of their subcommittee chairs. On other committees, enforcement of the rule meant there were not enough members able and willing to take subcommittee assignments, which forced the abolition of some subcommittees. A total of ten Senate committees were compelled or chose to eliminate at least one subcommittee that year.

The number and jurisdiction of subcommittees changes far more frequently than those of full committees. Within the limits set by chamber or party rules, committees are free to change the structure of their subcommittees as they see fit. Change occurs most frequently when there is a change in subcommittee leadership or rapid turnover in membership, or, as happened twice in the Senate during the 1980s, after a change in party control. New issues often stimulate committees to create a new subcommittee or realign subcommittee jurisdictions. New issues that fall under the jurisdiction of several committees, such as energy, the environment, and international trade, are especially likely to motivate committees to alter subcommittee jurisdictions and names as they move to claim legislative jurisdiction over those issues.

As the evidence on bill management suggests, subcommittees have gained great importance in committee decision making in the House but retain a more varied and sometimes ambiguous role in the Senate. Written jurisdictions, guaranteed staff, and required bill referral grant House subcommittees a degree of independence from full committee chairs that is not found on most Senate committees. The patterns in the House have led some observers to label House decision making "subcommittee government," at least as it appeared in the late 1970s. The next chapter will demonstrate how important it is to place committees in a broader institutional context before accepting such generalizations. The question here is the degree to which subcommittee government is a fair characterization of how committees operate internally.[18]

SUBCOMMITTEE ASSIGNMENTS

Much of the independence of present-day subcommittees derives from the process by which they are appointed. Before the 1970s, full committee chairs appointed subcommittees and their chairs. The democratization of committee procedure in the 1970s made the subcommittee assignment process a matter of self-selection. In the House, chamber rules are silent on subcommittee assignment procedures, so party rules and practices govern the allocation of subcommittee assignments. House Democrats' rules provide for a process of self-selection in order of seniority, in which every member gets a choice before anyone gets a second choice.[19] House Republicans leave the process to the ranking minority member of each full committee, but most of the ranking members have established a process similar to that of House Democrats.[20] In the Senate, committee rules often mandate a process guaranteeing members a first (or second) subcommittee choice before any other member receives a second (or third) choice, and all party contingents operate that way even in the absence of a formal rule. Consequently, committee members are no longer dependent on the full committee chair for desirable subcommittee assignments and generally may act without fear that they are putting their subcommittee assignments in jeopardy.

Members gained more subcommittee assignments in the 1960s and early 1970s. As rank-and-file members demanded assignment to subcommittees that served their political goals, the number and size of subcommittees gradually increased, and the typical member gained more subcommittee seats. In the House, the average number of assignments per member grew from 2.5 in the 88th Congress (1963-1964) to 4.0 in the 94th (1975-1976). More assignments meant more meetings to attend, which created scheduling conflicts for rank-and-file members, and for chairs entailed difficulties in obtaining quorums for meetings. In the 1970s, the Democratic Caucus limited each of its members to five subcommittee assignments, although it since has granted numerous exemptions to allow members six subcommittees. The exemptions sometimes were granted so that members could serve on subcommittees handling problems vital to their constituencies or to retain expertise or a particular ideological balance on particular subcommittees.[21] House Republicans have no formal limit but are constrained by the number of subcommittee seats allocated to them by the majority party Democrats. In recent congresses, the average number of subcommittee assignments per member has hovered just under four in the House.

Subcommittee assignments have expanded in the Senate as well. Between the mid-1960s and mid-1970s, the number of subcommittee assignments held by the average senator increased from 6.6 to 9.5. In 1977, the Senate adopted limits on the number of subcommittee assignments a senator could hold (eight for most senators), which brought down the average to just under seven.[22] This forced a contraction in the number of subcommittees because some committees found that there were not enough eligible senators to fill all of their subcommittees. However, when the Republicans gained control of the Senate in 1981, they added several new subcommittees and began to grant exemptions to the limits on subcommittee assignments. By 1983, the number of senators serving on more than eight subcommittees was thirty-two, roughly one-third of the Senate. As we have noted, some new restraint was exercised in the following congresses, so the average senator has held about seven subcommittee assignments in recent congresses.

Even with new limits on subcommittees, and the limits on the number of full committee assignments noted in Chapter 3, members today find themselves stretched to the breaking point as they endeavor to meet all of their commitments. The problem was illustrated in this *New York Times* story:

> In one room of the Dirksen Senate Office Building yesterday morning, the Foreign Relations Committee, of which Senator Claiborne Pell is the ranking Democrat, was quizzing Secretary of State George P. Shultz on proposed arms sales to Jordan. Down the hall, the Labor Committee, on which the Rhode Island Senator is the No. 2 Democrat, was holding a hearing on requiring manufacturers to list salt content on food labels. Across the street, in the Russell Building, an education subcommittee was meeting on a subject dear to Mr. Pell's heart: financing for Federal scholarships for poor students, known as Pell grants for their chief Congressional sponsor.
>
> Just after 10 o'clock Mr. Pell rushed into the hearing on salt labeling, announced that he was expected momentarily at the Foreign Relations Committee and began reading a statement on the urgent need for Pell grants. After a minute or two, mercifully, Senator Howard M. Metzenbaum, Democrat of Ohio, nudged him and whispered in his ear.
>
> "I apologize deeply," Mr. Pell said, smiling sheepishly. Then he rose, waved his hand and fled as Senator Metzenbaum explained to the bewildered audience: "There are too many hearings going on at the same time." [23]

Despite the scheduling problems members face, however, they dislike the idea of more stringent limits on assignments because they value the political opportunities and influence associated with service on multiple committees and subcommittees.[24]

VARIATION IN SUBCOMMITTEE STRUCTURE

Committees of all types—large and small, policy- and constituency-oriented, active and less active—have been prompted or required to create subcommittees. Nevertheless, the size and diversity of a committee's jurisdiction is related to the number of subcommittees it establishes.[25] This is most obvious at the extremes. The appropriations committees have the most comprehensive jurisdictions, the most complex agendas and political environments, and the most subcommittees. The rules, administration, and veterans' affairs committees are low in both jurisdictional fragmentation and number of subcommittees. Not surprisingly, policy committees average better than one subcommittee more than constituency committees in both chambers.

THE PATH OF LEGISLATION

The presence of numerous subcommittees and subcommittee assignments, even when bolstered by rules that grant subcommittees some independence from parent committees and their chairs, does not guarantee a decision-making pattern that is properly labeled "subcommittee government." Independence in activity does not necessarily provide autonomy in decision making, although it is probably a necessary condition for autonomy. Even active, seemingly independent subcommittees remain the creatures of parent committees that may ignore or amend their recommendations and alter their jurisdictions and duties.

Committees have developed a variety of roles for their subcommittees, which makes it inappropriate simply to characterize committees as centralized or decentralized. One way to examine the functions of subcommittees is to trace the path taken by individual measures. Virtually all legislation passed by Congress is first referred to or considered by a committee, where hearings may be held, legislative language is drafted and modified, and a vote is taken to report it to the floor. As subcommittees have gained greater independence, a similar process has been carried out increasingly at the subcommittee level before full committee action. That is, in many cases, subcommittees assume the initial responsibility for discussing and designing legislation, thereby setting the agenda for subsequent stages in the legislative process. The extent to which these responsibilities have shifted to

TABLE 4-4   Percent of Measures Referred to and Reported from Committees that Were Referred to Subcommittee or Subject to a Subcommittee Hearing, Selected Congresses (1969-1988)

	Congress		
	91st (1969-1970)	96th (1979-1980)	100st (1987-1988)
House			
Referred	35.7	79.8	84.6
Reported	75.4	80.0	79.7
Senate			
Referred	41.5	41.1	42.3
Reported	40.0	44.8	46.3

Source: Committee calendars.

Note: The table excludes House and Senate appropriations committees because they do not produce committee calendars comparable to those of other committees. It also excludes matters related to nominations and commemorative legislation. Final committee calendars were not available for the 100th Congress for four committees: House Armed Services, House Post Office and Civil Service, Senate Rules and Administration, and Senate Veterans' Affairs. The column for the 100th Congress includes tallies for the 99th Congress for those four committees.

subcommittees can be seen in the number of measures referred to or reported from subcommittees.

Consider the House first (Table 4-4). The percentage of legislation referred to House subcommittees more than doubled between the 91st Congress (1969-1970) and the 96th Congress (1979-1980), and it maintained a high level in the 100th (1987-1988). Until the 1970s, many full committee chairs did not bother to refer legislation to a subcommittee if it was not likely to be taken up by the full committee. This meant, of course, that full committee chairs retained control of legislation they opposed. But since 1975, when the 1973 Subcommittee Bill of Rights was implemented in most House committees, subcommittees have become the dungeons in which most legislation dies in the House.

There is much less change in the path taken by legislation eventually reported to the House floor. Even in the late 1960s, most legislation brought to the floor had been referred to subcommittee at some point in committee deliberations, if only for a hearing. It is obvious that subcommittees had become quite important by that time. Moreover, since the reforms in the mid-1970s, not all reported legislation has been referred to subcommittee. Several House committees have adopted rules to keep certain types of legislation at the full committee, as they are free to do under House and Democratic Caucus rules. The Ways and Means Committee keeps legislation amending the income tax sections of the Internal Revenue Code at the full committee; Interior and Insular Affairs retains matters pertaining to native American Indians for the full committee; and Foreign Affairs requires that the markup of foreign assistance and Peace Corps authorization be conducted by the full committee. In addition, many House committees routinely hold Senate bills sent to the House at the full committee, particularly late in a session when there is little chance of further action or when similar legislation already has been reported to the floor.

In contrast to the House, the Senate's pattern shows little change. A majority of both referred and reported legislation is not sent to sub-committee, and most Senate committees do not routinely refer legislation to subcommittee. Rather, legislation remains on the docket of the full committee, even when a subcommittee chooses to hold a hearing and write legislation on the subject.

Within the aggregate pattern of the Senate there is tremendous variation, far more than in the House. Because the Senate and the Senate parties do not have rules governing the referral of legislation to subcommittees, Senate committees have adopted a wide range of rules and practices to govern subcommittee referral. Many Senate committees have no formal rule on the subject, leaving referral to the chair's discretion or established practice. Other Senate committees have adopted rules that are quite specific. The Judiciary Committee, for example, requires that "except for matters retained at the full committee, matters shall be referred to the appropriate subcommittee or subcommittees, except as agreed by a majority vote of the Committee or by the agreement of the Chairman and the Ranking Minority Member."[26] In contrast, the Finance Committee's rule states that "all legislation shall be kept on the full committee calendar unless a majority of the members present and voting agree to refer specific legislation to an appropriate subcommittee."[27] Another, Energy and Natural Resources, explicitly reserves some issues, such as nuclear waste and natural gas pricing, for the full committee while placing the remainder in the hands of its subcommittees.[28]

SUBCOMMITTEE MEETINGS AND HEARINGS

An additional indicator of the function of subcommittees is the frequency of full committee and subcommittee meetings and hearings. Most formal meetings of committees and subcommittees are *markups*,

TABLE 4-5 Percent of Committee Meetings and Hearings Held by Subcommittees, Selected Congresses (1955-1988)

	Congress			
	86th (1955-1956)	91st (1969-1970)	96th (1979-1980)	100th (1987-1988)
House				
Meetings	45.6	47.9	56.1	52.0
Hearings	72.3	77.0	90.7	95.1
Senate				
Meetings	27.1	30.6	19.1	18.6
Hearings	77.7	79.6	65.2	64.4

Source: Daily Digest of the *Congressional Record*.

Note: House Appropriations excluded because it does not report its meetings in the Daily Digest. The table excludes meetings and hearings on nominations.

sessions at which legislation is considered in detail and perhaps reported to the full committee or the floor. The relative frequency of full committee and subcommittee markups indicates the degree of reliance on subcommittees for drafting the details of legislation. *Hearings* are sessions in which committees or subcommittees receive testimony from witnesses—administration officials, interest group representatives, independent experts, and constituents. Hearings often assist committees in gathering information about policy problems and solutions, but they also sometimes serve as platforms to publicize a cause. Thus, while hearings have less direct impact on the content of legislation, they can be important tools in building majority coalitions for or against legislation.

The pattern of meetings and hearings (Table 4-5) confirms the chamber differences that we noted above. The percentage of House meetings and hearings held by subcommittees increased greatly during the 1970s and has held steady since then. All House committees with legislative subcommittees now have a rule that authorizes the subcommittees to meet, hold hearings, conduct investigations, and report legislation to the full committee on matters within their jurisdictions.[29] In fact, nearly all House committees reserve the conduct of hearings for the subcommittees. Even full committee chairs pursue most of their own interests through hearings of the subcommittees they chair rather than by using the full committee. This arrangement allows a division of labor within committees and the pursuit of simultaneous hearings on a range of subjects. No committee members are excluded by this process because they are allowed to sit with any subcommittee during hearings and to question witnesses.

The key change in the House concerns the frequency of subcommittee meetings or markups. During the 1970s, enough committees were compelled to change their decision-making practices to shift the percentage of meetings held by subcommittees from just under 50 percent to just over that amount, a level that has been maintained since that time. Full committees still meet frequently, of course, because they must approve legislation recommended by subcommittees. As a result of the changes of the 1970s, the typical decision-making pattern in House committees has three stages: subcommittee hearings, subcommittee markup, and full committee markup. The degree to which the full committee rejects or modifies subcommittee recommendations cannot be discerned from these data, but the pattern of meetings suggests that full committees meet nearly as often as subcommittees to consider legislation.

In contrast, a long-standing two-stage process remains typical in Senate committees: subcommittee hearings and full committee markup. Most Senate committees, but not all, operate on the assumption that subcommittee markups are an inefficient use of senators' scarce time when full committee markup follows anyway. In fact, the percentage of meetings held in subcommittee in recent congresses remains lower than the House percentage of more than thirty years ago. Fewer than one in five Senate committee meetings is a subcommittee meeting.

The general view of subcommittees in the Senate is so different that its Rules and Administration Committee seriously suggested in 1988 that it would be advisable for the Senate to adopt a rule barring subcommittee markups. As of early 1990, the Senate has not acted on the package, but the recommendation reflects widespread concern among senators that there are too many demands on their time to tolerate subcommittee markups. Attendance at subcommittee markups has proven to be a serious problem, and many committees have stopped subcommittee markups of their own accord.[30]

SUBCOMMITTEES IN CONFERENCE

In addition to their greater role in initiating legislation within committees and managing legislation on the floor, House subcommittee members gained a greater role in conference committees during the 1970s. Participation in conference is critical to the power of subcommittee members. Conferences normally are the last stage at which the details of major legislation are modified before the legislation is finally approved and sent to the president. When subcommittee members are confident that they will be appointed to the conference, they can gauge strategy in committee and on the floor with the knowledge that they will be responsible for negotiating with the other chamber and thus may have the opportunity to reshape the legislation before it is finally enacted.

The conference role of subcommittees is a product of the role of subcommittees within committees. As the initiators of much legislation, House subcommittee chairs and members are quite natural choices for conference delegations. Their role has been enhanced further by a 1977 rule that "the Speaker shall name members who are primarily responsible for the legislation and shall, to the fullest extent possible, include the principal proponents of the major provisions of the bill as it passed the House." Although these instructions leave the Speaker with substantial discretion and reliant upon the recommendations of the full committee chair in most cases, members of the subcommittee with appropriate jurisdiction usually meet such conditions easily and are appointed to conferences.[31]

Six House committees have taken an additional step by adopting rules designed to limit the full committee chair's discretion in recommending conferees to the Speaker. Three committees, Education and Labor, Foreign Affairs, and Ways and Means, explicitly require the chair to recommend members from the appropriate subcommittee or subcommittees. The other three committees, Budget, Interior and Insular Affairs, and Public Works and Transportation, explicitly grant to the majority party members of the committee the right to approve or reject the chair's recommendations.

The net result of the changes in intracommittee decision-making patterns during the 1970s was a substantial increase in the number of House conference delegations dominated by members of the *sub*committee of appropriate jurisdiction. Table 4-6 indicates that the number of House conference delegations dominated by subcommittee members was about equal to the number that appeared to be appointed without regard to subcommittee membership. The delegations categorized as "full committee delegations" generally included a handful of the most senior members of the full committee. It is important to note, however, that subcommittee membership appeared to be the organizing principle for about half of the House delegations, even before reforms imposed a more decentralized decision-making process on most House committees.

By the late 1970s, the democratization of decision-making practices within committees was transparent in the composition of conference delegations. Three-fourths of the House delegations were either the nearly exclusive province of subcommittee members or combined a set

TABLE 4-6 Number of Conference Delegations Structured by Full Committee and Subcommittee Membership

	Congress		
	89th (1965-1966)	96th (1979-1980)	99th (1985-1986)
House			
Subcommittee delegations	72	109	50
Full committee delegations	60	33	76
Deliberately mixed delegations	8	21	21
Ambiguous cases	1	1	0
Total	141	164	147
Senate			
Subcommittee delegations	74	77	21
Full committee delegations	55	59	27
Deliberately mixed delegations	1	17	5
Ambiguous cases	8	4	0
Total	138	157	53

Source: Final Calendar of the House of Representatives, selected Congresses

Note: The table is based upon the membership in the majority party's delegation. In the case of multiple-committee delegations, each committee's conferees are counted separately. Subcommittee delegations are those in which either (1) all of the conferees came from a single subcommittee or (2) all but one conferee, the full committee chair, came from a single subcommittee. Mixed cases are those on which several subcommittee members are appointed, usually in order of seniority, and two or more other committee members are included. Nearly all other cases are categorized as full committee cases—cases in which members from several subcommittees, if the committee had subcommittees, are appointed. This category may include instances in which members from two or more subcommittees are chosen because of the subcommittee membership. Consequently, the table understates the role of subcommittee membership. The ambiguous cases involve sets of members who were the most senior members of both the full committee and one or more subcommittees. Conferees who did not sit on a committee originating the legislation are ignored. The figures for the 99th Congress are correct: The small number of Senate delegations is due to omnibus legislating, while the much larger number of House delegations is due to the use of exclusive and additional conferees for omnibus measures.

of subcommittee members with other committee members. Among the full committee delegations, seniority was less consistently observed.

The proportion of subcommittee-oriented delegations fell during the 1980s, however, as the total number of delegations declined precipitously (see Table 4-6). The causes of this pattern cannot be explored in detail here, but two mutually reinforcing developments appear to be responsible. First, a much smaller policy agenda in the 1980s, associated with severe constraints on federal spending, reduced the number of small measures emanating from subcommittees that otherwise would have been the subjects of subcommittee-dominated conferences. Second, strategic considerations led committees to package small measures into larger measures, or even to include them in omnibus reconciliation bills (see Chapter 5), reducing the number of delegations composed of the members of a single subcommittee. These factors are reflected in the number of delegations that were a part of a larger conference delegation for a multiple-committee bill, such as a reconciliation bill. In the 1979-1980 period, only twenty of the delegations in Table 4-6 were appointed for the consideration of certain sections or titles of bills, but that number was seventy-seven in 1985-1986. Of those seventy-seven, only twenty-four were unambiguously appointed for subcommittee membership. Generally speaking, the others were composed of members from several subcommittees and were led by the full committee chair.

The Senate and its committees lack formal rules instructing the Senate's presiding officer or committee chairs on the subject of who should be appointed to conferences, although the presiding officer is directed by a largely unenforceable rule that conferees should be supportive of the Senate position. As in the House, lists provided by full committee chairs usually guide the presiding officer. Moreover, in the Senate, too, there is a strong tendency and substantial demand to name subcommittee members to conferences. Even if a separate subcommittee markup was not held, members from the relevant subcommittee still tend to take greater interest in the issue (they may have sat through several subcommittee hearings on the bill) and to take the lead in full committee consideration on the bill. Furthermore, unlike the House, where it is virtually impossible to challenge the Speaker's choices, the Senate formally votes on its conferees, which enables a senator to object to or even filibuster the appointment of conferees. Seldom is a subcommittee member who is a principal author of the bill or important provisions excluded from the Senate conference delegation when he or she seeks appointment.

Several features of the Senate pattern of change in the composition of conferences are notable. Like House delegations, Senate delegations frequently were organized by subcommittee membership in the mid-

1960s. Surprisingly, Senate delegations were somewhat more likely than House delegations to exhibit a subcommittee orientation in the mid-1960s. But by the late 1970s, while the House became far more subcommittee-oriented, the Senate showed virtually no change and, on balance, was therefore less subcommittee-oriented than the House. In the 1980s, the same forces operating in the House appear to have operated in the Senate, making its delegations less subcommittee-oriented than they had been in the 1970s.

The record of subcommittee representation in conference delegations cautions against simplistic interpretations of the role of subcommittees. Even in the House, where subcommittees' independence is more firmly established, subcommittee membership does not structure conference appointments in many situations. Subcommittees are not autonomous creatures in the legislative process.

OTHER COMMITTEE SUBUNITS

In addition to their standing subcommittees, committees occasionally create other subunits. Most but not all committees allow the chair to create an ad hoc subcommittee to handle a matter that falls in the jurisdiction of more than one subcommittee. Unfortunately, there is no reliable record of the frequency with which such ad hoc arrangements are employed, but the relative ease of altering subcommittee jurisdictions keeps the number very small. Committee rules generally imply that the ad hoc subcommittees dissolve upon completing action on the specific matters assigned to them.

The use of task forces, special panels, and units with similar names has gone beyond isolated efforts to handle issues cutting across subcommittee jurisdictions, particularly in the House. For example, the House Committee on Education and Labor maintained a task force on pension issues for several congresses in the 1970s, effectively creating another chair and allowing committee members to exceed their subcommittee assignment limit.[32] House Ways and Means used a set of task forces to devise parts of the massive tax reform package eventually enacted in 1986. House Budget employs a fairly permanent set of task forces to study parts of the budget and budget process in lieu of standing subcommittees with authority to write legislation. House Armed Services added "panels" on defense policy, weapons acquisitions policy, and other topics in the mid-1980s. Even members not serving on Armed Services participated on these panels, which gave Chairman Aspin a means to demonstrate his responsiveness to the views of fellow party members on a few highly salient issues. The Armed Services panels have no legislative jurisdiction, although they have conducted hearings that normally are the province of standing subcommittees.[33]

There are no consistent implications of the ad hoc arrangements for the distribution of power within committees. In some cases, as in the Ways and Means Committee's effort on tax reform, task forces represented a way for Chairman Rostenkowski to create a division of labor without sacrificing his role in devising and packaging the legislation. In other cases, such as for the panels on Armed Services, the arrangement reflected the assertiveness of rank-and-file members in and out of the committee. In most cases, the legislative actions of task forces or panels are preliminary to subcommittee action and do not substitute for subcommittee consideration and markup.

COMMITTEE STAFF

Staff assistants also are a conspicuous feature of the internal world of committees. Committee staffs are among the most controversial features of the congressional committee systems. Some observers hold that the expansion of committee staffs in recent decades has helped members cope with burgeoning work loads. Committee staffs, along with personal staffs and the support agencies, help Congress to compete with the expertise of the executive branch and to scrutinize the claims of special interests. Others complain that enlarged committee staffs have damaged committee operations. They argue that large staffs overload committees with make-work, make possible endless hearings that take administration officials away from their duties, insulate members from each other, and enable committees and subcommittees to pursue topics beyond their legitimate jurisdictions. Most important, they contend, committee staffs wield too much power as they negotiate and make innumerable decisions about the details of legislation on behalf of their bosses. The popular press has characterized committee staff as "the new power elite," "the new senate barons," "governors on the Hill," and "shadow government." [34] Former Rules Committee chair Richard Bolling (D-Mo.) put it this way: "Some staffing is disastrous, but the key is whether they do useful work. You can have a staff where 50 percent are stirring the pot and they're not putting anything in the pot. They're just stirring. On the other hand, you can have a staff that makes a committee function."[35] Whatever one's view of staff, it is clear that committee staffs are powerful and play a more important role in Congress today than they did two or three decades ago.

Committee staffs both reflect and condition the power of committees and the distribution of power within them. Most professional staff aides to committees are well educated (most have post-baccalaureate degrees) and bring some professional or policy expertise to their jobs. In a few cases, they are the most expert policy specialists in their fields, in or out of government. Beyond the administrative tasks of arranging meetings and hearings and managing the paperwork associated with legislating, committee staffs influence the agenda-setting decisions of chairs, often advocate or even champion legislative proposals, conduct investigations, negotiate on behalf of committees and their chairs, and work to build coalitions in committee, on the floor, and in conference. The assistance of quality staff aides can give a committee or subcommittee chair a substantial advantage over competitors in legislative politics.[36]

TYPES OF COMMITTEE STAFF

The era of strong congressional committees had its heyday after the 1946 Legislative Reorganization Act reorganized the committee systems and granted each standing committee the authority to hire four professional staff assistants and six clerical aides. The 1970 Legislative Reorganization Act increased to six the number of professional assistants each committee could hire, but in 1974 the House increased the number to eighteen professional assistants and twelve clerical aides, where it remains today.[37] Minority party control of at least two professional staff assistants on each committee was guaranteed by the 1970 act, and both chambers later adopted rules guaranteeing even larger staffs to the minority party. The House gives the minority party control over one-third of professional and clerical staffs, and the Senate requires that staff be allocated to the minority party in proportion to the number of minority party members on each committee.[38]

The House strengthens the independence of subcommittees by guaranteeing, in rules adopted in the early 1970s, that both the chair and ranking minority member of each standing subcommittee may appoint at least one staff member.[39] Unless authorization for additional staff is obtained from the House, subcommittee staff come out of the allocation guaranteed to the full committee, which directly reduces the number of staff under the control of the full committee chairs and ranking minority members. As we will see, this rule dramatically altered staffing patterns in House committees. In many cases, subcommittee staffs have grown quite large, fifteen to twenty aides in a handful of cases, far beyond the minimum required by House rules.

Committees may request funding for staff support beyond that authorized by law. Known as "investigative" or "temporary" staff, these staff members have become a regular part of the operations of most committees, and funding is routinely provided for a significant number of them. Conflict arises whenever funding for such additional staff must be approved—annually in the House and biennially in the Senate. During the 1980s, when spending became an overriding political issue, some contraction in the number of temporary staff occurred on congressional committees.

Another type of staff, "associate staff," represents a cross between committee staff and the staff in members' personal offices. The Senate initiated the practice on a large scale in 1975, when it authorized each senator to hire up to three people to assist him or her on committee business. In most cases, associate staff work out of members' personal offices and often are difficult to distinguish from the legislative assistants that appear on senators' personal office budgets.

In the House, the three prestige committees—Appropriations, Budget, and Rules—authorize each of their members to hire one staff assistant at committee expense to assist them with their committee duties. The rationale is that the work load of these committees is so heavy and complex (and important, their members argue) that they require special assistance. Except for the Committee on Rules, these associate staff members are housed in the personal offices of members and, like their Senate counterparts, often become involved in activities not related to their committee duties. In fact, House Rule XI explicitly excludes the three committees from its requirement that committee staff not be assigned to or engage in work other than committee business.

GROWTH AND DISTRIBUTION OF COMMITTEE STAFF

The growth of committee staff is shown in Figure 4-1. Gradual expansion in the 1950s and 1960s turned into an explosion in the 1970s. The growth is a product of several factors. Committees requested and received more staff to manage larger legislative and investigative work loads. Congress also sought to bolster its capacity to compete with the executive branch and its store of expertise. And individual chairs viewed larger staffs as an important resource for expanding the number of issues they could address, the number of hearings they could organize, and the number of bills they could write, all of which enhanced their personal influence and political careers. Finally, and most important, the expansion was in part the product of creating new staffs for subcommittees and the minority party.

The surge in the size of committee staffs during the 1970s was much greater in the House than in the Senate. While the total number of House committee staff more than tripled between 1969 and 1979, Senate committee staff grew by only 80 percent or so (Table 4-7). The different rates of increase are due primarily to the tremendous expansion of

FIGURE 4-1   Growth of House and Senate Committee Staffs (1891-1987)

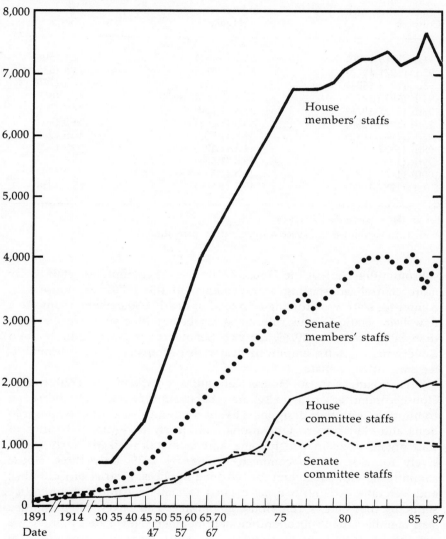

Source: Norman J. Ornstein, Thomas E. Mann, and Michael J. Malbin, *Vital Statistics on Congress 1989-1990* (Washington, D.C.: Congressional Quarterly Inc., 1990), 133.

TABLE 4-7 Percent of Committee Staff Allocated to Subcommittees, Selected Congresses (1969-1990)

Congress	Percent of Committee Staff Allocated to Subcommittees	
	House	Senate
91st (1969-1970)	23.2 (461)	42.1 (504)
92d (1971-1972)	27.7 (575)	44.6 (635)
93d (1973-1974)	36.4 (664)	40.5 (775)
94th (1975-1976)	32.8 (1,083)	32.1 (859)
95th (1977-1978)	38.8 (1,250)	27.7 (869)
96th (1979-1980)	43.0 (1,608)	34.5 (902)
97th (1981-1982)	39.8 (1,507)	32.5 (906)
98th (1983-1984)	44.2 (1,479)	40.8 (922)
99th (1985-1986)	45.8 (1,566)	41.4 (863)
100th (1987-1988)	45.8 (1,545)	37.3 (790)
101st (1989-1990)	45.2 (1,600)	38.7 (834)

Source: Congressional Staff Directory.
Note: Total committee and subcommittee staff in parentheses.

subcommittee staff in the House while Senate committees retained far more centralized staffing arrangements. In the 1970s, as House subcommittee staff was growing by a total of nearly 650 percent, thanks to a new Democratic Caucus rule, Senate subcommittee staff grew by less than 50 percent. In 1979, just two Senate committees, Judiciary and Government Affairs, employed nearly three-fourths of the subcommittee staff of the Senate.

The changes in the House were quite remarkable. In 1970, twelve House committees had no separate subcommittee staff. Of the seven committees with staff designated as subcommittee staff, only Appropriations and Government Operations had clearly decentralized forms of staff organization in which some staff members worked nearly exclusively for a single subcommittee chair. By 1979, only three House committees with subcommittees (Armed Services, District of Columbia, and Veterans' Affairs) had not created formally separate subcommittee staffs. By that time, seven House committees had fewer full committee staff members than subcommittee staff members. Nevertheless, there is a natural limit to how much staff can shift from full committee to subcommittee. Some administrative staff (bill, publications, and calendar clerks, for example) and at least a small professional staff to support the activities of the full committee chair and ranking minority member exist on even the most decentralized committees.

House committees, operating under requirements that committee staff be shared with subcommittees and the minority, now have very similar distributions of staff between the full committee and sub-committees. But there are still a few cases where the full committee chair, through the senior full committee staff, exercises substantial control over at least the majority party staff of the committee and subcommittees. On the Science, Space, and Technology Committee, for example, the top full committee staff has traditionally scrutinized the hiring of subcommittee staff professionals to ensure technical competence and good coordination with the full committee staff. Ways and Means chair Dan Rostenkowski, after becoming chair in 1981, reduced the number of staff appointments subcommittee chairs could make to those required by House rules. He makes it clear, through the senior full committee aides, that even subcommittee staff is responsible to the full committee chair and staff.

Senate committees, because they are not constrained by chamber or party rules requiring separate subcommittee staffs, continue to vary widely in the manner in which they staff subcommittee activities. Some Senate committees, such as Governmental Affairs, Judiciary, and Labor, are much like House committees in allowing subcommittee leaders to appoint their own staff. Others, such as Banking, do not appoint separate subcommittee staffs but assign certain subcommittee responsibilities to full committee staff assistants. In such cases, the staff assistant has two bosses, the full committee chair and the subcommittee chair. And in others, such as Agriculture, there is little meaningful differentiation among committee staff by subcommittee and usually little separate subcommittee activity, particularly with respect to drafting legislation. Three Senate committees with legislative jurisdiction—Rules and Administration, Select Intelligence, and Small Business—do not have subcommittees or subcommittee staff.

Since the late 1970s, the balance of committee and subcommittee staff has remained quite stable in the House, at least in the aggregate. Individual committees, particularly in the Senate, shift the balance from time to time as new chairs seek to alter the distribution of resources within their committees. In fact, the proportion of subcommittee staff increased somewhat under Republican control of committees (97th-99th Congresses) as Republican subcommittee chairs became more demanding of perquisites for their leadership posts. But the aggregate staffing patterns in the House and Senate chambers continue to parallel the patterns observed for bill management, the path of legislation, and meetings and hearings: the House is more subcommittee-oriented than the Senate.

OTHER VARIATIONS IN COMMITTEE STAFF

Within the constraints set by statute, chamber, and caucus rules, the character of committee jurisdictions and agendas also shape decisions about how to organize and utilize staff. The most obvious influences are the size and diversity of a committee's jurisdiction. Large, diverse jurisdictions are associated with large committee staffs. The appropriations, commerce, judiciary, and labor committees of the two chambers have very large staffs, even at the full committee level, reflecting the work load of these committees. The post office, rules, small business, and veterans' committees have very small staffs. Overall, the rank-order correlation between jurisdictional fragmentation and staff size was .81 in the House and .76 in the Senate (on a 0-to-1 scale) in 1982.[40]

In general, the prestige and policy committees have larger, more diverse jurisdictions and therefore require more staff assistance. Members' personal goals reinforce these differences. The activism found on policy committees leads subcommittee chairs to demand large staffs of their own. The greater emphasis on common interests on constituency committees allows their subcommittee chairs to rely on smaller and more centralized staffs. Thus, in the House, policy committees such as Banking, Energy and Commerce, Judiciary, and Government Operations have very large full committee staffs and large subcommittee staffs, while Agriculture, Armed Services, Merchant Marine and Fisheries, and Small Business have small and much more centralized staffs.

The distinction between policy and constituency committee staffs is not nearly so clean in the Senate, where members rely more on personal and associate staffs, but even there some differences can be found. For example, the change from Republican to Democratic control of the Senate in 1987 had consequences for staffs that varied greatly between committees. Wholesale changes occurred on many committees, but one constituency-oriented committee chair, Quentin Burdick (D-N.D.) of the Environment and Public Works Committee, hired ten Republican staff members for his own majority staff. The traditional bipartisanship and local orientation of Environment and Public Works made it possible for the Republican appointees to the staff to serve the needs of Democrats as well.[41] In contrast, when Richard Lugar (R-Ind.) took over the chair of the policy-oriented Foreign Relations Committee from fellow Republican Charles Percy (R-Ill.) in 1985, Lugar replaced most of Percy's staff with his own people who had worked for him before and whose commitment to his more conservative policy perspectives could not be questioned.[42]

In addition to the organization of staffs, the relationship between members and staff varies with the political goals of the members. David

Powerful Committee Staff

Capitol Hill's "Mr. Housing" has called it quits. He virtually concedes defeat to the budget cutters. Gerald R. McMurray, who has had a hand in crafting just about every major housing law enacted in the past two decades, has resigned as staff director of the House Banking Subcommittee on Housing and Community Development.

The unabashed populist and liberal Democrat said he is weary of battling conservatives for money to spend on programs that house the poor. A student of President Lyndon B. Johnson's Great Society days, during which he came to Capitol Hill, McMurray expects the frustrations he experienced during the tightfisted Reagan era to continue pretty much unabated under President Bush.

"I'm tired of fighting a battle that I just don't think I'm ever going to win," he said. "Eight years in the trenches were just beginning to wear on me. Fighting a losing battle just ground me down."

As the subcommittee prepared to mark up another McMurray-influenced housing bill Nov. 1, Chairman Henry B. Gonzalez, D-Texas, announced his aide's decision to join the Federal National Mortgage Association as vice president for housing initiatives. McMurray, 47, said he will get a "comfortable" increase over his $82,500-a-year salary and a chance to combat housing problems more directly.

Everyone in the packed hearing room gave the staff director a standing ovation. Several members said they were grateful to McMurray for guiding them through the labyrinth of federal housing laws and programs and helping them craft their own contributions to the federal code. "You've been Mr. Housing for the 10 years that I've been here," said Rep. Charles E. Schumer, D-N.Y., turning to McMurray to add, "Thank you."

McMurray has been a guiding force behind about two dozen major bills addressing urban and rural housing and development issues since joining the Housing Subcommittee in July 1967, including the landmark Housing and Community Development Act of 1974 and the Housing and Urban Development Act of 1968. A Capitol Hill employee since June 1964, he has been the subcommittee's staff director for the past 18 years.

Some members appeared concerned that McMurray's timing could hamper work on the housing reauthorization bill now in the works. "I am distressed by this news; I don't like it," said Del. Walter E. Fauntroy, D-D.C. Gonzalez said, "He will be sorely missed."

But McMurray, who leaves Dec. 1, said, "Nobody is irreplaceable."

Gonzalez said Frank T. DeStefano, a 14-year veteran with the subcommittee, would take charge of the panel's staff of eight.

Some sources said they had heard McMurray was frustrated by Gonzalez' sometimes eccentric style. They also said they had heard that McMurray lately had a hard time getting Gonzalez' ear. McMurray discounted such talk. "Gonzalez has always been like that," McMurray said. "I'm used to it."

Source: Phil Kuntz, " 'Mr. Housing' Bows Out," *Congressional Quarterly Weekly Report*, November 4, 1989, 2950.

E. Price, then a political scientist and now also a member of the House, described two primary roles for committee staff.[43] Staff "professionals" view their roles as supportive of corporate committee goals, so they are geared toward serving the entire membership. Turnover in the membership or in chairs may not have implications for their jobs. "Entrepreneurs" tend to be linked to a single member and that member's legislative goals. When their boss changes position, say from one subcommittee chair to another, they nearly always move, too.

Professionals are found disproportionately on constituency committees. Such staff members frequently come from the department or agency that administers the programs within their committees' jurisdictions or from positions with interest groups representing the constituencies receiving the programs' benefits. The clarity and homogeneity of the legislative goals of constituency committees make it possible for staff aides to develop a professional relationship with most members, which in turn helps staff members survive as committee and subcommittee chairs come and go.

In contrast, staff activists who constantly survey the political landscape for new issues and eagerly pursue extensive hearings and investigations are well suited to policy-oriented members. They may be dangerous to a member more exclusively concerned about preserving program benefits for a narrow constituency. It is common for policy-oriented members to recruit energetic staff with strong views and ideological commitments similar to their own so that they can reap the benefits of staff activism. But exhaustion and frustration tend to produce higher turnover among such staff aides, and turnover in the chair more frequently compels them to leave.[44] Furthermore, entrepreneurial staff assistants often make a name for themselves and are attracted by offers from interest groups, associations, law firms, or executive agencies (see the box on p. 155).

PATTERNS OF SUBCOMMITTEE ORIENTATION

The discussion of committee leaders, subcommittees, and staff suggests that House committees are fairly similar in the degree to which they have decentralized legislative responsibilities while Senate committees, lacking many of the formal constraints on committee procedure that exist in the House, continue to exhibit greater variety in their internal decision-making processes. To summarize these differences and illustrate the variety of orientations toward subcommittees, a composite measure has been constructed for each standing committee. The measure simply is the mean of the following indicators: (1) the percentage of

TABLE 4-8 Subcommittee Orientation of House Committees

| | Congress | | |
Committee	91st (1969-1970)	96th (1979-1980)	100th (1987-1988)
Prestige Committees			
Appropriations	n.a.	n.a.	n.a.
Budget	n.c.	n.s.	n.s.
Rules	n.a.	n.a.	n.a.
Ways and Means	0	44	33
Policy Committees			
Banking	30	78	69
Education and Labor	41	65	56
Energy and Commerce	42	79	71
Foreign Affairs	39	52	50
Judiciary	62	78	70
Government Operations	77	70	64
Constituency Committees			
Agriculture	51	57	55
Armed Services	60	58	46
Interior	53	63	63
Merchant Marine	59	62	52
Public Works	37	75	58
Science, Space, & Technology	50	68	71
Small Business	n.a.	n.a.	35
Veterans' Affairs	33	38	44

Source: See text.

Note: Subcommittee orientation is the mean of the percentage of measures managed by subcommittee chairs, percentage of reported measures subject to subcommittee referral or hearings, percentage of meetings held in subcommittee, and percentage of staff allocated to subcommittees. *Abbreviations:* n.a.—not available because not all of the four component indicators are available; n.c.—not a standing committee; n.s.—no legislative subcommittees.

measures considered on the floor that are managed by a subcommittee chair, (2) the percentage of measures reported to the floor that were referred to a subcommittee or on which a subcommittee hearing was held, (3) the percentage of meetings (primarily markups) that were subcommittee meetings, and (4) the percentage of staff specifically allocated to subcommittees.[45]

TABLE 4-9 Subcommittee Orientation of Senate Committees

| Committee | Congress | | |
	91st (1969-1970)	96th (1979-1980)	100th (1987-1988)
Policy Committees			
Budget	n.c.	n.s.	n.s.
Foreign Relations	9	10	1
Governmental Affairs	46	43	34
Judiciary	51	37	40
Labor and Human Resources	60	50	32
Mixed Policy/ Constituency Committees			
Armed Services	29	34	21
Banking, Housing, and Urban Affairs	32	20	27
Finance	3	9	6
Constituency Committees			
Agriculture, Nutrition, and Forestry	25	43	20
Appropriations	n.a.	n.a.	n.a.
Commerce, Science, and Transportation	38	32	39
Energy and Natural Resources	45	36	32
Environment and Public Works	19	31	33
Other			
Rules and Administration	16	0	2
Veterans' Affairs	n.c.	0	0

Source: See text.

Note: Subcommittee orientation is the mean of the percentage of measures managed by subcommittee chairs, percentage of reported measures subject to subcommittee referral or hearings, percentage of meetings held in subcommittee, and percentage of staff allocated to subcommittees. *Abbreviations:* n.a.—not available because not all of the four component indicators are available; n.c.—not a standing committee; n.s.—no legislative subcommittees.

The composite measure of subcommittee orientation shows the differences between the House and Senate once again (Tables 4-8 and 4-9).

House committees had an average subcommittee orientation of 47 percent in 1969-1970, 62 percent in 1979-1980, and 57 percent in 1987-1988. In contrast, the respective levels for the Senate were 26 percent, 25 percent, and 20 percent. Relative to their positions in the late 1960s, all but one of the fourteen House committees examined became more subcommittee-oriented by the late 1970s. Appropriations remained highly subcommittee-oriented. Budget has not adopted legislative subcommittees. And Rules conducts all of its business on its most important responsibility, writing special rules, at full committee. In sharp contrast, eight of the twelve Senate committees for which complete data are available became less subcommittee-oriented during the 1970s.

The index of subcommittee orientation declined for most committees between 1979-1980 and 1985-1986. In most cases, this is due to a decline in proportion of meetings held by subcommittees and in the proportion of reported measures receiving subcommittee referral or hearings. This pattern appears to be associated with the move to more omnibus bills, particularly reconciliation bills. Because of time constraints and political considerations, committees often incorporate legislation in their reconciliation packages without following the usual procedure of conducting subcommittee hearings and markups before full committee action. Legislating in this fashion undercuts the role of subcommittees.[46]

The variation in subcommittee orientation also is related to the goals of committee members, at least in the House. In 1969-1970, policy and constituency committees of the House had nearly identical scores on the subcommittee orientation index—48.5 and 47.5, respectively. But by 1979-1980, after the period of reform, policy committees became decidedly more subcommittee-oriented than constituency committees, on average—70.3 and 59.3 respectively—and the difference has held up since that time. Thus, change in the subcommittee orientation of House committees was greater among policy committees than constituency committees. It is on policy committees that activist, policy-oriented members have found independent subcommittees most useful.

No similar differences between committee types appear in the Senate. Senators, who have more committee assignments and parliamentary prerogatives on the floor, are less dependent upon subcommittees for achieving personal political goals. As Table 4-9 indicates, there is tremendous variation among committees of each mix of member goals.[47]

THE IMPLICATIONS OF SUBCOMMITTEE GOVERNMENT

"Subcommittee government" is a more appropriate description of the internal decision-making processes of House committees than Senate committees. House subcommittees have developed a more thoroughly institutionalized role. This role is established not only in the rules of the House and Democratic Caucus, but also in the interests of individual representatives. Representatives with sufficient seniority to chair a subcommittee ordinarily chair only one. That position gives them additional staff, control over hearings on matters under their sub-committee's jurisdiction, and the power to initiate or block legislation in the absence of actions by the full committee.

By contrast, a Senate subcommittee is only one of two or three subcommittees that a typical majority party senator chairs. The typical senator is less dependent on any one subcommittee or subcommittee chair for legislative livelihood than the typical representative. The tremendous demands on senators' time make senators less likely to insist that their subcommittees be active, effective decision-making units. As a result, the importance of Senate subcommittees is more variable. On several Senate committees, subcommittees play no formal role in writing legislation. And over the last decade or so, reliance on subcommittees has declined on some Senate committees. Rather than developing an entrenched role in committee decision-making processes, Senate sub-committees have proven to be a component of a very individualistic decision-making process.

The independence acquired by House subcommittees and their chairs during the past three decades has had some negative conse-quences, as well, for rank-and-file members, full committee chairs, party leaders, and the policy process itself.[48] The number of meetings and hearings House members are expected to attend has increased greatly, approaching but not yet matching senators' work loads. There is a widespread feeling among representatives that they lack control over their own legislative lives. Now they are less able to choose carefully their legislative priorities and specialize in a narrow subject matter as they have in past years. They have become more dependent on committee and personal staffs, and somewhat less dependent on close working relationships with colleagues.

Subcommittee independence has developed at the expense of the full committee chairs' power. On most House committees, full commit-tee chairs can do very little to block a determined subcommittee chair's effort to hold hearings, recommend legislation, and place the legislation on the full committee's agenda. They now lack the firm control of the flow of legislation to subcommittees, of committee staff, and of the agenda that many Senate chairs retain. House chairs are now more dependent on personal skills to lead their committees than on their formal powers; accommodation and responsiveness are now more characteristic of their actions.

For majority party leaders in the House, the rise of independent subcommittees has been a mixed blessing. No longer confronted with committee chairs who enjoy dictatorial control over their committees, party leaders now have more avenues of access to committee members and more ways to influence committee decisions. But a more open and democratic process also means that more members place demands on party leaders. More members must be consulted and accommodated, many of whom are not nearly as well known to party leaders as committee chairs tend to be.

Shifting the responsibility of originating legislation to subcommittees has had several other implications for House policy making. First, weaker "institutional memory" for past policies and political maneuvers often results from the fairly high turnover among subcommittee chairs. As members choose more highly coveted chairs as they gain seniority, subcommittees lose the experience and expertise that their chairs developed. And subcommittee staff assistants often move with chairs to their new job.

Second, the small size and relatively small jurisdictions of most subcommittees often narrow the range of political interests represented at the initial stage of writing legislation. Narrowness of interest is reinforced by the process of subcommittee self-selection that operates in both chambers. The greater bias of the interests represented in subcommittee may, in turn, provoke more intense conflict in full committee and on the floor than would occur if more representative groups populated subcommittees.

Third, while subcommittees provide for a greater division of labor among members and increase the capacity of Congress to consider many issues simultaneously, they also add a step to the legislative process and create an additional obstacle to legislative action. Active subcommittees tend to increase the points at which jurisdictional conflicts arise between committees. Even intersubcommittee conflict over jurisdiction within a single committee occasionally complicates policy making.

Such undesirable consequences of independent subcommittees should be kept in perspective. They are more serious in the House than the Senate, and even in the House the substantive role of subcommittees varies. Clientelism and parochialism may be magnified by independent subcommittees, but many interests that were locked out by autocratic full committee chairs now have several avenues of access to committees. It is important to recognize that subcommittee chairs cannot dominate committee decision making the way some full committee chairs once did. On controversial issues, subcommittee chairs cannot guarantee party leaders that legislation will be reported to the floor in a particular form at a particular time. The allocation of subcommittee assignments by self-selection means that subcommittee chairs have no more control than full committee chairs over the composition of their subcommittees—far less control than most full committee chairs enjoyed before the reforms of the 1970s. Subcommittee chairs are not assured of control of their own subcommittees' policy decisions. Hence, the independence of subcommittee chairs does not guarantee subcommittee autonomy. Subcommittee chairs are dependent on the support of a majority of the full committee, which often is difficult to obtain.[49]

CONCLUSION

No longer are committees the personal fiefdoms of their chairs. Full committee chairs remain powerful players, but they now are more accountable and responsive to their committee colleagues, party caucuses, and parent chambers. These changes are more conspicuous in the House, where they were forced through more deliberate and sweeping reform efforts. But in the Senate, too, chairs now seldom wield the autocratic authority that at least a few chairs did forty years ago.

During the last twenty years, House committees have become more formally decentralized, while Senate committees continue to show a very mixed pattern. Reliance on subcommittees to hold hearings and devise the initial drafts of legislation is now nearly universal in the House, although there are important exceptions. If anything, the Senate is moving in the opposition direction. Some Senate committees have reduced their reliance on subcommittees for drafting legislation, and it has even been proposed that subcommittees should be limited to the function of conducting hearings. "Subcommittee government" therefore is an accurate depiction of decision-making patterns within most House committees but very few Senate committees.

Within each chamber committees continue to exhibit important differences. Characteristics of committee jurisdictions, the nature of committees' policy environments, and members' personal political goals shape the decision-making processes within committees. Thus, House committees such as Energy and Commerce, Education and Labor, and Ways and Means, all operating under identical restrictions imposed by chamber and caucus rules, have developed distinctive patterns of leadership, subcommittee orientations, and staffing arrangements. Nevertheless, because of the more restrictive character of chamber and party rules in the House, House committees exhibit greater similarity in internal decision-making processes than do Senate committees.

NOTES

1. Technically, the parent chambers elect heads of full committees (and other committee members), but they rely on the majority party to nominate a member for each chair. House Rule X(6) provides that "one of the members of each standing committee shall be elected by the House, from nominations submitted by the majority party caucus, at the commencement of each Congress, as chairman thereof." Senate Rule XXIV requires that "the Senate, unless otherwise ordered, shall by resolution appoint the chairman of each [standing] committee and the other members thereof. On demand of any senator, a separate vote shall be had on the appointment of the chairman of any such committee and on the appointment of the other members thereof."
2. For more detail on these subjects, see Steven S. Smith and Christopher J. Deering, *Committees in Congress* (Washington, D.C.: CQ Press, 1984), chap. 6.
3. Smith and Deering, *Committees in Congress*, pp. 197-198.
4. *Congressional Quarterly Weekly Report*, February 9, 1985, 287.
5. C. Lawrence Evans, *Influence in Senate Committees* (Ph.D. dissertation, University of Rochester, 1987), chap. 4.
6. Ibid., chap. 5.
7. Richard L. Hall, "Participation and Purpose in Committee Decision Making," *American Political Science Review* 81 (March 1987): 115; and Lawrence Evans and Richard L. Hall, "The Power of Subcommittees," *Journal of Politics* (forthcoming).
8. For additional background, see Christopher J. Deering, "Subcommittee Government in the U.S. House: An Analysis of Bill Management," *Legislative Studies Quarterly* 7 (November 1982): 533-546.
9. A recent development in the House is the more frequent appearance of the majority leader as a bill manager. This is a by-product of the greater frequency of multiple committee bills orchestrated by the central party leadership (a subject addressed in more detail in Chapter 5). Bills on drugs, education, trade, and other issues have been stimulated by the leadership, drafted by multiple committees, and then packaged into a single measure for consideration on the floor. The majority leader managed several of these bills during the 1980s, although the number is small relative to the large volume of measures considered on the floor (the tally for the majority leader is included in the "Others" category in Table 4-2). As we will see in the next chapter, this development is indicative of a general trend toward a more centralized decision-making process and less autonomous committees in the House.
10. Dole often shared bill management duties with his whip, Alan Simpson. One-third of the leader-managed measures were managed by Simpson in the 99th Congress. Byrd was far more self-reliant.
11. It also should be noted in Table 4-3 that House Democrats have exhibited a trend toward increasing support for party positions since the mid-1970s (as have House Republicans). The trend is due primarily to the increasing party support among southern Democrats, although northern Democrats have become more supportive of party positions as well. In the 1980s, the gap between northern and southern Democrats remained, but was much smaller than in the 1970s. In light of these trends, the increase in party support among full committee chairs is quite remarkable, for it far exceeds the increases found among southern Democrats.

12. Not-so-veiled threats are reported occasionally. In 1989, for example, John P. Murtha (D-Pa.), a new defense appropriations subcommittee chair, was put on notice that liberals in his party would be scrutinizing his behavior. See Richard E. Cohen, "Calling the Tune on Military Spending," *National Journal*, March 11, 1989, 605.

13. At the time of his election in 1985, Aspin is reported to have assured colleagues that he would modify his position on the controversial MX missile, which he had supported. He later was criticized for reneging on his promises, although Aspin contended that he never promised to alter his MX position. On his original election and his colleagues' concerns, see Steven V. Roberts, "Democrats Defy House Leaders; Price Loses Post," *New York Times*, January 5, 1985, 1, 7; and Nadine Cohodas and Diane Granat, "House Seniority System Jolted; Price Dumped, Aspin Elected," *Congressional Quarterly Weekly Report*, January 5, 1985, 7-9. On Aspin's initial defeat for reelection as chair, see Jacqueline Calmes, "Aspin Ousted as Armed Services Chairman," *Congressional Quarterly Weekly Report*, January 10, 1987, 83-85.

14. In contrast, the three instances of successful challenges in 1975 represented broad dissatisfaction with the incumbent chairs, and in each case the next most senior Democrat was elected.

15. See Dale Tate, "Retrenchment Too: Use of Omnibus Bills Burgeons Despite Members' Misgivings: Long-Term Impact Disputed," *Congressional Quarterly Weekly Report*, September 25, 1982, 2379-2383; and Allen Schick, "The Whole and the Parts: Piecemeal and Integrated Approaches to Congressional Budgeting," paper prepared for the Task Force on the Budget Process, House Committee on the Budget, Serial No. CP-3 (Washington, D.C.: U.S. Government Printing Office, 1987).

16. See, for example, Allen Schick, "The Ways and Means of Leading Ways and Means," *The Brookings Review* (Fall 1989): 23.

17. Jacqueline Calmes, " 'Professor' Runs the Show at House Banking," *Congressional Quarterly Weekly Report*, September 8, 1984, 2203-2205.

18. For more background on the emergence of powerful subcommittees, see Roger H. Davidson, "Subcommittee Government: New Channels for Policy Making," in *The New Congress*, ed. Thomas E. Mann and Norman J. Ornstein (Washington, D.C.: American Enterprise Institute, 1981), 99-133; Steven Haeberle, "The Institutionalization of Subcommittees in the U.S. House of Representatives," *Journal of Politics* 40 (1978): 1054-1065; and Lawrence C. Dodd and Richard L. Schott, *Congress and the Administrative State* (New York: John Wiley & Sons, 1979).

   For background on the role of subcommittees on various standing committees, see David N. Farnsworth, *The Senate Committee on Foreign Relations* (Urbana: University of Illinois Press, 1961); Richard F. Fenno, Jr., *Congressmen in Committees* (Boston: Little, Brown, 1973); Richard F. Fenno, Jr., *The Power of the Purse: Appropriations Politics in Congress* (Boston: Little, Brown, 1966); George Goodwin, Jr., *The Little Legislatures* (Amherst: University of Massachusetts Press, 1970); Ralph K. Huitt, "The Congressional Committee: A Case Study," *American Political Science Review* 48 (1954): 340-365; Charles O. Jones, "Representation in Congress: The Case of the House Agriculture Committee," *American Political Science Review* 55 (1961): 358-367; John D. Lees, *The Committee System of the United States Congress* (New York: Humanities Press, 1967); John Manley, *The Politics of Finance: The House Committee on Ways and Means* (Boston: Little, Brown, 1970); William Morrow, *Congressional*

Committees (New York: Scribner's, 1969); Norman J. Ornstein and David W. Rohde, "Shifting Forces, Changing Rules and Political Outcomes: The Impact of Congressional Change on Four House Committees," in *New Perspectives on the House of Representatives*, 3d ed., ed. Robert L. Peabody and Nelson W. Polsby (Chicago: Rand McNally, 1977), 186-269; Norman J. Ornstein and David W. Rohde, "Revolt from Within: Congressional Change, Legislative Policy, and the House Commerce Committee," in *Legislative Reform and Public Policy*, ed. Susan Welch and John G. Peters (New York: Praeger, 1977), 54-72; Ralph Nader Project, *The Agriculture Committees* (New York: Grossman, 1975); Ralph Nader Project, *The Money Committees* (New York: Grossman, 1975); David E. Price, *Who Makes the Laws?* (Cambridge, Mass.: Schenkman, 1972); David E. Price, *The Commerce Committees* (New York: Grossman, 1975); Catherine E. Rudder, "Committee Reform and the Revenue Process," in *Congress Reconsidered*, ed. Lawrence C. Dodd and Bruce I. Oppenheimer (New York: Praeger, 1977), 117-139; and Randall Strahan, "Agenda Change and Committee Politics in the Postreform House," *Legislative Studies Quarterly* 13 (May 1988): 177-197.

19. Three House committees—Banking, District of Columbia, and Public Works and Transportation—have rules requiring that majority party members (Democrats) receive an equal number of subcommittee assignments.

20. In practice, House Republican ranking members have some flexibility. They often suggest certain arrangements of subcommittee assignments to strengthen the party's position or retain experienced members on critical subcommittees.

21. At the start of the 100th Congress in 1987, the Democratic Caucus barred waivers of the subcommittee limitation rule, except in two situations: (1) members serving on three full committees by serving on the less popular District of Columbia, House Administration, or Judiciary committees; and (2) members serving on a full committee with a temporary appointment (for one congress).

22. Senate Rule XXV(4) limits each senator to no more than three subcommittees on the two major committees on which he or she may sit and to no more than two on the one minor committee on which he or she may sit.

23. "Right Pell, Wrong Pew," *New York Times*, October 11, 1985, A22.

24. The multiplicity of committee and subcommittee assignments has created more than scheduling problems for some members. Members' attendance records at committee meetings and hearings have been raised as issues in campaigns. The Senate Committee on the Judiciary changed its rule on attendance record keeping in 1987 as a reaction to criticism of one of its members during his 1986 campaign for reelection. The rule provides that attendance at hearings will be recorded only if members are given advance notice. See Ward Sinclair, "Absence-Minded Panel Stops Taking Attendance: Records Have Become Campaign Issue," *Washington Post*, March 5, 1987, A25.

25. Smith and Deering, *Committees in Congress*, 131.

26. Judiciary Committee Rule V(3), 101st Congress, *Congressional Record*, February 23, 1989, S1712.

27. Finance Committee Rule 16, 101st Congress, *Congressional Record*, February 28, 1989, S1854.

28. *Congressional Record*, February 22, 1989, S1594. Energy and Natural Resources' rule includes the follow parenthetical statement: "In addition, other issues are retained in the Full Committee on an ad hoc basis. Generally, these are

issues which (1) require extremely expeditious handling or (2) substantially overlap two or more subcommittee jurisdictions, or (3) are of exceptional national significance in which all Members wish to participate." Thus, as on many Senate committees, the full committee chair retains substantial discretion about whether to refer legislation to subcommittee.

29. House committees uniforely require that subcommittees consult with the full committee chair in order to avoid scheduling conflicts. Energy and Commerce is the only House committee with an even stricter requirement. Its rule requires the *approval* of the full committee chair when scheduling meetings and hearings, although this has not been a significant problem for subcommittees of the committee.

30. The use of subcommittees on most Senate committees did not change much with the change in party control of the Senate from Democratic to Republican in 1981 and back to Democratic in 1987. On the 1981 switch in majority status, see Roger H. Davidson and Walter J. Oleszek, "Changing the Guard in the U.S. Senate," *Legislative Studies Quarterly* 9 (November 1984): 635-663.

31. See Chapter 6 for more discussion of the selection of conferees. Also see Lawrence D. Longley and Walter J. Oleszek, *Bicameral Politics: Conference Committees in Congress* (New Haven: Yale University Press, 1989), 178-186.

32. The 1981 rule of the House Democratic Caucus limiting the number of subcommittees has made it more difficult to create such semipermanent task forces.

33. It should be noted that House Armed Services has had more difficulty than other committees in developing a subcommittee arrangement that suits the needs and policy perspectives of its members. The committee is torn between organizing its subcommittees according to narrow categories used to structure the Department of Defense budget and structuring the subcommittees by broad policy questions or defense missions (such as readiness or regional defense). Over the years the committee has used various combinations, producing overlapping jurisdictions and intersubcommittee conflict. See Nelson Schwartz, "Will Readiness, Seapower Panels Survive Reorganization of House Armed Services?" *Roll Call*, October 16, 1988, 12-13.

34. See, respectively, *Business Week*, March 27, 1987, 90; *Washington Post*, January 18, 1981, A1; and *Washington Post*, February 12, 1980, A1; also Hedrick Smith, *The Power Game: How Washington Works* (New York: Ballantine Books, 1988), chap. 10.

35. Quoted in Irwin B. Arieff, "Growing Staff System on Hill Forcing Changes in Congress," *Congressional Quarterly Weekly Report*, November 24, 1979, 2631.

36. For background on congressional committee staffs, see Joel D. Aberbach, "The Congressional Committee Intelligence System: Information, Oversight, and Change," *Congress and the Presidency* 14 (Spring 1987): 51-76; and Joel D. Aberbach, *Keeping a Watchful Eye: The Politics of Congressional Oversight* (Washington, D.C.: Brookings Institution, 1990); David W. Brady, "Personnel Management in the House," in *The House at Work*, ed. Joseph Cooper and G. Calvin Mackenzie (Austin: University of Texas Press, 1981), 164-177; Christine DeGregorio, "Professional in the U.S. Congress: An Analysis of Working Styles," *Legislative Studies Quarterly* 13 (November 1988): 459-476; Susan Webb Hammond, "The Management of Legislative Offices," in *The House at Work*, ed. Cooper and Mackenzie, 186-189; Gladys M. Kammerer, *The Staffing of the Committees of Congress* (Lexington: University of Kentucky Press, 1949);

Kenneth T. Kofmehl, *Professional Staffs of Congress* (Lafayette, Ind.: Purdue Research Foundation, 1962); Harrison W. Fox, Jr., and Susan Webb Hammond, *Congressional Staffs: The Invisible Force in American Lawmaking* (New York: The Free Press, 1977); Michael J. Malbin, *Unelected Representatives: Congressional Staff and the Future of Representative Government* (New York: Basic Books, 1980); David E. Price, "Professionals and 'Entrepreneurs': Staff Orientations and Policy Making on Three Senate Committees," *Journal of Politics* 33 (May 1971): 316-336; Robert H. Salisbury and Kenneth A. Shepsle, "Congressional Staff Turnover and the Ties-That-Bind," *American Political Science Review* 75 (June 1981): 381-396; and Steven S. Smith and Christopher J. Deering, *Committees in Congress*, chap. 7.

37. House Rule XI(6) grants two committees, Appropriations and Budget, authority to hire as many staff assistants as they deem necessary, subject to approved appropriations.

38. Committees may elect to maintain nonpartisan staffs without distinguishing between majority and minority party staffs. The choice rests with the minority party contingents on each committee, which may demand staff of their own.

39. House Rule XI makes this guarantee for up to six subcommittees on each committee.

40. Smith and Deering, *Committees in Congress*, 209. The statistic is Spearman's *r*, a correlation coefficient for ordinal rankings.

41. The *New York Times* implied that retention of the Republican appointees was part of a deal to gain the ranking Republican senator's support for a clean water bill. See "Patronage Wrinkle I," *New York Times*, January 7, 1987, A18. Even if there was such a deal, however, it was made possible only because the new chair found the Republican appointees compatible with his own plans.

42. John Felton, "Lugar Moves to Put Stamp on Foreign Relations," *Congressional Quarterly Weekly Report*, January 12, 1985, 84-85.

43. Price, "Professionals and 'Entrepreneurs'."

44. Smith and Deering, *Committees in Congress*, 215-216.

45. Bill management data are taken from the 99th Congress (1985-1986), and the others are taken from the 100th Congress (1987-1988).

46. Omnibus legislating has little effect on the distribution of staff. It may actually increase the relative frequency of bill management by subcommittee chairs on some committees, as measures otherwise managed by the full committee chairs are included in larger packages.

47. As useful as an overall index of subcommittee orientation has proven, a caution is in order. In our effort to draw general characterizations of committee practices, we do not mean to imply that each subcommittee of a committee is treated identically. Variations in the salience and controversy of subcommittee jurisdictions, along with factors such as personal skills and human relations, shape the relationship between subcommittees and their parent committees. It certainly would be fallacious to assume that the general patterns we have reported accurately represent the experience of individual subcommittees. An excellent treatment of the experiences of House Ways and Means subcommittees can be found in Randall Strahan and R. Kent Weaver, "Subcommittee Government and the House Ways and Means Committee," paper delivered at the annual meeting of the Southern Political Science Association, Memphis, Tenn., November, 1983. Neverthe-

less, we are confident that a more detailed analysis would support the view
that variation in subcommittee orientation between House committee types
and between the chambers exceeds the variation within most committees.
Reliance on subcommittees for initiating legislation, patterns of bill management, and the independence of subcommittee staff do not vary greatly
within most committees.

48. See Davidson, "Subcommittee Government," and Norman J. Ornstein, "The
    House and Senate in a New Congress," in *The New Congress,* ed. Mann and
    Ornstein, 367-369.
49. For examples of the limits of subcommittee chairs' power on an important
    committee, see Ronald Brownstein, "Trench Warfare," *National Journal,*
    September 14, 1985, 2047-2053, on the problems of a House Energy and
    Commerce subcommittee chair in gaining the approval of his subcommittee
    and committee for legislation authorizing the Superfund, a federal program
    to fund the cleanup of hazardous wastes; and Christopher Madison, "Midair
    Collision," *National Journal,* October 7, 1989, 2491, on the problems faced by
    another Energy and Commerce subcommittee chair in clean air legislation.

CHAPTER 5

Committees, Parties, and the Parent Chambers

Committee power has come under attack during the past two decades. While committees remain central to nearly all congressional policy decisions, they no longer operate as autonomously as they once did. Change has been most dramatic in the House of Representatives, where committees traditionally have dominated policy making more completely than in the Senate. But in both chambers decision making has become much less committee-centered.[1]

This chapter details the challenges to the function of the House and Senate committee systems. First, three perspectives on committee power are described. These perspectives suggest propositions about the degree of committee autonomy that exists in Congress. Then we examine important developments that altered the role of committee power during the past two decades: party activism, referral of legislation to committee, floor amending activity and roll-call voting, committee control of conference committees, and elaboration of the congressional budget process. As we will see, committees retain great power in Congress, although they do not control legislative outcomes to the extent they once did.

PERSPECTIVES ON COMMITTEE POWER

Decision-making processes in Congress represent an interaction of committees, parties, and the parent chambers. The relative importance of committees, parties, and the chamber floors in policy making varies from time to time. To develop an appreciation of the potential importance of each for policy outcomes, it is useful to consider three alternative perspectives on, or interpretations of, committee power: autonomous committees, party-dominated committees, and chamber-dominated committees.[2] Each perspective is a highly stylized view of congressional decision making grounded in certain aspects of actual practice. After reviewing the three perspectives, we will consider conditions that lead Congress to adopt decision-making patterns that approximate one perspective or another.

The *autonomous committees perspective* holds that the members of each committee determine policy within their jurisdiction, irrespective of the policy preferences of the parent chamber and parties. Fully autonomous committees would have monopoly control over setting the agenda for their parent chamber. That is, they would have the ability to exercise negative power (blocking legislation by refusing to report it to the floor) and positive power (proposing legislation that the chamber is compelled to consider). Complete autonomy also requires that alternatives to committee recommendations be ineligible or routinely defeated and that committee recommendations be adopted.

While congressional committees have never been completely auton-omous, the autonomous committees perspective is very close to the one propounded by observers who emphasize Congress's decentralized features. Supporting this perspective are the following observations: those members whose constituencies care most about the jurisdiction of a committee are assigned to the committee and dominate its decisions; once assigned to a committee, the "property right" norm allows them to retain a seat on the committee as long as they want it; and members not assigned to the committee defer to the committee when its legislation comes to the floor, primarily because there is little political incentive to take an interest in the legislation. Therefore, in this view, policy is a product of the preferences of committee members and their constituen-cies, and reflects their biases. The perspective depicts each chamber as a set of fairly autonomous, mutually deferential committees, and allows little real policy role for the floor, the parties, or party leaders.

The *party-dominated committees perspective* emphasizes the vital role of the parties in each chamber. In this view, committee members are agents or instruments of their parties. The parties have the capacity to shape the composition and policy outlook of their committee contingents because they control appointment decisions. In addition, committees are depen-dent on party leaders for scheduling their legislation for floor consider-ation, among other things, which gives party leaders an additional source of leverage with committees. These ties between the party and committee members create an implicit contract that constrains committee behavior. As a result, the majority party has effective control over committee decisions. And because committee recommendations are constrained by the views of the majority party, committees lack autonomy.[3]

The *chamber-dominated committees* perspective emphasizes that com-mittees are agents or instruments of their parent chambers. According to this view, committees are created to meet the needs of the chamber for a division of labor, the development of expertise, the acquisition of information, and the organization of a supporting staff. The charters of most committees are found in the rules of their parent chamber, which may abolish or restructure committees at any time. Most important, committees must obtain majority support on the floor for their legislation and so must anticipate floor reactions to their recommendations. Rather than viewing committees as autonomous, this perspective considers committees to be highly constrained by chamber preferences. Committees are granted discretion only within narrow ranges of policy options and over legislative detail. This discretion may give committees leverage over individual noncommittee members, but it does not grant autonomy over matters of importance to chamber majorities.[4]

Each of the three perspectives has attractive features. A committee-dominated system allows Congress to manage a large work load by providing a division of labor and encourages the development of expertise among committee members, who know that their work will be respected and approved by others. A party-dominated system allows for the emergence of strong party leadership, which can supervise the development of coherent, timely policy, and makes it possible to hold a party accountable for congressional decisions. A chamber-dominated system seems quite democratic because it preserves the equality of the members and allows all members to have an active voice in all important decisions.

None of these perspectives fully captures the nature of the relationships among committees, parties, and the parent chambers. Rather, each exaggerates the importance of certain features of congressional rules and practices. But there is more than a grain of truth in each model. For example, self-selection and the property-right norm are important to committee assignments, but the parties do exercise great care in the appointment of members to a few committees. On most pieces of legislation, many members are quite indifferent and willingly defer to committees, but in many areas party leaders and the parent chambers show little deference. In fact, the exercise of committee discretion, party influence, and chamber influence is visible in some degree on most major bills passed by Congress.

CONDITIONS SHAPING THE ROLE OF COMMITTEES

The fundamental issue, then, is the degree to which the House and Senate rely upon committees, parties, and the floors of the parent chambers to make authoritative decisions for the institution. Because of our focus on the role of committees, we will view this issue as a question of the extent to which committee decisions are constrained or checked by the parties and parent chambers. Constraints on committee decisions are determined by the character of Congress's policy agenda, the distribution of policy preferences, and the institutional context. The effects of these factors can be summarized in several propositions.

THE POLICY AGENDA. The nature of the issues or policy problems that Congress faces affects how Congress makes decisions and the reliance it places on standing committees. In general, it seems reasonable to argue, *the larger the agenda, the more separable the issues, the more issues recur frequently, and the less salient the issues, the more Congress relies on committees and the less it relies on the parties or the parent chambers to make decisions.* Large agendas require a division of labor to handle the work load and a system of powerful committees provides it. If the issues are not interconnected, then a system of committees handling mutually exclusive issues works well. Furthermore, if similar issues are raised frequently, then fixing committee jurisdictions can be done without concern that some committees will become superfluous over time and that their members will become inactive and powerless. Moreover, if most issues concern only a few members, committees can make decisions without serious challenge on the floor. Conversely, more narrowly defined agendas, interrelated issues, rapidly changing policy problems, and widespread interest in most legislation undermine committee autonomy and encourage active party and chamber involvement on most matters.

DISTRIBUTION OF POLICY PREFERENCES. When most members take an active interest in policy decisions, the alignment of members on important issues shapes the role of committees as well. The alignment of members, of course, is primarily a function of constituency preferences, although forces internal to Congress—the persuasiveness of a party leader, for example—can make a difference at times. But whatever the cause, *if the majority party is highly cohesive on the issues and most issues are salient, it will be in a position to impose policy decisions by virtue of having enough votes to win, and a system of party-dominated committees will develop.* If the majority party lacks sufficient cohesiveness, majority coalitions— perhaps different coalitions on different issues—may assert themselves on the floor and determine policy outcomes. That is, *when the majority party lacks cohesiveness and most issues are salient, a system of chamber-dominated committees will develop.*

INSTITUTIONAL CONTEXT. Finally, it is worth remembering that the House and Senate are very different institutions. The root of many of their differences is size: the House is much larger than the Senate. There is greater demand for strong leadership and observance of formal rules in the larger, more unwieldy House. In the Senate, there is greater tolerance of individual initiative and greater resistance to committee- or party-imposed policy decisions. That tolerance is represented in the rules of the Senate that protect the individual senator's right to offer amendments on any subject and conduct extended debate. Such rules preserve the bargaining leverage that individual senators have when dealing with committee and party leaders. To generalize, *a chamber-dominated system will be more common in the Senate*, where floor procedures allow individual members to challenge committee and party actions more effectively. Therefore, *changes in policy agendas and political alignments that encourage more committee-dominated or party-dominated decision making are not reflected as rapidly in the Senate as in the House.*

DECLINING COMMITTEE POWER

Changes in the policy agenda and political alignments have led to a decline in committee autonomy in recent decades. The developments within Congress that contributed to this decline are detailed in the remainder of this chapter. But these developments had origins outside of Congress. A few words about the external sources of declining committee power are in order here.

The character of the congressional policy agenda changed in important ways during the 1960s and 1970s as new issues appeared on the congressional agenda.[5] Energy, the environment, consumer protection, civil rights, and many other issues that had not been subject to national debate or had been suppressed now emerged, creating new demands for congressional action. These issues failed to fit neatly into the jurisdictional confines of a single committee, and many, like energy and the environment, became interconnected in new ways. Moreover, as the agenda grew in size it also became less predictable and recurrent. Issues died and new ones were born in more rapid succession. More members, particularly recently elected ones, insisted on having a voice in decisions concerning the wide range of new issues before Congress.

Under such circumstances, a system of fairly autonomous committees was inconvenient, to say the least. Outsiders to committees resented the dominance of senior committee members on policy decisions, and committees found themselves in conflict with other committees seeking jurisdiction for new, complex issues facing Congress. As noted in Chapter 2, many of the reforms of the 1970s were motivated by these changes in the policy problems Congress faced.

By the late 1970s and 1980s, concern about the federal budget deficit began to dominate policy making. Most other domestic policy issues were set aside or reinterpreted largely in terms of their budget consequences. The congressional agenda contracted, and the remaining issues, largely surrounding budgetary decisions, concerned all members.

While the policy agenda was expanding and then shrinking, the political alignments among members shifted.[6] In the 1970s, fights over how and where to expand the role of the federal government continued to divide congressional Democrats. Liberal northern Democrats generally favored an expanded federal role and were opposed by much more conservative southern Democrats. Republicans also experienced similar divisions within their ranks. But due to electoral changes and a new agenda, the party coalitions proved far more cohesive in the 1980s. In many southern states, conservative Republicans were elected in place of conservative Democrats. The remaining southern Democrats in Congress were more supportive of their party leaders, and the new southern Republicans proved highly partisan, making both parties more homogeneous. In addition, the budget cuts of the 1980s put Democrats from all regions on the defensive and produced more party-line votes.

Thus, by the mid-1980s a more consolidated and interconnected policy agenda, along with more partisan political alignments, had dramatically altered the context in which committees operated. The propositions set out in the previous section suggest that committees would not be granted as much autonomy under such conditions. The legislative work load contracted, core budget decisions constrained other policy decisions, and the parties were in a position to act more cohesively on key policy decisions. A process once dominated by fairly autonomous committees and maintaining weak parties became a system ripe for stronger parties.

Development of stronger parties and weaker committees is exactly what came to pass in Congress during the 1980s. As the propositions suggest, the decline in committee power was greater in the House than in the Senate, where committees had less autonomy to lose, but a decline in committee autonomy is noticeable in the Senate as well. As this chapter details, however, not all committees have experienced the same changes, and, in the case of the House, some steps have been taken to stop or even reverse the decline in committee autonomy. Nonetheless, the place of the House and Senate committee systems in the legislative process has changed in ways that make them less central to policy outcomes than they were three or four decades ago.

We now turn to the developments within Congress associated with the decline in committee autonomy. Several developments have reshaped the role of congressional committees: (1) the revitalization of the

Democratic caucuses in the House and Senate and developments in their organizations that affect committee activity, (2) multiple referral of legislation in the House, (3) changing patterns of floor amendments and new floor procedures, (4) conference practices, and (5) new and frequently modified budget procedures.

THE ACTIVITY OF THE PARTY CAUCUSES AND LEADERS

The vital role congressional parties play in making committee assignments gives the parties a source of influence with their committee contingents. But of the four congressional party organizations, only House Democrats have adopted a formal set of rules to govern the behavior of party members in their capacity as representatives of the party on standing committees. Senate Democrats recently have rejuvenated their party committees and sought to improve central coordination of committee decision making.

The single most prominent source of declining congressional committee autonomy was the revitalization of the House Democratic Caucus in the late 1960s and its activism, particularly in the 1980s. The Democratic Caucus was an engine for the reform of committee procedures in the 1970s, and it has become the arena for frequent policy debates, occasionally serving as a forum for criticizing the recommendations or strategies of committee leaders.[7] In 1989, for example, Democrats used a caucus meeting to chastise Ways and Means Democrats who opposed the leadership's position on the capital gains tax rate.

The most direct assault on committee autonomy by the Democratic Caucus concerned the committee assignment process. Two key changes, both implemented in 1975, transformed the relationship between standing committees and the majority party: (1) the shift of committee assignment authority to the Steering and Policy Committee, a party committee chaired by the Speaker, and (2) the requirement that committee chairs (and Appropriations subcommittee chairs) stand for election in the Democratic Caucus. Democrats now had to lobby the leadership directly for coveted committee assignments, and committee chairs were forced to pay closer attention to the policy and procedural preferences of the party.

The clear winner in these changes was the Speaker, who became central to the committee assignment process and could play an important role in the election and reelection of committee chairs. The clear losers were the chairs, who had been well insulated from challenges to their reappointment. Successful challenges to four full committee chairs and one Appropriations subcommittee chair, along with threats to unseat others and occasional discussion of incorporating more sub-committee chairs under the rules, have undermined this traditional source of committee autonomy.

More generally, the high level of activity of the Democratic Caucus and its various organizational units has introduced new actors into the environments of major standing committees. By participating through party organs, rank-and-file Democrats not sitting on the committee of origin gain legitimacy and often secure timely information that en-hances their influence. On major measures, these developments have substantially reduced committee autonomy in prefloor deliberations. Participation in caucus activities is now so widespread and affects so many important issues that its effects are difficult to isolate and measure. The important point is that their party has provided rank-and-file Democrats avenues of influence through the party that did not exist in the 1960s.

In the Senate, Majority Leader George Mitchell (D-Maine) has rejuvenated the role of party organs in Senate decision making since gaining his post in 1989.[8] Under former majority leader Robert Byrd (D-W.Va.), the Democratic party conference and its committees had little role. Byrd preferred to deal personally and directly with committee chairs and bill managers, and he held few meetings of the conference, Policy Committee, or whips. Mitchell changed course, as he had promised, after being elected majority leader. He shared important party posts with more Democrats, encouraged the new party leaders to help set a direction for the Senate on important issues, and began to call more regular meetings of the party conference. In 1989, after Byrd had retired from his post as majority leader to chair the Appropriations Committee, the conference played an important role in promoting his antidrug plan over competing plans, including one sponsored by an Appropriations subcommittee chair.[9] Nevertheless, Senate Democrats, like House and Senate Republicans, impose no formal rules on committee operations and have not changed their committee assignment procedures in material ways in recent decades.

MULTIPLE REFERRAL IN THE HOUSE

A development of direct bearing on the autonomy of individual committees is the referral of legislation to more than one committee. In 1974 the Speaker of the House was granted the authority to send legislation to committees jointly or sequentially, or by splitting it into parts. Before 1974, the Speaker had been required to assign legislation to the single committee that had predominant jurisdiction for the contents of a bill, a practice that guaranteed monopoly referral rights to a single committee in each policy area. Under the current rule, the Speaker is encouraged to recognize overlapping jurisdictions and the desirability of coordinating the decisions of committees on complex issues. In fact, in recent congresses, about a quarter of the work load for the average House committee is multiple referred legislation.[10] By the 1980s, nearly one in five bills important enough to warrant a special rule originated in two or more committees. In the Senate, multiple referral always has been possible but remains far less common than in the House, perhaps because it is so easy for committees to protect their jurisdictional interests by seeking to amend legislation on the floor.

Multiple referral has several important implications for committee autonomy in the House.[11] First, sharing jurisdiction with other committees directly undermines the autonomy of a committee (see the box on p. 178). The multiple referral rule has encouraged committees to stake jurisdictional claims on a wide variety of issues and almost guarantees that conflict between committees will frequently arise. Since the mid-1970s, many committees have developed informal understandings about areas of shared jurisdiction that reduce open conflict, but these arrangements represent perforations in the autonomy of the committees that once enjoyed sole jurisdiction over those issue areas. In some policy areas, then, interdependence has replaced autonomy in intercommittee relations.

Second, conflict between two or more committees enhances the importance of others in shaping policy. Sometimes that conflict spills onto the House floor, where votes on a series of amendments may impose a resolution on the contesting committees. And party leaders may be encouraged to intercede between committees in order to avoid open conflict on the floor between fellow partisans of different committees. Committees have recognized, however, that they may be better off resolving their differences before the legislation goes to the floor. The Rules Committee has encouraged such prefloor compromises by granting special rules limiting floor amendments and by allowing a compromise version to be taken to the floor as a substitute for the competing committee proposals.[12] The process may help committees fend off unfriendly floor amendments, but it also sometimes involves compromises of committee positions that might not otherwise have been necessary.

Finally, and perhaps most important, the multiple referral rule and associated practices substantially strengthen the Speaker's influence on committee decisions. The Speaker determines, without appeal, the original referral of legislation to multiple committees. Moreover, since

Multiple Referral
Undermines a Committee's Autonomy

A House Merchant Marine and Fisheries subcommittee Oct. 3 approved a bill that would end years of effort by Merchant Mariners to expand their status as active-duty veterans of World War II.

The measure now goes to the Veterans' Affairs Committee, where action is unlikely. "I think frankly it will fall into the black hole of Calcutta, never to be seen again," a Merchant Marine Committee staffer said. Military veterans' groups oppose the bill.

The legislation (HR 44), introduced by Jack Fields, R-Texas, and approved by the Merchant Marine Subcommittee by voice vote after no debate, would extend eligibility for certain benefits to seamen who served from Aug. 15, 1945, to Dec. 31, 1946. Those benefits—such as the right to have an American flag on their caskets and to use Department of Veterans Affairs hospitals—are already offered to Merchant Mariners who served between Dec. 7, 1941, and Aug. 15, 1945—the date the Japanese surrendered.

But sponsors of the bill argued that the 1945 cutoff date is arbitrary and out of keeping with benefits received by military veterans' groups under the G.I. bill, which defines World War II as ending in 1946.

The Pentagon has long opposed extending these benefits to Merchant Mariners; the secretary of the Air Force did so reluctantly on Jan. 19, 1988, for the period ending with the Japanese surrender, but only after the U.S. District Court of the District of Columbia called a denial of benefits arbitrary.

The Merchant Marine, which transported military equipment during the war but did not carry guns, incurred a higher proportion of casualties during World War II than any branch of the armed forces other than the Marine Corps, according to the Maritime Administration. So far 72,000 people—some of them widows or surviving relatives of Merchant Mariners—have applied for the certification. Of the 3,882 applications denied, about three-quarters would be eligible for benefits under the legislation extending eligibility to 1946.

Source: Alyson Pytte, "A Few Good Merchant Marines," Congressional Quarterly Weekly Report, October 7, 1989, 2633.

1981, the Speaker also may re-refer a measure after it has been amended by a committee so as to affect another committee's jurisdiction. Thus, the Speaker is central to the process of resolving intercommittee conflict when it arises and may take the initiative to structure a multiple committee arrangement when it suits policy purposes. Speakers have taken such an initiative on many important pieces of legislation in recent years, including legislation on international trade, drug importation and abuse, homelessness, South African apartheid, and oil spills—

all issues on which House Democrats wanted to make an emphatic policy statement.

Furthermore, the Speaker may set deadlines on committee decisions when legislation is subject to multiple referral. When the referral is sequential, a series of deadlines normally are set. When the referral is joint, the Speaker may designate a primary committee and set deadlines on the secondary committees. And informally, the Speaker may announce the intention to proceed with a bill at a certain time and require that committees report legislation by a certain time if they want to contribute to a large package. In designing such arrangements, the Speaker is in a position to confer advantage on some committees, speed or delay committee action for strategic purposes, and send strong signals about policy preferences.

In sum, the new and still evolving techniques of multiple referral substantially reduce both the traditional negative and positive sources of committee power. On the negative side, committees receiving a referral subject to a deadline established by the Speaker effectively lose the option of reporting no legislation. If a committee fails to report its recommendations by the specified deadline, the Speaker is free to discharge the committee. On the positive side, more committees have access to legislation, but they now must formally share responsibility to determine the content of legislation taken to the floor. The net result of the increasing number of areas where committees share jurisdiction is declining autonomy, increasing interdependence among committees, and greater control of committee actions by the majority party leadership.

FLOOR ACTIVITY

In Chapter 1, negative and positive forms of committee power were distinguished. Traditionally, the ability of committees to attract support on the floor and to fend off unfriendly amendments has rested on sources of positive power—the ability to induce others to accept committee recommendations even when they oppose the recommendations. In most circumstances, it was noted, positive power is the product of extraprocedural resources of committees. Committee leaders usually have an advantage in information about policy substance and political circumstances. The advantage is acquired from personal experience, formal hearings, relationships with interest groups and executive agencies, expert staff assistance, and close ties to the party leadership. Committees' specialized staffs place committee members in a better position than others to define issues to their advantage, monitor the activity of their opponents, and respond promptly to opponents' political maneuvers. Due to their standing relationships with lobbyists and executive officials, committee leaders usually are in a good position to orchestrate external pressure on their colleagues.

These sources of positive power were reinforced by informal norms, at least before the 1960s.[13] An *apprenticeship* norm provided that new members refrain from active participation in policy making until they had served several years and gained political and policy experience. Through apprenticeships, members would gain expertise and earn the respect of their colleagues. A *specialization* norm provided that members should concentrate their efforts on matters under the jurisdiction of their assigned committees and matters directly affecting their constituencies. Apprenticeship and specialization together implied that experienced committee members should dominate policy making. In practice, this meant that committee recommendations, which were the handiwork of senior committee members, deserved *deference*. That deference, in turn, was *reciprocated* when other committees' legislation was on the floor. Apprenticeship, specialization, deference to committees, and intercommittee reciprocity formed a coherent set of informal norms that enhanced the autonomy of committees in policy making.[14]

Many of these committee advantages have weakened since the 1950s. During the last four decades, Congress has distributed more resources to rank-and-file members. Even the most junior minority party members now have substantial personal staffs and office budgets; improved office technology for information retrieval and dissemination; expanded access to strengthened support agencies, such as the Congressional Research Service and the General Accounting Office; and more relationships with experts in the swelling community of interest groups in Washington. As the resources of rank-and-file members expanded, the net informational advantage for committees diminished and the rationale for deferring to committees when their recommendations were brought to the floor weakened. Moreover, many of the new interest groups and growing constituencies placed demands on members to champion their causes when legislation affecting their interests reached the House and Senate floors, which increased the pressures on members to offer floor amendments. And just as important, many new members were elected to Congress with an established commitment to have an immediate impact on policy. By the early 1970s, few members considered deference to committee recommendations a viable norm.

Weakening committee autonomy is reflected in the record of floor amending activity since the mid-1950s.[15] Amending activity increased in both chambers during the 1950s and 1960s and surged upward in the 1970s.[16] A spectacular surge in House floor amending activity between 1971-1972 and 1973-1974 coincided with the adoption of recorded electronic voting in the Committee of the Whole, which appears to have increased the political incentives for members to offer floor amendments. But the increase in floor amending activity is not merely a function of the congressional work load, since the *proportion* of measures adopted in the House and Senate that were subject to at least one floor amendment also increased in the 1960s and 1970s.

Not all floor amendments are unfriendly to committee recommendations. To the contrary, some amendments—a fairly constant 10-15 percent of all amendments—are *second-degree amendments* (that is, amendments to amendments) supported by committee members and designed to weaken the effect of unfriendly first-degree amendments.[17] More important, many amendments—probably a majority of all first-degree amendments—represent legislative contributions that committee members find acceptable. And yet the increase in floor amendments represents weakening committee autonomy if for no other reason than that it reflects a shift in the location of policy initiative from committees to outsiders.

COMMITTEE DIFFERENCES

As expected, the pattern of change in floor amending activity is not identical for all committees. Consider the House first. The number of floor amendments per measure that were offered to each House committee's legislation in selected congresses since the 1950s is reported in Table 5-1. The table demonstrates that the surge in House amending activity occurred disproportionately among prestige and policy committees. That is, the most powerful committees witnessed the greatest increase in threats to their autonomy. The move to limit House floor amendments is visible for most committees in the drop in floor amendments between the 96th Congress (1979-1980) and the 99th (1985-1986).

A committee that stands out in Table 5-1 is House Appropriations. The two appropriations committees long have been the leading committees in floor amending activity, measured on a per bill basis. In part this is due to the fact that they report relatively few separate bills. Each bill is fairly important and must, in some form, be considered each year. The appropriations committees, unlike most other committees, do not have the luxury of reporting dozens of noncontroversial measures. In addition, because their bills cover most federal spending, many substantive controversies find their way into debates on appropriations bills. Spending decisions themselves often are controversial, of course, and

TABLE 5-1 Number of Floor Amendments per Measure in the House, by Committee (Selected Congresses)

	Congress				
	84th (1955-1956)	88th (1963-1964)	92d (1971-1972)	96th [a] (1979-1980)	99th [a] (1985-1986)
Prestige Committees					
Appropriations	2.6	2.4	3.6	9.5	4.4
Budget	—[b]	—	—	16.5	0.5
Rules	—	—	—	—	0.1
Ways and Means	0.1	0.1	0.2	0.8	3.1
Policy Committees					
Banking, Finance, and Urban Affairs	0.6	0.8	2.2	7.2	10.2
Education and Labor	2.1	6.6	4.1	3.0	2.1
Energy and Commerce	0.4	0.8	1.1	3.0	0.4
Foreign Affairs	0.3	2.9	0.9	10.1	3.4
Government Operations	0.8	0.9	0.7	2.7	0.3
Judiciary [c]	0.2	1.5	0.8	3.4	0.4
Constituency Committees					
Agriculture	0.4	2.0	1.0	2.2	4.1
Armed Services	0.3	0.4	0.8	2.6	19.1
Interior and Insular Affairs	0.2	0.5	0.4	0.9	0.2
Merchant Marine and Fisheries	0.1	0.0	0.4	1.0	0.2
Post Office and Civil Service	0.6	1.3	0.3	0.5	0.1
Public Works and Transportation	0.3	0.3	2.3	2.1	1.8
Science, Space, and Technology	—	1.2	0.7	3.1	0.9
Small Business	—	—	—	1.7	0.0
Veterans' Affairs	0.2	0.1	0.1	0.1	0.1

Source: Congressional Record; Final Calendar of the House of Representatives.

[a] For the 96th and 99th Congresses, only amendments to measures that were referred to three or fewer committees are included.

[b] Less than 0.05 amendments per measure.

[c] The number of amendments per measure for Judiciary is very low because of the large number of noncontroversial commemorative measures that it reports to the floor.

they are made even more so when they are used as vehicles for legislative provisions that might not survive the scrutiny of the authorizing committees.

A notable exception to the overall pattern of proportionately smaller increases in amending activity among constituency committees is House Armed Services, historically no more than an average constituency committee with respect to floor amendments. The traditional deference to the executive branch and the committee that generally reflected the policy preferences of the executive branch disappeared during the 1970s in the aftermath of the Vietnam War. In the 1980s, sharp differences between the Democratic House and the Reagan administration regarding defense policy and spending, as well as other priorities, sharpened the differences between Armed Services and the Democratic majority. This is reflected in the very high level of amending activity on Armed Services measures in the 99th Congress (1985-1986), which was fairly typical of the congresses of the 1980s. The Senate's Committee on Armed Services shows a similar pattern.

As in other areas, differences between committee types are not as tidy in the Senate as in the House. Nevertheless, the major policy committees face a large number of floor amendments and, with the obvious exception of Appropriations, display larger increases in the 1970s than constituency committees.

The House Response to the Surge in Floor Amendments

Committees did not sit idly by and gladly suffer unfriendly amendments. In some cases, second-degree amendments watered down unfriendly amendments. In others, the committee relied upon its monopoly control of the conference delegation to strip away unfriendly provisions in conference. In yet other cases, unfriendly floor action was avoided by making concessions to opponents in advance.

These tactics were no match for the forces stimulating unfriendly floor amendments and did not alleviate the logistical problems of preparing for large numbers of amendments, particularly on major bills. This was perceived to be a more serious problem in the House, where committee autonomy traditionally was stronger than in the Senate. Eventually, the majority party Democrats of the House were motivated to pursue new strategies: an increased use of suspension of the rules, and an expanded use of special rules to restrict and structure amending activity in the Committee of the Whole.[18] Both procedures had been used for decades, but new conditions led House Democrats to discover new uses for them.

TABLE 5-2   Number of Floor Amendments per Measure in the Senate, by Committee (Selected Congresses)

	Congress				
	84th (1955-1956)	88th (1963-1964)	92d (1971-1972)	96th (1979-1980)	99th (1985-1986)
Policy Committees					
Budget	— a	—	—	20.3	33.0
Foreign Relations	1.1	2.4	3.7	2.2	4.8
Governmental Affairs b	0.2	0.1	1.4	0.7	0.4
Judiciary c	0.1	0.2	0.1	0.3	0.2
Labor and Human Resources	0.1	1.8	5.1	3.0	1.4
Mixed Policy/ Constituency Committees					
Armed Services	0.2	0.3	1.7	1.8	10.8
Banking, Housing, and Urban Affairs	0.9	1.1	2.4	6.5	0.4
Finance	0.7	1.1	10.1	2.7	12.7
Constituency Committees					
Agriculture, Nutrition, and Forestry	1.1	1.4	0.6	1.4	12.1
Appropriations	2.7	3.6	3.1	11.8	17.9
Commerce, Science, and Transportation	0.2	0.4	1.3	1.1	1.0
Energy and Natural Resources d	0.1	0.2	0.3	1.3	0.4
Environment and Public Works	0.5	0.2	2.0	1.4	2.5
Veterans' Affairs	1.0	0.0	—	3.1	0.9
Other					
Rules and Administration	0.5	0.2	0.6	0.2	0.6

Source: *Congressional Record; Final Calendar of the House of Representatives.*

a Fewer than 0.05 amendments per measure.
b Governmental Affairs was previously named Government Operations. In the 84th, 88th, and 92d Congresses, only amendments for Government Operations are included.
c The number of amendments per measure for Judiciary is very low because of the large number of noncontroversial commemorative measures that it reports to the floor.
d Energy and Natural Resources was previously named Interior and Insular Affairs.

The rule providing for a motion to *suspend the rules* limits debate to forty minutes, bars amendments, and requires a two-thirds vote to adopt (simultaneously) the motion and measure. Use of the procedure by a committee requires the cooperation of the Speaker, who must recognize a representative of the committee before the motion can be made. The procedure was designed to expedite the consideration of minor legislation. And before 1973, motions to suspend the rules were in order only two days each month. By 1977, the majority party Democrats had amended the rule to allow suspension motions two days each week. As a result, the number of measures considered under suspension increased from fewer than 200 between 1967 and 1972 to more than 400 in three of the four congresses between 1977 and 1984.[19] Thus, committees more frequently enjoyed insulation from unfriendly floor amendments. One by-product of this development was greater discretion for the Speaker in determining when and how legislation is considered on the floor. Such discretion occasionally has given the Speaker some leverage to gain policy concessions from committees seeking to avoid the floor amending process. But even suspension has its limits as a mechanism for circumventing the floor because it requires an extraordinary majority for passage: two-thirds of those present and voting.

Starting in late 1979, the House majority party leadership and the Rules Committee began to employ special rules more frequently to restrict floor amendments in some way. *Special rules* (usually simply called "rules," sometimes called "special orders") are resolutions from the Rules Committee that provide for floor consideration of legislation and, by supplementing or supplanting the standing rules of the House, may structure the amending process in the Committee of the Whole. They are necessary for most major legislation and so offer a regular opportunity for the Rules Committee to bar amendments, order the consideration of amendments, or even allow amendments that otherwise would violate the rules of the House. They also give majority party leaders, who effectively control the Democratic contingent on the Rules Committee, an opportunity to structure floor consideration of legislation in a manner that meets the needs of the party and of the standing committees that the party controls. In late 1979, the majority leadership decided to make more frequent use of restrictions on floor amendments.

Special rules long had been used to limit amendments on tax and social security measures from the Committee on Ways and Means. In fact, tax bills from Ways and Means generally received *closed rules*—rules that barred amendments altogether. The justification for this special treatment was that those Ways and Means measures were very complex substantively and very fragile politically. The decision to expand the use

of restrictive rules to measures originating in other committees represented a clear break with the past practice of preserving each member's
right, under the standing rules, to offer germane floor amendments in
the Committee of the Whole.

The change in the content of special rules in the 1980s was
dramatic. Between 1975-1976 and 1981-1982, the percentage of special
rules that restricted amendments in some way increased from 15.7 to
28.8 percent: in 1985-1986, 44.6 percent of all special rules limited
amendments. By the mid-1980s, nearly everyone assumed that a controversial measure would receive a special rule that restricted and structured amending activity to some degree. In fact, in 1985-1986, 65 percent
of floor amendments were offered under special rules that limited or
structured amending activity in some way, up from just over 13 percent
in 1979-1980.[20]

Restrictions on amendments have taken many forms. Some restrictive rules merely require that eligible amendments must be printed in
the *Congressional Record* in advance, giving committee bill managers and
party leaders time to react to the proposals. But in many cases restrictive
rules bar amendments to certain sections or even specify the particular
amendments that would be in order in the Committee of the Whole. In
the 1980s, between two-thirds and three-fourths of special rules identified the particular amendments that would be in order, up from one-
third or less in the congresses of the mid-1970s. Furthermore, special
rules were used to alter relations among amendments, such as barring
second-degree amendments or allowing third-degree amendments, in
order to make the consideration of an amendment contingent on the
adoption or rejection of another amendment, and to adopt an amendment to a bill without a separate vote on the amendment, among other
things.

Special rules need not bar unfriendly amendments altogether in
order to achieve a committee's goal of preventing the adoption of such
amendments. For example, in March 1989 the Rules Committee approved a rule for a controversial minimum wage bill that allowed a vote
on an amendment supported by the Bush administration but opposed by
Education and Labor Committee Democrats. The rule required that the
vote on the administration-backed amendment occur before a vote on
yet another compromise amendment supported by the committee's
Democrats and provided that the last one approved would be adopted.
As a consequence, the rule made it possible for a few conservative
Democrats to vote as a part of a majority for both amendments and still
preserve the committee position.[21]

The innovations in special rules were, in most instances, the fruit of
a partnership between the majority party leadership, Rules Committee

Democrats, and the committee originating the legislation (see the box on p. 188). Majority leaders and the Rules Committee often cared most about an orderly, efficient, and predictable consideration of legislation, while committee leaders sought to reduce uncertainty about the timing, sources, and content of unfriendly amendments to their bills. Indeed, committee bill managers began to demand advantageous special rules once they learned of the possibilities. To a large degree, then, restrictive rules helped House committees regain some of the autonomy they had lost during the 1970s.

Nevertheless, in some cases majority party leaders take charge of designing a rule and impose a structure on floor debate to suit party needs, even when party needs are inconsistent with committee interests. Party leaders regularly play a central role in crafting rules for budget resolutions and reconciliation bills that are very important to the party and the chamber. Prominent bills that involve conflict between two or more committees are particularly apt to draw the majority party leadership into the process of designing a special rule. Intercommittee conflict that spills onto the floor may undermine a bill's chances, a situation that the leadership may want to avoid. And intercommittee conflict often reflects conflict within the party that the leadership must step in to resolve. By employing a special rule to protect some provisions from amendment, order amendments, and authorize amendments that might otherwise violate House rules, the leadership is in a position to guarantee that compromises will be honored or to minimize the damage in cases where it is not possible to resolve conflict informally before the bill reaches the floor. All such cases create opportunities for the leadership to influence the outcome by controlling an important procedural tool. Thus, while special rules usually are a product of the majority party leadership and committee majorities working together, there are times when the expanded and more flexible use of restrictive rules has increased the influence of the majority party leadership at the expense of committee autonomy. It is reasonable to hypothesize that the leadership's new uses of special rules have caused committees to anticipate more carefully the reaction of the majority party and its leadership and to become more responsive to leadership and party policy preferences in writing legislation.

Not all committees require the protection of special rules that restrict amendments. The prestige committees and, to a lesser extent, the policy committees request and often receive special rules that limit amendments.[22] In fact, only a few committees, the prestige committees, routinely receive restrictive special rules. Their legislation is almost always controversial and perceived as vital to the interests of the majority party. A large part of it is necessary legislation (budget bills,

The House Rules Committee and Special Rules

The last time Joe Moakley faced a difficult election, his opponent assailed him as an "old-style politician, a backroom-type person." The critique was no doubt taken as high praise by the Boston-Irish Democrat who, following the May 30, 1989, death of Rep. Claude Pepper, is to become the chairman of the influential House Rules Committee. [Moakley became acting Rules chairman in March after Pepper, the chairman since 1983, took ill.]

Upon entering the House in 1973, Moakley declared, "I'd like to be a Tip O'Neill-type guy if I could." He succeeded—first as a protégé and then as a top lieutenant of Speaker Thomas P. O'Neill Jr. of Massachusetts.

A party stalwart, Moakley is affable and quick with a joke. He joined Rules in 1975 and has often displayed a keener interest in politics than policy. "He's just a nuts-and-bolts Democrat," says David E. Bonior, a Michigan Democrat and Rules Committee member.

Rules is among the most powerful committees in the House. Often described as the gatekeeper to the floor, the committee works in concert with the leadership to control the flow of legislation and set the terms of its floor debate.

The committee writes a "rule" that, subject to approval of the full House, scripts floor action for each piece of legislation. This fixes the actual language of the measure to be considered; what, if any, amendments can be offered; the time allowed for debate, etc. . . . The way an issue is framed often determines whether a coalition will hold on the floor and how an issue will play in the press.

Speaker Jim Wright, D-Texas, often used the Rules Committee to limit amendments and debate on the legislation high on his agenda. This not only irritated Republicans, more than once it cost the Democrats enough of their own votes to lose control of a measure.

Bart Gordon, a Rules Committee Democrat from Tennessee, says Moakley several times cautioned the leadership against forcing an issue on the floor, was ignored and "it wound up he was right."

Adds Gordon: "His strength is understanding the mood of the House and how to get things done."

Moakley has at times agitated for more open debate. He once became incensed at a committee chairman who wanted a "closed rule"—that is, no amendments—on a three-sentence measure. "I think we should all be distressed by the rising number of rule requests that seek restrictions for no justifiable political reasons," he said.

The operative word may be "political," for with few exceptions Moakley has done the leadership's bidding. For example, in 1987 the committee took testimony for 90 minutes on the rule for a controversial welfare-reform measure. Moakley, reading from a prepared text, then promptly moved to adopt a restrictive rule sought by his friend, Dan Rostenkowski of Illinois, the chairman of the Ways and Means Committee.

Source: Chuck Alston, " 'A Nuts-and-Bolts Democrat,' " *Congressional Quarterly Weekly Report*, June 3, 1989, 1305.

continuing appropriations resolutions), and much of it is considered under severe time constraints. All of these factors help to justify limiting amendments. The majority of committees receive a restrictive special rule for only a small fraction of the legislation they report to the floor.

Thus, innovations in special rules have helped the House committees that suffered most from the surge in amending activity regain some of their autonomy. At a minimum, restrictive special rules reduce the uncertainty about what amendments will be offered on the floor. In some cases, the restrictive provisions even allow committees to avoid unfriendly amendments that may have put their legislation in danger. But the degree to which restrictive special rules preserve committee autonomy should not be exaggerated. Normally, the Rules Committee believes that it is obligated to provide for the consideration of amendments representing the major alternatives on significant issues. If it failed to do so, the Rules Committee would risk having the rules it reports rejected by a majority. Nevertheless, particularly on those few measures of paramount importance to the majority party, special rules have proven to be a useful tool in clearing the minefield of amendments that would await committee proposals on the floor.

Innovations in special rules, however, have not allowed committees to recover all of the autonomy that is threatened by a more active parent chamber. First, not all unfriendly floor amendments are barred by restrictive rules. To the contrary, most rules still allow the important alternative proposals to receive a vote. Second, special rules must be adopted by majority vote on the floor. The House has rejected special rules from time to time—an average of once every four months in the 100th Congress—when a majority did not like the alternatives the rules made available.[23] And finally, committees sometimes must make policy concessions to the majority party leadership and Rules Committee Democrats in order to obtain a protective rule. To a significant degree, then, House committees no longer are in the business of picking their own fights. Leaders and Rules members help to shape the battle for them in designing special rules.

THE SENATE RESPONSE TO THE SURGE IN FLOOR AMENDMENTS

The floor amendment stage is particularly troublesome for Senate committees. In most cases, Senate rules do not bar amendments that are not germane or relevant to the subjects addressed in a bill reported from committee. Thus, senators may seek to attach an amendment on any subject, even the text of a whole bill, to a bill before the Senate. In July 1989, for instance, a senator used a bill to authorize the activities of the State Department as a vehicle for an amendment that would keep it easy to evict tenants from public housing for drug abuse.[24] The absence of a general germaneness rule makes it very easy for senators to circumvent Senate committees by bringing issues directly to the floor.

In contrast to the House, however, no Senate strategy to control floor amending activity and enhance the autonomy of the committees has emerged. Efforts to make it easier to block nongermane amendments, which allow senators to circumvent committees and prevent unlimited debate, thus giving individual senators substantial blocking power, have failed. Adjustments in the cloture rule have made it marginally easier to limit debate and impose a germaneness requirement on remaining amendments, but cloture still requires an extraordinary majority (three-fifths of all senators) that limits its utility as a tool for managing the floor. In only one area, budget measures, has the Senate moved effectively to limit debate and amendments. The effect of budget politics on committee autonomy is considered below.

Lacking new formal rules and facing an ever-present threat of filibusters, Senate leaders turned to unanimous consent agreements to structure amending activity and bring debate to a close whenever they could. *Unanimous consent agreements,* as the name implies, are agreements adopted by the Senate that require unanimous approval. These agreements may supplement or even supplant the standing rules of the Senate, in much the same way that special rules do in the House. As a result, unanimous consent agreements may be used to restrict or order the consideration of amendments and to specify times for votes, limit debate, and provide for a final vote on measures. They are useful tools for adding some predictability to the flow of business on the Senate floor and often streamline the consideration of measures and amendments. But because the agreements require unanimous consent, any senator who wants to preserve his or her privileges under the standing rules can prevent restrictions from being imposed. In general, therefore, there is no way for a majority of senators to insulate committee bills from unfriendly or nongermane amendments whose sponsors are committed to offering them.

The possibility of objecting to unanimous consent requests to limit debate and amendments gives senators a source of leverage with floor and committee leaders. An objection to a prospective unanimous consent request is known as a *hold* in the Senate. Holds are communicated privately to the floor leaders and usually have the effect of preventing floor action on a bill. Floor leaders may call a senator's bluff now and then, but they generally cannot afford to risk creating a legislative logjam by calling for the consideration of a bill and stimulating a filibuster. Consequently, the increased dependence on unanimous consent agreements to streamline floor debate reinforced the obstructionist power of individual senators. That power, in turn, creates bargaining leverage for individual senators with proponents of measures, particularly committee and subcommittee chairs. Thus, as the House was moving with special rules to recover some of the autonomy its committees had lost to the floor, the Senate was moving in the direction of further entrenching individualism at the expense of committee autonomy.

CONFERENCES

Decision-making processes within each chamber affect not only committee autonomy, but also the manner in which differences between House and Senate versions are resolved. This postpassage stage creates opportunities for members to alter the legislation before it is sent to the president. The changing role of subcommittees in conference delegations and the importance of conferences for the power of subcommittee members was noted in Chapter 4. The assumption made there, however, was that committee members—whether or not they organized by subcommittee—have dominated conferences for more than a century and a half. But committee domination of conferences has weakened somewhat in the last two decades.

The procedures for resolving House-Senate differences on legislation grant committee members important advantages. These advantages are the product of three features of those procedures. First, most controversial legislation goes to a conference committee after initial House and Senate passage. The differences between the chambers are usually too important and complex to be resolved through informal discussions and an exchange of amendments between the chambers. Second, conference delegations are composed, usually exclusively, of members of the committees that originated the legislation. Conference appointments are made by the Speaker and the presiding officer of the Senate, who generally rely on lists provided by committee chairs. And third, the primary products of conference negotiations, conference reports, are given special treatment when they are sent back to the two chambers. A conference report is returned to the chambers after a majority of conferees from each chamber have signed it. But amendments may not be offered to the report from the House or Senate floor— the report must receive a simple up-or-down vote.[25]

The conference process endows committee members, as conferees, with important sources of negative and positive power. On the negative side, conferees may strip away unfriendly provisions added on the floor as long as the modified measure is acceptable to the other chamber's conferees and to a majority of both chambers. In some cases, committees may even repeal provisions they originally favored in order to punish members who voted against them on the floor.[26] Because this negative power constitutes a sort of veto after the floor stage, it has recently been referred to as the *ex post veto*.[27]

On the positive side, conferees may take advantage of conferences to introduce provisions not included in the original committee bills reported to the House and Senate floors, subject to the condition that House and Senate majorities will support the conference report. The ability to include new provisions is limited by House and Senate rules that limit conferees to subjects addressed in at least one of the chambers' bills and that restrict the conference agreement to the scope of the differences between the bills. These rules must be enforced by a point of order and majority vote when the conference report is considered in the House or Senate. Many new provisions are tolerated or simply go undetected. Moreover, the House and Senate versions may differ in so many ways—as when one chamber adopts a substitute version—that the scope of the differences is broad enough to allow any provision remotely related to the subjects addressed in either bill to be included in the conference report.

The strategic importance of the conference stage was well illustrated in the 1989 fight over clean air legislation in the House. Two long-term opponents on the issue, Energy and Commerce Committee chair John Dingell (D-Mich.) and Health and the Environment Subcommittee chair Henry Waxman (D-Calif.), managed to work out a compromise on emissions standards for cars and light trucks. Critical to the deal was an agreement to abide by the terms of the compromise on the floor and in conference. Without such an agreement, a compromise in committee would mean little as both sides sought advantage through floor amendments and conference negotiations. Only by promising not to take advantage of each other at subsequent stages could Dingell and Waxman find a compromise at the committee stage in their best interest.[28]

The strategic advantages bestowed upon committee members by the conference process exist for both House and Senate committees. In fact, in many circumstances, the ex post veto is just as viable in the Senate as in the House. Senate committees may suffer during initial floor debate from nongermane amendments, unlimited debate, and the absence of protective special rules, but they may recover in conference much of what they lost. And yet Senate conferees do operate under a constraint that House conferees do not: senators may filibuster a conference report and force supporters of the report to garner an extraordinary majority to overcome the filibuster and bring the report to a vote.[29] Thus, threatened filibusters often give individual Senate nonconferees leverage that their House counterparts do not have.

Several developments in the conference process, particularly in the House, suggest that committee autonomy at the conference stage is not as strong as it was in the 1950s and 1960s: (1) changes in the rules and practices related to the composition of conference delegations, (2) new rules governing the procedures and discretion of conferences, and (3) increases in the challenges to conference recommendations on the House and Senate floors. We will consider each of these in turn.

COMPOSITION OF CONFERENCE COMMITTEES

The appointment of conferees often is a critical point in the legislative process because the conferees are usually the last group of members who may alter the details of the legislation. The appointment of conferees is the responsibility of the Speaker of the House and the presiding officer in the Senate, but they generally follow the recommendation of the appropriate committee chair and ranking minority member. Many behind-the-scenes conflicts occur concerning committee leaders' recommendations as the contending factions seek advantage.[30] Sometimes party leaders must step in to referee these disputes, especially in the House where the Speaker has a formal role to perform in the appointment process.

Under a rule adopted in 1946, the Speaker and the Senate's presiding officer are obliged to appoint conferees who have demonstrated support for the measure in their chambers. In practice, the rule is difficult to enforce.[31] Determining which members support the legislation, and to what degree, is nearly impossible. In the 1950s and 1960s the rule usually was ignored.

In the 1970s the House moved to tighten the conference appointment rule, reflecting the view that committee chairs should not be able to exercise unchecked discretion in naming conferees. House rules adopted in 1975 and 1977 require that "the Speaker shall appoint no less than a majority of members who generally supported the House position as determined by the Speaker" and that "the Speaker shall name members who are primarily responsible for the legislation and shall, to the fullest extent possible, include the principal proponents of the major provisions of the bill as it passed the House." Thus, the new rules implied that members who did not sit on the committee originating the legislation but who sponsored important provisions in the House-passed version were entitled to appointments to the conference. And they also gave members a firmer basis for appealing the committee chair's recommendations to the Speaker. The Senate has not adopted similar rules.

Changing attitudes about rights to participate in conference deliberations produced major changes in the number and type of members appointed. In the 1950s and 1960s, the modal conference was composed of five representatives and five senators, usually the three most senior majority party members and the two most senior minority party members from the committee, or sometimes the subcommittee, of each chamber. The mean size in 1963-1964 was just 5.8 in the House and 6.4 in the Senate. By 1979-1980, the mean was 10.5 in the House and 9.2 in the Senate, excluding the large conferences for reconciliation bills and a few other measures originating in multiple committees. In 1985-1986, that mean had increased further to 11.8 in the House and 10.1 in the Senate. In those two years, 71.2 percent of all House conference delegations and 43.1 percent of Senate delegations had 11 or more members, up from just 2.4 percent and 4.5 percent, respectively, in 1963-1964.

The expansion in delegation size was largely the result of reaching deeper into committees for conferees. In the House, this has meant including nearly all subcommittee members on most delegations. In the Senate, where the average committee has only seventeen or eighteen members, a majority of full committee members gain appointment to most conferences. In fact, the expansion of conference delegations has reinforced the democratization of intracommittee politics that occurred in the 1960s and 1970s. Because a majority of each chamber's delegation must approve the conference report, a few senior committee members cannot dictate conference outcomes. Nor do a few senior members monopolize information about what took place in conferences, making it easier for the parent chambers to learn about what happened and to hold the conferees accountable.

Committee outsiders also gained a greater voice in conferences after the new House rules were adopted. In 1971-1972, only 2 of 150 House conference delegations included members not sitting on the committee originating the legislation, but in 1979-1980 the number of such delegations increased to 27 of the 154 delegations. Senate delegations also seldom included committee outsiders before the 1970s, with the exception of a few members of authorizing committees who were ex officio members of appropriations conferences specified in a Senate rule. The rule was dropped in 1977. But the Senate continues to appoint fewer outsiders to conferences than does the House. In 1979-1980, only eight Senate delegations included outsiders; in 1985-1986, only eleven included outsiders.

The expansion of delegation size and the addition of more committee outsiders made conference negotiations more difficult and time-consuming in many cases. Committee leaders and staff were forced to consult with more members, delegations often were less cohesive, and committee outsiders often had little long-term commitment to maintaining good working relations with committee members from the other chamber. It did not take long for committee leaders to look for ways to limit the role of some conferees, particularly committee outsiders. Limitations have taken two forms.

One way to limit the role of conferees is to appoint them as *additional conferees* for the consideration of specified subjects or sections. The additional conferees then serve as voting members of the conference delegation for only those subjects or sections. *General conferees* participate in all matters, including those for which additional conferees are appointed. Conference agreements on the specified subjects or sections require the support of a majority of conferees, general and additional, who have jurisdiction. The additional conferees may be committee outsiders with an interest in only a few subjects or sections, so the arrangement may be acceptable to them. The general conferees retain unfettered control on all other matters.

A second way to limit the role of conferees is to appoint them as *exclusive conferees* for certain subjects or sections. Exclusive conferees are the sole negotiators for their chamber on those subjects or sections. General conferees are not allowed to vote on those subject or sections, unless they also are named among the exclusive conferees for the specified subjects or sections; only a majority of the named exclusive conferees may approve a conference agreement on the specified subjects or sections. Thus, exclusive conferees have a virtual veto over policy within their jurisdiction and the entire conference report that depends upon House-Senate agreement on all items. The relative influence of committee and noncommittee members on an exclusive subconference therefore depends on the number of each that are appointed and the policy preferences they hold.[32]

The appointment of *limited-purpose conferees,* additional or exclusive, was rare before the late 1970s. Since then, about half of the instances of limited-purpose conferees have involved measures originating in multiple committees. In fact, such uses of limited-purpose conferees represent an effort to reduce intercommittee conflict and preserve committee autonomy. By assigning the members of a committee with jurisdiction over just one section of a bill as exclusive conferees, as is usually the case, that committee retains control of negotiations with the other chamber while the other committees are not hampered by interlopers on their sections. The process sometimes makes it more difficult to trade provisions in one section for provisions in another section, but it is more likely to produce coherent legislation than the alternative of considering separate bills, each from a different committee. Complex arrangements of additional and exclusive conferees became standard practice in the 1980s for large, multiple committee conferences on budget reconciliation, trade, and drugs, to name a few.

The use of limited-purpose conferees to limit the role of committee outsiders is now common in both the House and Senate. In 1985-1986, for example, nineteen of the twenty House appointment orders involving committee outsiders limited the outsiders' role in some way, up from ten of twenty-one in 1979-1980. In the Senate, restrictions were used in five of the six cases of outsider appointments in 1979-1980 and in all ten cases in 1985-1986. Thus, while committee outsiders now have a much more important role in conference deliberations than they did traditionally, that role has been circumscribed by innovations in conference appointment practices.

The developments in the appointment of conference delegations have produced many strange conferences. The 1989 conference on the savings and loan bailout bill was composed of eight senators from two committees (five from Banking, three from Finance) and ninety-four House members from five committees, including all fifty-one members of the House Banking Committee. The Senate Banking chair, Donald Riegle (D-Mich.), deliberately kept his delegation small to facilitate negotiations on the large, complex bill. The participation of the three Finance conferees was limited to negotiations on the bill's tax provisions. House Banking chair Henry Gonzalez (D-Texas) felt that he had to include nearly all members who wanted a voice in the conference. Even so, Gonzalez, with the consent of the Speaker, was able to structure the House conferees into subgroups for particular sections of the bill. Several of the subgroups were stacked with members who shared Gonzalez's point of view on key issues. Because the five Senate Banking conferees faced negotiations with many House subgroups, most of the negotiations were left to staff supervised by the committee chairs and ranking minority members, leaving many of the members in the dark about the details of discussions. Despite complaints about the composition of the conference and how the conference was run, the report eventually was adopted by both Houses.[33]

CONFERENCE PROCEDURES AND DISCRETION

New rules governing conference appointments in the House were a part of an effort to make conference committees more responsive to the parent chamber. Concern about conference representation extended to the Senate as well, but, as we will see, there it produced less dramatic changes in formal rules. Two additional sets of rules that affect the autonomy of committees in conference warrant attention.

First, the two chambers moved in 1975 to open conference meetings to the public. Previously, most conference meetings had been held in closed sessions. The rationale in most cases was that closed sessions

eliminated grandstanding and facilitated compromises on difficult issues. Closed sessions also meant that outsiders, even other members of
Congress, were in a weak position to evaluate the performance of
conferees. The new rules required that conference meetings be open to
the public unless the conferees of either chamber voted in open session
to close the meeting for that day. But the House, not pleased with the
decisions of a few conference delegations, required in 1977 that the
House itself must approve closing conference meetings.

Since 1977, most formal meetings of conferences have been held in
public session. The major exception has been conferences on legislation
dealing with national security matters, and in those cases, explicit
permission for members of Congress to attend is included in the motion
to allow a closed meeting. Nevertheless, conferees have found ways to
circumvent the rules. Just as before the new rules, informal meetings of
committee leaders and staff resolve most issues in complex conferences.
In some cases, very small meeting rooms are used to limit the number of
outsiders who may attend. For example, the 1989 conference on the
savings and loan industry bill met in a room so small that no television
cameras were allowed; only reporters were allowed into the room, and
they had to stand—the general public could not attend.[34] In a few cases,
the two delegations have met in separate rooms so that their meetings did
not constitute formal conference sessions. Negotiations were then carried
out by having staff members shuttle between the rooms or by arranging
hallway meetings of two or three members.

A second set of rules concerns the exercise of discretion by conferees.
An issue particularly troubling to the House has been the addition of
provisions on new subjects in conference. Such nongermane additions
eliminate an opportunity for the chambers to amend the new provisions
before they are faced with a take-it-or-leave-it decision on the entire
conference report. The problem is most difficult when one chamber
adopts a substitute version of the other chamber's bill that differs in
structure and scope as well as content. The long-standing rule that the
conference report must be restricted to the scope of the differences
between the chambers is not very limiting in such cases. The problem
became more severe in the 1960s as substitutes became more common.

Both chambers had long-standing rules barring nongermane modifications of the legislation in conference. The House, however, generally
resisted nongermane provisions more strenuously, particularly those
added by the Senate to a House bill, consistent with its traditionally
stronger concern for germaneness and the jurisdictional territories of
committees. In 1971 the House sought to strengthen its rule barring the
addition of new subjects in conference by requiring that "the introduction of any language in [the conference] substitute presenting a specific

additional topic, question, issue, or proposition not committed to the conference committee by either House shall not constitute a germane modification of the matter in disagreement." But this rule, like the Senate's less specific rule, must be enforced by a successful point of order. And a point of order is a very blunt instrument because it defeats the entire conference report. The risk for members objecting to the nongermane provisions was that a new conference report might be less acceptable in other ways or that it would not be possible to negotiate a new version with the other chamber. Thus, in 1972, the House granted itself the right to "surgically" remove nongermane provisions added by the Senate or the conference committee. The rule allows the House to vote separately on a nongermane provision after a successful point of order has been made against the provision.

These and other related developments were a part of the reform efforts to limit the control of committee chairs and a few senior committee members over conference outcomes.[35] The House moved more aggressively than the Senate because the House, particularly its liberal Democrats, was most concerned about the power of a few conservative chairs to thwart the will of the majority party and the House itself. Much of that concern dissipated by the late 1970s after many of the conservative chairs had been replaced by members more in tune with the party and as the composition of conference delegations themselves began to change.

ROLL-CALL VOTE CHALLENGES TO CONFERENCES

The 1970s efforts to curb committee autonomy in conference through rules changes were accompanied by more frequent challenges to conference recommendations. During the 1950s and 1960s, the vast majority of conference reports were approved by the House and Senate by voice votes. Only one in five, in the case of the House, and one in ten, in the Senate, faced a recorded vote on the motion to adopt the report. Even fewer conferences were subject to motions to instruct the conferees to adhere to a specified policy position or to recommit the report to conference.

By the end of the 1960s, more and more recorded votes occurred on the various motions related to conference deliberations, especially in the House. In 1969-1970, more than 34 percent of the reports were subject to a recorded vote on adoption in the House, compared with just 7 percent in 1955-1956. In the Senate, the frequency increased from 2 percent in 1955-1956 to more than 15 percent in 1969-1970. Voting procedures cannot account for the increase, of course, because no changes in voting procedures had been adopted by that time. The frequency of challenges continued to increase during the 1970s, reaching a peak of 61 percent in the House during 1977-1978 and 27 percent in the Senate during 1981-1982. Recently, there has been a surge in motions to instruct conferees sponsored by House Republicans. Republicans have turned to this tactic as a way to force votes on difficult issues, establish a party position of symbolic value, and increase the pressure on conferees to adhere to a House-passed version.[36] Successful motions to instruct are not binding on conferees, but they make compromises on the chamber's position very conspicuous and sometimes more difficult to justify.

Few challenges to conference reports succeed. Conferees, of course, anticipate the reaction of the two chambers and often act in advance to make sure the conference report will be acceptable to a majority in both chambers. Nevertheless, conference reports are defeated from time to time. Sometimes a defeat is due to an error in judgment on the part of the conferees. In 1989, for example, a conference report on a supplemental appropriations bill was defeated in the House, much to the surprise of the conferees and the majority party leadership.[37] Despite the fact that the bill included appropriations for veterans' medical facilities that were about to close for lack of funding, Republicans voted against the bill to avoid a subsequent vote on whether it should include antidrug funds, and some Democrats voted against it because they disapproved of certain extraneous projects that were included in the bill. But whatever the reasons for objecting, conference reports run into trouble frequently enough to put conferees on notice that the parent chambers will not defer to the conferees on important matters.

Several indicators—changing conference delegation composition, new formal constraints, and more floor challenges—suggest that committee autonomy in conference can no longer be assumed. A prescriptive norm of deference to conference recommendations no longer exists. Committees have responded, of course: they have sought restrictions on outsiders' participation in conference deliberations, found ways to cheat on the open meeting rule, and so on. But the necessity of playing such games reflects how much the rules have changed. As committee outsiders have become more assertive and less indifferent to conference negotiations, the autonomy of committees at the postpassage stage has weakened considerably.

COMMITTEES AND BUDGET POLITICS

During most of this century, committees set the agenda for their parent chambers. While committees always have had to concern themselves about various formal constraints, particularly time deadlines set in law for the expiration of programs or spending authority, they have had few formal constraints imposed on them by their parent chambers concerning the substance of the legislation they are to report. The necessity of gaining floor majorities and the support of the president have imposed constraints, of course, but formal strictures on policy substance generally have been lacking, which has given committees the freedom to make their own choices.

Committees, of course, dislike formal restrictions. The imposition of enforceable constraints in advance of committee action would greatly alter the sequence of decision making in Congress and reduce committee power. The adoption of the Congressional Budget and Impoundment Control Act in 1974 created the possibility of rearranging the normal sequence and placing the initiative for policy change in the hands of members not serving on the committees of relevant jurisdiction. That threat was realized in the 1980s when budget deficits became very large, stimulating procedural innovations. Committees resisted developments that put their power in jeopardy, but they were not able to avoid significant erosion in their autonomy.

Three components of budget and spending legislation must be understood to appreciate the implications of budget politics for autonomy. First, *reconciliation instructions* provide orders to committees to recommend legislation that achieves specified spending savings. Second, appropriations caps, often called *302(b) allocations,* after a section of the 1974 Budget Act, provide spending guidelines for appropriations bills. And third, *continuing resolutions* provide budget authority for federal programs when regular appropriations bills are not passed by the beginning of the fiscal year. Developments in each of these areas during the 1980s redistributed power among the parent chambers, party leaders, and committees, as well as among the various committees.

RECONCILIATION

As envisioned in 1974, the new budget process was designed to supplement and coordinate the decisions of the standing committees. A first budget resolution was to be adopted in May, setting targets for spending and revenues for the next fiscal year. Individual authorization, appropriations, and revenue bills would be passed during the summer months, to be followed in September by a second budget resolution. The second budget resolution could be used to order modifications in the decisions of the summer months by requiring certain committees to report legislation that achieved specified spending savings or revenue enhancements. Such *reconciliation* legislation—so named because it reconciled the differences between decisions of the summer months and the provisions of the second budget resolution—was to be adopted before October 1, the beginning of the new federal fiscal year. Responsibility for writing the budget resolutions and supervising the reconciliation process fell to a new budget committee in each chamber. If reconciliation instructions are included in a budget resolution, responsibility for devising the detailed legislation that achieves the specified savings rests with the individual committees.

During the 1970s, the decisions of the summer months on appropriations and authorization legislation were allowed to stand under the terms of second budget resolutions, despite the fact that many of those decisions were not consistent with the targets of the first budget resolutions. Second budget resolutions merely ratified the decisions of the summer months, and reconciliation instructions were not imposed, with the one exception of instructions to a few Senate committees in 1979. Although the Senate's Budget Committee was more aggressive than the House committee, the new budget process proved to be accommodating rather than threatening to the interests of the appropriations and authorizing committees.[38]

Large budget deficits dramatically altered the context of budget politics in the 1980s and produced an important change in the sequence of congressional decision making. In 1980, an unexpectedly large deficit led both chambers to include reconciliation instructions in the first budget resolution in order to give the budget process new teeth. By including reconciliation instructions in the first resolution, the various committees were constrained to abide by the instructions before they had an opportunity to report legislation more to their liking. Moreover, by revealing how they had devised the reconciliation figure for each committee, the budget committees were indicating which programs might be cut to achieve the specified level of spending savings. Committee chairs protested this infringement on their jurisdictions, arguing that the budget committees had no business making suggestions about individual programs within the jurisdiction of authorizing committees. The budget committees insisted that taking programs into account was the only way to devise reconciliation instructions appropriate to each committee. An amendment to the resolution that would have deleted the reconciliation instructions was easily defeated. Reconciliation has been a central component of the budget process ever since.[39]

The 1980 reconciliation instructions were quite mild in comparison to those imposed in 1981, after Ronald Reagan became president and the Republicans gained control of the Senate. Congressional Republicans, motivated by the new administration, employed reconciliation instructions for fifteen House committees and fourteen Senate committees in the first resolution to achieve substantial spending cuts in many domestic programs. Committees with the largest jurisdictions were hit the hardest. In the House, where Republicans were in the minority, the instructions were written by Republican members and staff, assisted by administration officials, and passed with the help of conservative Democrats. The reconciliation bill that was adopted later was the work of the same group. Many majority party members, particularly committee chairs, vowed that they would not allow reconciliation procedures to be used again to undermine the role of committees.

After 1981, support for more deep cuts in domestic programs waned, and so reconciliation lost much of its bite. Nevertheless, reconciliation instructions continued to be included in the first budget resolution. The House, in fact, decided that the use of reconciliation instructions in the first resolution obviated the second budget resolution; it dispensed with separate action on second resolutions. Committees with jurisdiction over the largest programs continued to be affected more than others. One scholar estimated that programs under the jurisdiction of House Ways and Means and its counterpart, Senate Finance, shouldered over half of the spending savings imposed by reconciliation instructions.[40]

By the mid-1980s, then, the budget process had been substantially revised, at least in practice, placing the decisions on individual pieces of appropriations and authorizing legislation a step behind the adoption of meaningful budget resolutions. The potential existed, as was realized in 1981, that the autonomy of the appropriations, authorizing, and revenue committees could be eviscerated by first budget resolutions written by the budget committees and party leaders and approved by the parent chambers. But stalemate on the shape of the budget prevented such a disaster for congressional committees between 1982 and 1985.

In the meantime, many committees found reconciliation legislation a convenient vehicle for unrelated authorization legislation. As necessary legislation, reconciliation bills were a way to guarantee that authorization legislation opposed by the other chamber would get to conference.[41] In addition, reconciliation legislation usually went to the floor in the House with a special rule that restricted amendments, giving the authorizing committees some insulation from unfriendly floor amendments that they might not have if they reported separate legislation. In the Senate, reconciliation bills are protected from nongermane amendments and subject to a limit on debate. While Senate rules do not protect reconciliation bills from germane amendments, the limit on debate allows committees to include provisions that otherwise might be subject to a filibuster, thereby giving Senate committees an ounce of autonomy they would not have if the provisions were handled in separate legislation. Thus, while the restructured budget process threatened committee autonomy, many House and Senate committees actually gained some insulation from their parent chambers through the reconciliation process.

Frustration over continuing high deficits finally led to a more drastic step in 1985: the Gramm-Rudman-Hollings procedure, named after its primary Senate sponsors.[42] The procedure provided for across-the-board spending cuts—a process labeled *sequestration*—if certain deficit reductions were not attained in each of the following five years. The purpose of the sequestration procedure is to motivate Congress and the president to achieve deficit reduction, thereby reinforcing the reconciliation process. For most committees, it was thought, failure to achieve the deficit reductions and suffer across-the-board spending cuts would impose a worse outcome than an adequate deficit reduction that they devised for themselves.

The Gramm-Rudman-Hollings rules are particularly tough on Senate committees. Under these rules, reconciliation bills are protected from "extraneous" provisions, due to a provision called the "Byrd rule," after its inventor Sen. Robert Byrd, and identical rules adopted in subsequent years. The rule makes it easier to enforce a point of order that a provision is not related to the central purposes of reconciliation (cutting spending and raising revenues). The reason is that sixty votes must be obtained to override the ruling of the presiding officer on such a point of order (the same number is required to invoke cloture to stop a filibuster). Therefore, a committee seeking to include extraneous provisions in its reconciliation package must either avoid a point of order or have enough support to overturn the decision of the presiding officer. The Byrd rule limits the ability of committees to attach legislation to reconciliation bills and therefore reduces the value of reconciliation bills as a means for preserving committee autonomy (see the box on pp. 204-205).[43]

The Gramm-Rudman-Hollings procedure increased the political stakes in writing the first budget resolution, compelling party and budget committee leaders to negotiate with the administration over an acceptable plan of action.[44] Members of individual committees do not have much effect on whether or not an adequate deficit reduction plan is achieved. A few committee leaders, particularly those of the money committees, play an important role in these negotiations, but they share with party and budget committee leaders the responsibility to make decisions that directly affect the jurisdiction of their committees. The process severely limits the ability of committees to act freely on matters falling under their jurisdiction and sometimes forces them to report legislation they dislike.

In 1989, nearly all of the advantages that committees found in the reconciliation process were lost as Senate party leaders negotiated a

Senate Committees under Gramm– ...

When Senate Republicans expressed distress at the Democrats' use of a procedural rule to block floor action on a capital gains tax cut, it recalled a comic moment from the cinema classic *Casablanca*. It is the scene where Claude Rains as Capt. Renault announces that he is closing a nightclub because he is "shocked, shocked" to learn that there is gambling on the premises. A croupier then hands him the cash from his evening's winnings.

In fact, the 60-vote (three-fifths of the Senate) threshold has been regularly employed by both parties as a last-ditch defense when outvoted on a bill. Since Democrats re-established control of the Senate in 1987, there have been more than 100 such floor votes.

The number 60 took on its magic in the mid-1970s. The Congressional Budget Act of 1974 required 60 votes to waive its restrictions on when and how measures that raise or spend money could be brought to the floor.

Then in 1975, the long battle to weaken the filibuster weapon saw some success in the aftermath of Watergate with the result that senators have been able to cut off debate with 60 votes (rather than two-thirds of those present and voting). A decade later, the Senate adopted the Gramm-Rudman anti-deficit law, requiring 60 votes to waive certain provisions of that act as well.

...Between them, cloture votes and Budget Act or Gramm-Rudman waivers have made the pursuit of 60 votes a rather commonplace event.

The single issue that spawned the most such votes was the attempt at campaign finance reform in the 100th Congress. The Democratic leadership tried to invoke cloture eight times, each time winning a majority but falling shy of 60.

In the 100th and 101st Congresses, efforts to waive provisions of the Budget Act or of Gramm-Rudman have come along slightly more than once a month, on average. Of these, just about three-fifths have failed.

reconciliation bill stripped of extraneous legislation. Objections to committee plans to incorporate tax, health, child care, and other provisions in the reconciliation bill threatened to kill the reconciliation bill, which would have forced permanent across-the-board spending cuts under the Gramm-Rudman-Hollings procedure. Rather than selectively eliminating the extraneous provisions, Senate party leaders chose to drop all such provisions and send the bill to conference. Only a few of the extraneous provisions incorporated in the House version survived the conference, so even House committees lost most of the advantages that packaging legislation in reconciliation measures had provided in previous years.

... *Rudman-Hollings: The 60-Vote Rule*

The most controversial are those that fail but achieve a majority.

Perhaps the most important came on Aug. 3, when Sen. Donald W. Riegle Jr., D-Mich., tried to waive the Budget Act so that $50 billion needed to finance the thrift bailout bill could be included in the budget (as the House and Senate conferees on the bill had decided to do).

Riegle's waiver motion got 54 votes, a clear majority. But President Bush opposed putting the cost on the budget, and all but one Republican joined in opposition (along with two Democrats). So Riegle's motion failed, the conference report on the mammoth bill was declared out of order and the conference committee had to reconvene.

Earlier in 1989, Sen. Bob Kasten, R-Wis., tried to waive the Budget Act to delay the effective date of tax code rules prohibiting discrimination between classes of employees in an employer's pension plan (Section 89). But Kasten was frustrated because his April 12 motion got only 56 votes (42 Republicans and 14 Democrats), four shy of what he needed. Kasten tried again on June 6 and received less than a majority.

More recently, Sen. Orrin G. Hatch, R-Utah, sought a waiver on Sept. 7, 1989, to set up a refundable tax credit for small businesses hit with costs for improving access for the disabled. Hatch got a majority among the 92 senators voting, but his 48 votes fell well below the 60 needed.

In the 100th Congress, Republicans raised the provisions of Gramm-Rudman to block a House-Senate conference report on a housing authorization bill. The chief sponsor, Sen. Alan Cranston, D-Calif., sought a waiver and got 57 votes. But he lost five Democrats (along with 38 Republicans) and so was denied the waiver.

Source: Ronald D. Elving, "60-Vote Rule: A Frequent Defense," *Congressional Quarterly Weekly Report*, October 14, 1989, 2695.

The politics of spending cuts has produced many odd legislative entanglements. In 1989, for instance, both the House Energy and Commerce Committee and the House Ways and Means Committee included provisions affecting the payment of physicians under Medicare in their reconciliation packages.[45] They could both receive credit for the savings that would be realized because they shared jurisdiction over the physician payment component of Medicare. Under the special way reconciliation legislation is packaged by the Budget Committee, the substantial differences between the versions of the two committees would not be worked out until the bill was in conference, where both House committees were represented. The Senate, of course, contributed

206 COMMITTEES IN CONGRESS

a version of its own, requiring a three-way negotiation over a major policy decision.

Contrary to what we might expect, a few authorizing committees have preferred the across-the-board cuts of sequestration to meeting their reconciliation targets. The major reason is their jurisdiction over self-financed programs. Self-financed programs whose budgets are dependent on special fees paid by clients of the program often are not affected by sequestration orders that affect appropriated funds. By refusing to reduce spending in these programs and thereby increasing the probability that across-the-board cuts will be ordered, authorizing committees with jurisdiction over such programs are forcing the cuts to be made elsewhere. Appropriations committee members have expressed dismay that these programs, and the committees that support them, gain insulation from budget cuts and force larger cuts in the programs under the jurisdiction of other committees, particularly the appropriations committees.[46]

APPROPRIATIONS CAPS

For the most part, reconciliation instructions affect the appropriations committees only indirectly. When other committees are required to modify the authorizing statutes for federal programs so as to reduce their costliness, the appropriators then adjust the appropriations bills accordingly. Yet, even when budget resolutions do not provide for reconciliation instructions to the authorizing and revenue committees, they must provide guidelines for appropriations decisions if they are to have any meaning.

Translating budget resolutions into guidelines for appropriations is not a straightforward process, however. Budget resolutions employ very broad functional policy categories (education, health, defense, and so forth) that do not have a one-to-one correspondence with the sets of departments and agencies that organize the thirteen separate appropriations bills. The 1974 Budget Act provided, in Section 302(b), that the appropriations committees must translate the functional allocations into appropriations allocations and report the result.[47] While there is substantial room for discretion on the part of the appropriations committees, most of the translation is accomplished by computer with the exercise of little discretion. Once the allocations have been made, it is possible to determine whether appropriations bills are consistent with the budget resolution, an accounting process known informally as *score keeping*.

During the 1970s, when first budget resolutions were nonbinding, the 302(b) allocation process created some friction between appropriations and budget committees.[48] The friction was greater in the Senate, where the Budget Committee was more assertive and the Appropriations Committee was more prone to exceed the allocations in the bills it reported. But in neither chamber was the allocation decision of the appropriators viewed as strictly binding. In fact, numerous appropriations bills passed that exceeded allocation ceilings that the appropriations committees set for themselves. Thus, other than operating on a faster schedule as provided in the Budget Act, the appropriations process changed very little, perhaps with the exception that appropriators now could use the 302(b) allocations as an argument against floor amendments proposing more spending.

The quickened pace of appropriations action in the 1970s did affect the autonomy of authorizing committees.[49] Appropriations bills often came to the floor before authorizing legislation affecting programs in the bills had passed. In order to appropriate without an authorization, House appropriations bills required protection from points of order, which was provided by special rules that waived points of order. Many authorizing committees complained bitterly about this development. And for good reason. Critical decisions affecting programs under their jurisdictions now were being made by appropriators in advance of action on their own bills.

Making the 302(b) allocations binding became an issue when federal deficits increased in the 1980s.[50] The designers of the budget resolutions in 1980, 1981, 1982, and 1983 took advantage of a provision in the Budget Act that allows the enrollment of appropriations bills to be deferred until after the second resolution and any reconciliation legislation has been adopted. By delaying enrollment (the last step before bills are sent to the president), Congress makes it possible to revise the bills at the last minute, without going through the entire bill process, if the bills add up to an amount inconsistent with budget decisions. The process encourages the appropriations committees to conform to the dictates of the budget resolutions. But political stalemate and delays in the consideration and adoption of many appropriations until after October 1, forcing the use of continuing resolutions, reduced the impact of the deferred enrollment provisions.

As a part of the 1985 Gramm-Rudman-Hollings package, more teeth were added to the 302(b) process. The new rules made the 302(b) allocations binding on individual appropriations bills by authorizing points of order against the individual bills when they are reported to the floor. Reflecting the relative strength of House appropriators in their chamber and their strategic position in the negotiations over Gramm-Rudman-Hollings, the new rules were more stringent for Senate Appropriations than House Appropriations. The Senate Appropriations Committee was forced to report bills that were under the limits for granting new spending authority (the technical term is *budget authority*), whether or not the spending was required by another law, as well as for actual spending *(outlays)*. The House committee was required to abide by the limit for new budget authority permitted but not outlays. Since that time, however, the House has insisted on measuring appropriations bills for their effects on outlays, so the Appropriations Committee has done so as well. One consequence of the 302(b) constraints is that appropriators have favored slow spending programs over fast spending programs in order to reduce the projected spending for the next year.

Thus, the 302(b) allocation process has added bite to budget constraints in recent years. In 1989, House Appropriations subcommittee chairs openly complained about the stringency of the constraints placed on them by the 302(b) process.[51] Efforts by some of them to camouflage spending were rejected by Budget leaders who were carefully scrutinizing the allocation decisions within Appropriations.[52] Not surprisingly, the tight constraints imposed by the process motivated some members to invent new techniques to protect their favored programs. A 1989 innovation of the Senate Budget Committee was to specify that a part of the budget authority allocated to the appropriations committees could be used only for housing programs and certain initiatives of the Internal Revenue Service. House conferees on the budget resolution blocked the plan, although the Senate Budget Committee included the instructions in its report.[53]

The more rigid constraints reduced the autonomy of the appropriations committees. But that is not the whole story. Appropriators retained control over the 302(b) allocations, which permit them to exercise at least some discretion in identifying the specific spending limits for each appropriations bill. Moreover, the constraints also applied to floor amendments to appropriations bills, which meant that appropriators could raise points of order against amendments that had the effect of pushing a bill beyond the limit. This is particularly important in the Senate, where appropriations bills have almost routinely been made more expensive through floor amendments. As a result, within the constraints imposed on them by the process, the appropriations committees gained more control over the details of their bills.

The remaining, and difficult, question is: Are the appropriations committees more powerful as a result of the binding 302(b) process? The answer has two parts. First, with respect to their ability to make decisions according to their own policy preferences and by processes that suit their own needs, the appropriations committees have lost a great deal of autonomy. They are constrained by budget decisions negotiated by party and budget committee leaders and imposed by the parent chambers. They are more constrained in their ability to meet the demands placed on them by their colleagues and constituencies. In the long run, this will substantially reduce the influence of the committees over their colleagues and constituencies.

Second, with respect to determining legislative details *within the constraints* of the binding 302(b) allocations, the appropriations committees gained some insulation from outside forces. When the committees do include in their bills funding for projects or programs desired by colleagues and constituencies, they are in a better position to protect them from unfriendly floor amendments. And they are in a better position, within the budget constraints, to set priorities as they see fit.

CONTINUING RESOLUTIONS

Congress uses continuing resolutions to provide funding for federal agencies and programs when the regular appropriations bill has not been enacted by the start of the new fiscal year.[54] Traditionally, continuing resolutions were short term—they expired in a few days or weeks when the regular appropriations bill was adopted. They also were very brief, usually providing for funding through a formula at the previous year's rate. And they concerned only the one or two regular appropriations bills that Congress and the president did not manage to enact. Continuing resolutions were considered unfortunate, largely innocuous necessities.

Budget conflict and the resulting strategies and delays associated with the appropriations process transformed continuing resolutions in the 1980s. Disputes between the House and Senate, and between Congress and President Reagan, delayed approval of budget resolutions and the appropriations bills dependent on the resolutions. Over half of the regular appropriations bills were not enacted by the start of the fiscal year in 1982, 1984, and 1985, and none of them were enacted in 1986 and 1987. The failures in 1986 and 1987 were encouraged by the Gramm-Rudman-Hollings procedure, which made points of order against the regular appropriations bills serious obstacles, particularly in the Senate. The key continuing resolutions of these years became full-year funding measures—obviously quite comprehensive, including hundreds of pages of text rather than just a formula—and took on great political importance. Omnibus continuing resolutions were avoided in 1988 and 1989, primarily because Congress and the administration agreed to a two-year budget plan in late 1987 that allowed appropriations bills to be considered and adopted on schedule.

These developments in the use of continuing resolutions had several implications for the autonomy of both appropriations and authorizing committees.[55] As for reconciliation and appropriations allocations, party and budget leaders assumed an active role in negotiating the broad contours of the resolutions. In fact, negotiations over continuing resolutions often were a by-product of negotiations over more general budget questions. In such negotiations, appropriators lacked the authority and the influence to negotiate on behalf of their chambers and parties on such important matters. Thus, at the most general level, reliance on continuing resolutions came at the price of sharing decision-making functions on appropriations with other members.

But in other ways—appropriations details and nonappropriations matters—reliance on continuing resolutions substantially increased the power of the appropriations committees at the expense of their parent chambers and the authorizing committees. Greater control over appropriations details is the product of several aspects of the way continuing resolutions are handled. First, because the massive continuing resolutions of the 1980s have been considered under severe time constraints, they are considered on the House floor under special rules that severely restrict or bar floor amendments. This possibility encourages appropriators to delay their regular bill and include it in the continuing resolution if they fear many unfriendly floor amendments. Second, the size of some continuing resolutions makes them difficult to challenge. They are so large that only a few elements receive much scrutiny on the floor. If they were considered as separate bills, days or weeks apart, more issues normally would be raised. And finally, the severe time constraints increase the difficulty of defeating the conference report on the continuing resolutions, giving the appropriators who are conferees a little greater leeway in writing the conference report. Conference reports on continuing resolutions are not insulated from defeat, of course (the House turned down one in 1983), but it usually is their aggregate cost and nonspending features, and not appropriations details, that get them into trouble.

An even more important concern to other members of Congress is the infringement of authorizing committees' jurisdictions by continuing resolutions. Unlike regular appropriations bills, continuing resolutions may include any kind of legislation, such as legislative authorizations not within the jurisdiction of the appropriations committees. Continuing resolutions of the 1980s became vehicles for carrying a great deal of authorizing legislation. In some cases, authorizing committees asked friendly appropriators to include their legislation in a continuing resolution in order to force the other chamber and the president to consider and agree to it. Many large authorizing measures were included in continuing resolutions in this way. In doing so, however, appropriators gained a voice in shaping legislation that they otherwise would not have had, particularly in conference. And the continuing resolutions gave appropriators—as well as other members through appeals to appropriators and through floor amendments—an opportunity to pursue legislative matters without the consent and cooperation of the affected authorizing committee.

Leaders of authorizing committees have complained, often with great bitterness, about the use of continuing resolutions for nonappropriations matters. Even when the policy outcome suits their needs, authorizing committees realize that they are not controlling those outcomes and may find future outcomes less satisfactory. They risk becoming supplicants to the appropriations committees on matters within their own jurisdictions. And the lobbyists and constituencies traditionally dependent on authorizing committees shift their attention to appropriators when the action shifts to continuing resolutions, further undermining the value of membership on the authorizing committees. In short, the long-term price of legislating through continuing resolutions for authorizing committees may be atrophy in their policy-making role.

BUDGET POLITICS IN RETROSPECT

The damage done to the autonomy of appropriations and authorizing committees was not nearly as profound as it could have been. The designers of budget resolutions have themselves been constrained by the necessity of obtaining majority support and agreement with the other chamber before imposing instructions and restrictions on committees. This constraint is severe. After all, both chambers are populated by members of those committees affected by the instructions and restrictions of budget resolutions. Budget makers have found their efforts to manage the deficit problem frustrated by the unwillingness of their chambers to accept the policy and institutional consequences of the proposed solutions.

Nevertheless, as partisan conflict over budget priorities intensified and produced policy stalemates among the House, Senate, and White House, both appropriations and authorizing committees lost autonomy. Party and Budget Committee leaders became central to resolving the conflict. Normal legislative procedures were ignored, set aside temporarily, and in some cases directly altered. All committees learned new legislative tricks to minimize the damage to programs they wanted to protect, but most could not avoid deep encroachments on their traditional autonomy. Appropriations committees, particularly the House committee, managed to preserve a degree of control over appropriation details under the 302(b) allocation procedure and even gained a greater role in authorizing legislation at times through skillful use of continuing resolutions. Authorizing committees appeared to suffer the most. Deficit politics limited new legislative initiatives and focused energy on preserving programs they supported. Reconciliation cut sharply into the traditional power of authorizing committees to block action on matters under their jurisdiction. Thus, in the quite unsettled power structure of Congress, leaders and budget committees fared well, appropriations committees survived but were injured, and authorizing committees took strong blows to their autonomy.

SUMMITS AND TASK FORCES

Two other developments of the 1980s are worth noting. The first is the use of domestic policy summits—meetings of committee leaders, the lieutenants of congressional leaders, and top executive branch officials designed to get over an impasse on an important policy problem. Summits have been used effectively to handle budget and social security problems. Once summit groups reach agreements, their recommendations carry tremendous weight in the legislative process. Most important, they shift the blame to those in Congress who might seek to alter or block the recommendation before it becomes law. Although committee reactions are a part of the calculations at summits, committees and their leaders find that their freedom to design legislation as they see fit is severely limited by the terms of summit agreements. Thus, while summits are uncommon and sometimes involve committee representatives, they have the effect of shifting the proposal power to party leaders and administration officials and reducing the blocking power of committees.

A device similar to summits is commissions, more formal bodies created by statute designed to find bipartisan solutions to difficult policy problems. Commissions on the federal deficit and comprehensive health care have been created in recent years, but neither has proved successful in finding bipartisan recommendations.

Leadership task forces are the second important development.[56] Since the late 1970s, Speakers have appointed task forces of twenty-five or thirty Democrats to assist the leadership in gaining House approval for most important legislation. Now a matter of routine, task forces represent whip systems specialized in both policy and political terms. The members appointed to task forces have a special interest in the legislation and often are chosen because of their relationship to the contending factions within the House. Most often they are used to help the party leadership secure a House majority for a measure reported from committee, and so they reflect a partnership between leadership and committee. But there have been several occasions when task forces have produced policy proposals themselves, usually in the form of floor amendments. In a few instances, with the blessing of party leaders, task forces have pressured committees to produce legislation to their liking or even written legislation themselves. In recent years, the Republican leadership also has begun to employ a few task forces, usurping some of the role played traditionally by committee Republicans and the party's Policy Committee.

A more recent development in the House is the creation of bipartisan task forces by the joint leadership in order to address issues of concern to both parties. In the first session of the 101st Congress (1989-1990), task forces on the reform of congressional ethics and campaign finance held many hearings and, in the case of congressional ethics, eventually devised legislation.[57] Partisan differences on campaign finance practices proved too deep for that task force to solve.

Senate majority leader George Mitchell has followed the House lead by creating several task forces of Senate Democrats to address issues that cross jurisdictional lines.[58] Contra aid, government ethics, and rural development were among the subjects for which task forces were created during 1989, Mitchell's first year as majority leader. Unlike the task forces of the House Democratic leadership, which usually do not devise legislation, the Senate Democratic task forces have the express purpose of formulating new legislation.

ADDITIONAL PERSPECTIVE
ON DECLINING COMMITTEE POWER

Before concluding that committees are no longer important to policy outcomes, it is important to develop a sense of proportion about the changes reported in this chapter. The review of the previous sections makes it appear that change in the role of committees has been sweeping. Hardly an aspect of committee power has remained untouched by one procedural change or another. In many respects, it appears that decision making is far more centralized than in the 1970s, particularly in the House, where formal rules shape the distribution of power more directly. And yet there are limits on the extent to which central leaders have reached into congressional decision making, even in the House. Many committees retain a great deal of autonomy. A quick review, from a different perspective, of the developments outlined in this chapter should make this point.

COMMITTEE ASSIGNMENTS. Party leaders do not take a very active interest, at least on behalf of the party, in assignments to many, if not a majority, of the House committees. Moreover, in the case of the House Democrats, it is important to keep in mind that there are nonleadership members of Steering and Policy to whom competitors for choice assignments must appeal for support. And in neither party has there been a serious challenge to the property right norm—that once members are assigned to a committee, it is their post to keep until they request a transfer. State, regional, factional, and other claims still play an important role in assignments.

MULTIPLE REFERRAL. There is a flip side to leadership control of multiple referral in the House. Most multiple referral is now routine and does not require the personal involvement of the Speaker. It represents established precedents about areas of shared jurisdiction among committees and so constitutes an institutionalized expansion of access to various policy areas more than regular leadership coordination or manipulation. Indeed, given the frequency of multiple referral in recent congresses, it could be no other way. Central party leaders do not have the time or interest to scrutinize each referral. The House must rely upon routine and direct committee-to-committee communication to manage most cases of overlapping jurisdictions and multiple referral. Thus, while the shift from single to multiple referral means that a committee has lost autonomy and another has gained access to an issue, the initiative, coordination, and policy direction generally remain within the committee system. It also is important to note that the vast majority of measures, even among major measures reported and passed, still are subject only to a single referral.

AMENDMENTS, SUSPENSION, AND SPECIAL RULES. The surge in amending activity did not affect all committees. Even committees considered to be in the middle of the pack in terms of policy significance, such as the banking and judiciary committees, did not experience significant increases in amending activity during the 1970s.[59]

In the House, the expanded use of suspension of the rules and restrictive special rules serves, rather than undermines, the interests of the majority party contingents on committees. And in the vast majority of cases, the expanded use represents an effort to facilitate the passage of the committee recommendation—that is, to preserve a degree of committee autonomy that might be at risk if committees were forced to bring measures to the floor under a procedure that left the measures fully open to amendment. For the most part, then, these developments represent a partnership of the majority party leadership and the party contingents of standing committees.

CONFERENCE DELEGATIONS.   In both chambers, the vast majority of conference delegations remain under the firm control of committee members. It appears that the chair's list of conference appointees is usually accepted by the appointing authorities in both chambers.

BUDGETING.   The actual damage to committee autonomy accomplished by reconciliation and 302(b) processes is much less than the potential or even intended damage. Fiscal trickery is now legend, but it also is real. Furthermore, budgeting is not a one-way street. Many committees have used reconciliation and continuing resolutions to package authorizations, which then are protected by the restrictive rules usually granted to such omnibus bills. In many cases, far more autonomy is granted to committees by this means than was granted before the advent of stricter budgeting in 1980. Such packaging is usually done at the initiative of the committees and often is criticized by central budget leaders. And perhaps most important, the fiscal conditions that spurred more centralized decision making are likely to change. Reduced defense spending, for example, may lessen the pressures on domestic spending and revenues, and allow Congress to grant more autonomy to authorizing committees.

SUMMITS AND TASK FORCES.   There are limits to how far central party leaders can tread on the jurisdictions of committees by employing summits and task forces to forge legislation. For example, in early 1989 many House Democrats were resentful about the highly centralized bargaining in a budget summit between administration and congressional leaders, and they later opposed another summit in the fall.[60] Task forces typically include key members of the relevant committee or committees and sometimes are dominated by them.

Committees have adjusted their own procedures in yet other ways to adapt to their contemporary institutional environment. For example, committees moved to insulate themselves from close scrutiny by lobbyists and outsiders by closing their markup sessions.[61] No systematic tally of closed meetings is available, although it appears that more House than Senate committees have regularly closed meetings in recent years. In both chambers, the defense committees and subcommittees frequently hold meetings concerning national security matters that are classified in private. But many others—ranging from the appropriations committees to the agriculture, education, foreign policy, and judiciary committees—have held closed markups on matters other than national security issues.

Finally, it bears noting that committees are themselves partly responsible for the institutional environment in which they operate, even though that environment now limits their autonomy more than it once did. In some situations, committees have preferred that control over policy outcomes be transferred to others, or at least that their own discretion be very conspicuously constrained, in order to avoid blame for damaging the interests of important constituency groups. The pressures of deficit reduction, for example, lead committees to seek political cover when program benefits must be limited. Pushing responsibility to a party or budget leader helps a committee maintain good relations with its constituency groups. In other situations, limited autonomy is the price paid by committees for having any influence over policy outcomes. Multiple referral, for example, works to the advantage of committees previously excluded from a role on certain issues, even when it means the central party leaders will play a more important role in setting the committees' agendas. Thus, some of the decline in autonomy is by committee choice and cannot be equated with lost power in all situations.

The developments of the past two decades have had mixed effects for committee autonomy. On balance, committee autonomy has declined and congressional decision making has become less committee-oriented, but the ability of committees to recover, often with the assistance of the majority party and its leadership, cannot be ignored. In many important ways, the primary responsibility of the majority party leadership continues to be to serve its party's committee contingents. Committees remain the principal, if not always fully autonomous, players in nearly all policy decisions.

CONCLUSION

Committee autonomy, when viewed over the long term, is in remarkable flux. Change in the role of committees is primarily the product of new policy problems and political alignments, as well as the character of the existing institutional arrangements. When interest in issues is highly fragmented, policy outcomes satisfy most members, and the issues bear little on party fortunes, autonomous committees are tolerated and even revered. When issues are more interrelated and few members are indifferent to outcomes, as appeared to be the case more frequently in the 1970s, committees are highly constrained by their parent chambers and must rely on formal procedural safeguards to preserve their control over legislative details. If the parties' electoral fortunes also are tied to those issues and decisions, as happened on budget matters in the 1980s, party leaders and their functionaries assume decision-making responsibilities that otherwise would fall to committees.

The *direction* of change over the last two decades or so—toward less autonomous committees and a less committee-oriented process—must not be confused with the *degree* of change. The changes reported in this chapter appear to be quite sweeping, particularly in the House. Many of the procedural sources of committee power seem to have been weakened. Developments affecting committee assignments, bill referral, floor debate, conferences, and the budget process reduced committee autonomy. And the informal norm of deference to committee recommendations certainly is much weaker now than it was in the 1950s and 1960s. But some care must be taken in drawing inferences from these changes. Most legislation comes from a single committee in each chamber, suffers few successful and important floor amendments, and does not require a conference. When a conference is necessary, it is managed by conferees chosen nearly exclusively from the committee of origin. Moreover, committees have devised a remarkable variety of legislative tricks to minimize the effect of budget constraints. With the creative use of special rules and omnibus measures in the 1980s, committees have actually recovered some of the autonomy they lost in the 1970s.

Nevertheless, both chambers have demonstrated a willingness to manipulate their procedures to meet current, and sometimes very short-term, needs. This is most evident in the use of special rules in the House, but the Senate, too, has altered its rules governing budget procedures. If committee power could ever be taken for granted, and it has been during most of this century, it no longer can be. In fact, there is a sense of instability or fluidity on Capitol Hill now that power is not clearly grounded in the committee systems.

The prospects for the future are difficult to forecast. They turn on factors external to Congress that shape its agenda and political alignments. For example, if budget constraints weaken and new domestic policy initiatives become more common in the 1990s, committees probably will gain a more central role in designing policy and develop more independence from party and budget committee leaders. But even if no significant change occurs in the character of agendas and political alignments, there will be continuing reliance on standing committees to fashion the details of legislation. The necessity of a division of labor to manage the immense work load, even—perhaps especially—under reconciliation and binding 302(b) allocation procedures, has led Congress to grant substantial discretion to committees. That organizational imperative is well established.

NOTES

1. On this theme, also see Roger H. Davidson, "The New Centralization in Congress," *The Review of Politics* 49 (Summer 1988): 345-363; Roger H. Davidson, "The Impact of Agenda on the Post-Reform Congress," paper presented at the 1989 annual meeting of the American Political Science Association, Atlanta, August 31-September 3, 1989; Kenneth A. Shepsle, "The Changing Textbook Congress," in *Can the Government Govern?* ed. John E. Chubb and Paul E. Peterson (Washington, D.C.: Brookings Institution, 1989), 264; Barbara Sinclair, "House Majority Leadership in the Late 1980s," in *Congress Reconsidered*, 4th ed., ed. Lawrence C. Dodd and Bruce I. Oppenheimer (Washington, D.C.: CQ Press, 1989), 3-7, 29; Barbara Sinclair, "The Changing Role of Party and Party Leadership in the U.S. House," paper presented at the 1989 annual meeting of the American Political Science Association, Atlanta, August 31-September 3, 1989; Steven S. Smith, *Call to Order: Floor Politics in the House and Senate* (Washington, D.C.: CQ Press, 1989).
2. The alternative models parallel Fenno's scheme for characterizing the political environments of committees. See Richard F. Fenno, Jr., *Congressmen in Committees* (Boston: Little, Brown, 1973), chap. 2. They also emphasize the locations in the legislative process that are central to the major styles of decision making noted by Smith. See Steven S. Smith, *Call to Order*, chap. 1.
3. For further elaboration of a similar model, see Gary W. Cox and Mathew D. McCubbins, *Parties and Committees in the U.S. House of Representatives* (manuscript).
4. For further elaboration of a similar model, see Keith Krehbiel, *Information and Legislative Organization* (manuscript).
5. Roger H. Davidson, "The Impact of Agenda on the Post-Reform Congress," paper prepared for the 1989 meeting of the American Political Science Association, August 31-September 3, 1989, Atlanta.
6. David W. Rohde, "Democratic Party Leadership, Agenda Control, and the Resurgence of Partisanship in the House," paper prepared for the 1989 annual meeting of the American Political Science Association, August 31-September 3, 1989, Atlanta.
7. Don Wolfensberger, "The Role of Party Caucuses in the U.S. House of Representatives: An Historical Perspective," paper prepared for the annual meeting of the American Political Science Association, Washington, D.C., September 1-4, 1988; and Diane Granat, "Democratic Caucus Renewed as Forum for Policy Questions," *Congressional Quarterly Weekly Report*, October 15, 1983, 2115-2119.
8. Richard E. Cohen, "Setting the Senate Democrats' Agenda," *National Journal*, February 25, 1989, 484; and Richard E. Cohen, "Making His Mark," *National Journal*, May 20, 1989, 1232-1236.
9. Jackie Calmes, "Fight Over Anti-Drug Funds Threatens Spending Bills," *Congressional Quarterly Weekly Report*, September 16, 1989, 2368-2369.
10. Roger H. Davidson, Walter J. Oleszek, and Thomas Kephart, "One Bill, Many Committees: Multiple Referrals in the U.S. House of Representatives," *Legislative Studies Quarterly* 13 (February 1988): 10.
11. See Melissa P. Collie and Joseph Cooper, "Multiple Referral and the 'New' Committee System in the House of Representatives," in *Congress Reconsidered*, 4th ed., ed. Dodd and Oppenheimer, 245-272.

12. For background on multiple referral and special rules, see Stanley Bach and Steven S. Smith, *Managing Uncertainty in the House of Representatives: Adaptation and Innovation in Special Rules* (Washington, D.C.: Brookings Institution, 1988), 18-23, 38-45, 59-61.

13. On norms, see Herbert B. Asher, "The Learning of Legislative Norms," *American Political Science Review* 67 (June 1973): 508-509; Richard F. Fenno, Jr., "The House Appropriations Committee as a Political System: The Problem of Integration," *American Political Science Review* 56 (June 1962): 310-324; Richard F. Fenno, Jr., "The Freshman Congressman: His View of the House," in *American Governmental Institutions: A Reader in the Political Process*, ed. Aaron Wildavsky and Nelson W. Polsby (New York: Rand McNally, 1968); Irwin Gertzog, "Frustration and Adaptation," paper prepared for the 1966 annual meeting of the American Political Science Association; Ralph K. Huitt, "The Morse Committee Assignment Controversy: A Study in Senate Norms," *American Political Science Review* 51 (June 1957): 313-329; Ralph K. Huitt, "The Outsider in the Senate: An Alternative Role," *American Political Science Review* 55 (September 1961): 566-575; Donald R. Matthews, *U.S. Senators and Their World* (New York: Vintage Books, 1960), chap. 5; David W. Rohde, Norman J. Ornstein, and Robert L. Peabody, "Political Change and Legislative Norms in the U.S. Senate, 1957-1974," in *Studies of Congress*, ed. Glenn R. Parker (Washington, D.C.: CQ Press, 1985), 147-188; Barbara Sinclair, "Senate Styles and Senate Decision Making," *Journal of Politics* 48 (November 1986): 877-908; Smith, *Call to Order*, chap. 5.

14. In addition to the empirical literature cited in note 13, there are several formal treatments of legislative norms that bear on the role of committees. See, for example, Robert Axelrod, *The Evolution of Cooperation* (New York: Basic Books, 1984); Emerson M. Niou and Peter C. Ordeshook, "Universalism in Congress," *American Political Science Review* 29 (May 1985): 246-258; Kenneth Shepsle and Barry Weingast, "Political Preferences for the Pork Barrel: A Generalization," *American Journal of Political Science* 25 (February 1981): 96-111; Kenneth Shepsle and Barry Weingast, "The Institutional Foundations of Committee Power," *American Political Science Review* 81 (March 1987): 85-104; and Barry Weingast, "A Rational Choice Perspective on Congressional Norms," *American Political Science Review* 23 (May 1979): 245-262.

15. On the problems associated with making inferences about committee power from the roll-call voting record, see Keith Krehbiel and Douglas Rivers, "The Analysis of Committee Power: An Application to Senate Voting on the Minimum Wage," *American Political Science Review* 32 (November 1988): 1151-1174.

16. The counts of amendments noted in this chapter exclude committee amendments, and so are not inflated by routine and substitute amendments offered by bill managers that represent committee recommendations. For more detail, see Smith, *Call to Order*.

17. On the use of second-degree amendments to preserve committee recommendations, see Smith, *Call to Order*, 183-187; Barry R. Weingast, "Floor Behavior in the U.S. Congress: Committee Power Under the Open Rule," *American Political Science Review* 83 (September 1989): 795-815; and Barry Weingast, "Fighting Fire with Fire: Amending Activity and Institutional Change in the Post-Reform Congress" (1989), Hoover Institution, mimeo.

18. Bach and Smith, *Managing Uncertainty*, chaps. 2, 3.

19. Stanley Bach, "Suspension of the Rules in the House of Representatives," report 86-103 GOV (Congressional Research Service, May 12, 1986).

20. See Bach and Smith, *Managing Uncertainty*, 75, 82.

21. *Congressional Record*, daily edition, March 22, 1989, H799-H806. The rule also did not allow a motion to recommit with instructions, allowing only a simple motion to recommit, and thus prevented the minority party from offering an amendment to the compromise version supported by the committee Democrats.

22. Bach and Smith, *Managing Uncertainty*, 116-117.

23. For example, in 1987 the House defeated a rule for a reconciliation bill that included a controversial welfare reform package because members objected to being denied an opportunity to amend the reform package. See *Congressional Quarterly Almanac* (Washington, D.C.: Congressional Quarterly, 1987), 555.

24. See Helen Dewar, "Bill Gives Senators a Chance to Play Secretary of State," *Washington Post*, July 20, 1989, A6-7.

25. For background on conference procedures and politics, see Lawrence D. Longley and Walter J. Oleszek, *Bicameral Politics: Conference Committees in Congress* (New Haven: Yale University Press, 1989).

26. This threat is common for committees whose bills contain projects important to the districts or states of individual members, such as the appropriations and public works committees. For a recent example, see Paul Starobin, "Can Anderson Bridge Gap to Fill His Wider Role?" *Congressional Quarterly Weekly Report*, April 29, 1989, 955.

27. See Keith Krehbiel, *Information and Legislative Organization*, chap. 6; Shepsle and Weingast, "The Institutional Foundations of Committee Power," 85-104; Keith Krehbiel, Kenneth A. Shepsle, and Barry R. Weingast, "Why Are Congressional Committees Powerful?" *American Political Science Review* 81 (1987): 929-945; Steven S. Smith, "An Essay on Sequence, Position, Goals, and Committee Power," *Legislative Studies Quarterly* 13 (May 1988): 151-176; and Smith, *Call to Order*, chap. 7.

28. See George Hager, "Energy Panel Seals Pact on Vehicle Pollution," *Congressional Quarterly Weekly Report*, October 7, 1989, 2621-2624.

29. Indeed, certain concessions with respect to conference negotiations may be necessary in advance to avoid a filibuster during initial Senate consideration.

30. A recent example is the selection of conferees on a 1989 appropriations bill that included provisions on counting illegal aliens in the 1990 national census. See Kim Mattingly, "House Census Vote Will Affect Reapportionment," *Roll Call*, October 9-15, 1989, 1, 24.

31. In the House, the Speaker's list of conferees can be altered only by unanimous consent, making it virtually impossible to challenge the Speaker. In the Senate, the list of the presiding officer (nearly always taken from the committee chair) may be modified by a debatable motion that must be adopted by majority vote.

32. A good example is the 1989 defense authorization conference. See Pat Towell, "Conference over Defense Bill: Test of Political Muscle," *Congressional Quarterly Weekly Report*, October 7, 1989, 2656.

33. John R. Crawford, "102 Conferees Appointed on S&L Bailout Bill," *Congressional Quarterly Weekly Report*, June 24, 1989, 1530; Kathleen Day and Sharon Warren Walsh, "Negotiations on S&L Bailout Bill Move Behind Closed Doors," *Washington Post*, July 19, 1989, F1; and Sharon Warren Walsh,

"House, Senate Staffs Work on S&L Bill," *Washington Post,* July 20, 1989, F2.

34. See Sharon Warren Walsh, "S&L Conference's Cramped Quarters Will Squeeze Out the Public, Media," *Washington Post,* June 22, 1989.

35. The rules of both chambers were changed in 1970 to allow minority opinions greater expression when conference reports are debated on the floor. The old practice of granting control over all debate time on the report to the chair of the conference delegation sometimes meant that little time was given to minority views. The new rules guaranteed equal time for the majority and minority. The House went a step further in 1985 when it adopted a rule that requires one-third of debate time to be reserved for an opponent of the report in the event that the majority and minority party bill managers support the report. The House also adopted in 1970 a rule requiring a layover period of three days for conference reports to give members an opportunity to review them. The requirement does not apply during the last six days of a session and may be waived by a special rule.

36. Janet Hook, "GOP Conference-Report Moves Often Serve to Split Party," *Congressional Quarterly Weekly Report,* October 21, 1989, 2765.

37. Don Phillips, "House Defeats Compromise Emergency Spending Bill," *Washington Post,* June 22, 1989, A7.

38. See Allen Schick, *Congress and Money: Budgeting, Spending, and Taxing* (Washington, D.C.: Urban Institute, 1980), chap. 8.

39. For a convenient summary of the 1980 budget battle in the House, see Barbara Sinclair, *Majority Leadership in the U.S. House* (Baltimore: Johns Hopkins University Press, 1983), 181-190.

40. Louis Fisher, "The Budget Act of 1974: Reflections After Ten Years," paper presented at the annual meeting of the Midwest Political Science Association, Chicago, 1985.

41. This was a strategy particularly useful to House committees controlled by Democrats who were faced with a Republican Senate and administration that were opposed to most new policy initiatives. But both House and Senate committees have taken advantage of reconciliation to force floor and conference consideration of legislation. For recent examples, see Ronald D. Elving with Jackie Calmes, "Tax, Health-Cost Disputes Slow Deficit Reduction," *Congressional Quarterly Weekly Report,* September 23, 1989, 2444-2445.

42. For background on Gramm-Rudman-Hollings, see John W. Ellwood, "The Politics of the Enactment and Implementation of Gramm-Rudman-Hollings: Why Congress Cannot Address the Deficit Dilemma," *Harvard Journal on Legislation* 25 (Summer 1988): 553-575.

43. Extraneous provisions, under the Byrd rule, are those that either do not make changes (or make only incidental changes) in outlays (spending) or revenues, increase the budget deficit when the reporting committee has not met its deficit reduction target, are not within the jurisdiction of the reporting committee, or increase the deficit after the final year covered by the bill by an amount greater than the savings achieved by the same title. In 1989, the rule played a central role in forcing Congress to consider capital gains tax legislation separately from reconciliation. See Ronald D. Elving, "What's in a Rule?" *Congressional Quarterly Weekly Report,* October 7, 1989, 2617. The rule sometimes works in favor of a committee because it can be used to block amendments that are opposed by a committee, although there are other ways to block such amendments.

44. For example, see David Rapp, "Negotiators Agree on Outlines of Fiscal 1990 Plan," *Congressional Quarterly Weekly Report*, April 15, 1989, 804-805.
45. Julie Rovner, "Ways and Means OKs Overhaul of Medicare Payment Plan," *Congressional Quarterly Weekly Report*, July 1, 1989, 1626-1627.
46. See Lawrence J. Haas, "Losing Its Punch," *National Journal*, December 30, 1989, 3107.
47. Public Law 93-344, Sec. 302(b).
48. Schick, *Congress and Money*, 447-462.
49. Ibid.
50. For background on making 302(b) allocations binding, see Allen Schick, "The Whole and the Parts: Piecemeal and Integrated Approaches to Congressional Budgeting," Report Prepared for the Task Force on the Budget Process, Committee on the Budget, U.S. House of Representatives, Serial No. CP-3 (Washington, D.C.: U.S. Government Printing Office, 1987), 20-21; and Joseph White, *The Functions and Power of the House Appropriations Committee* (Ph.D. dissertation, University of California, Berkeley, 1989), 460-492. The remainder of this section draws from White's excellent study.
51. Dan Morgan, "In College of 'Cardinals,' A Summer of Frustration: Freewheeling Spending Now Has High Price," *Washington Post*, June 30, 1989, A1, A14; Dan Morgan, "Power and the Purse: The Appropriations Committee," *Washington Post*, November 11, 1989, A10, A11; and Dan Morgan, "Pet Projects Pay the Price as Members Cross Chairman," *Washington Post*, November 20, 1989, A1, A4. Also see David Rapp, "Neal Smith: Digging in His Heels," *Congressional Quarterly Weekly Report*, May 27, 1989, 1239; and David Rapp, "With Fiscal '90 Allocations Set, Spending Bills Start to Move," *Congressional Quarterly Weekly Report*, June 17, 1989, 1458-1459.
52. For example, the Budget Committee chair, Leon Panetta, testified before the Rules Committee against a request of two Appropriations subcommittee chairs who were seeking a rule for a supplemental appropriations bill that would waive points of order against the bill for violating their 302(b) allocations. The Rules Committee supported Panetta and refused to grant the waiver. See David Rapp, "House Clears Supplemental After Midweek Revolt," *Congressional Quarterly Weekly Report*, June 24, 1989, 1525.
53. David Rapp, "Agreement on Fiscal 1990 Plan Puts Off Tough Decisions," *Congressional Quarterly Weekly Report*, May 13, 1989, 1104.
54. For historical background on appropriations and continuing resolutions, see Schick, "The Whole and the Parts," 33-39. This section draws heavily on Schick's discussion, as well as on White's discussion of House Appropriations in *The Functions and Power of the House Appropriations Committee*, 492-553.
55. For additional background, see Joe White, "The Continuing Resolution: A Crazy Way to Govern?" *The Brookings Review* (Summer 1988): 28-35.
56. Barbara Sinclair, "The Speaker's Task Force in the Post-Reform House of Representatives," *American Political Science Review* 75 (June 1984): 397-410.
57. Janet Hook, "Far-Reaching Rule Reforms Aren't Easy to Come By," *Congressional Quarterly Weekly Report*, September 23, 1989, 2437-2438.
58. Cohen, "Making His Mark," 1236; and David S. Cloud, "New Rural-Development Effort Has Strong Senate Support," *Congressional Quarterly Weekly Report*, May 20, 1989, 1189.
59. Steven S. Smith, "Revolution in the House," Brookings Discussion Papers, No. 5 (September 1986), table 12.
60. See Lawrence J. Haas, "Loading the Last Train," *National Journal*, August 5,

1989, 1980; and Haas, "Losing Its Punch," 3107.

61. See Jacqueline Calmes, "Fading 'Sunshine' Reforms: Few Complaints are Voiced as Doors Close on Capitol Hill," *Congressional Quarterly Weekly Report*, May 23, 1987, 1059-1060; Nadine Cohodas, "Panels OK Justice Department Authorization," *Congressional Quarterly Weekly Report*, April 11, 1987, 692; Spencer Rich, "Hill Panels' 'Sunshine' Starts Clouding Over," *Washington Post*, August 10, 1985, A4; Ward Sinclair, "Senate Panel Agrees to Cut Farm Programs," *Washington Post*, December 5, 1987.

CHAPTER 6

The Dynamic Committee Systems of Congress

The committee systems of the House and Senate are varied and dynamic. In fact, the central theme of this book has been that the place of committees in the decision-making process continues to vary within and between the chambers, as well as over time. We have described the evolution of the committee systems from sets of highly constrained, temporary committees into the highly independent, seemingly autonomous committees of the middle decades of this century. We have also examined the changing relationship between committees and the parties with respect to making committee assignments and the great variety in member goals and environments among committees. We have discussed variations in patterns of change in decision-making processes within committees. And finally, we have recounted developments of the last two decades that have recast the relationships among committees, parties, and the parent chambers and substantially reduced the autonomy of committees in policy making. This historical record suggests that there is little reason to believe that the current role of congressional committees will last for long. We will conclude, therefore, with an assessment of the future of congressional committees.

THE CURRENT STATE OF CONGRESSIONAL COMMITTEES

Committees continue to be central to congressional decision making because they serve the needs of both the institution and individual members.[1] The committee systems are vital to the well-being of Congress as an authoritative decision-making institution. Committees provide the division of labor required to handle a large and complex work load.[2] The parliamentary advantages granted to committees provide incentives for members to take their committee work seriously.[3] Knowing that their decisions often determine policy outcomes, committee members are encouraged to specialize, develop expertise, observe and appraise developments in Congress's environment, and craft legislation. Furthermore, jurisdictional divisions between committees separate issues into more manageable pieces, which may avert conflict that would arise if some issues were considered together. And committees provide avenues of access to Congress for constituents whose support, at least over the long term, is critical to the perceived legitimacy of the institution's decisions. For many observers, therefore, strong committees have been viewed as essential to a strong Congress.

For individual members, the division of jurisdictions among committees makes it possible for members to focus on issues that most affect their own interests and to ignore many others, which makes for greater efficiency in the achievement of personal political goals. This is accomplished at the expense of losing influence over decisions in other policy areas, but this price may be quite small. As long as members can gain assignments to those committees whose jurisdictions are most closely associated with their interests and as long as those interests are fairly stable, a decentralized system of committees will meet the political needs of most members.

This dual rationale for independent and autonomous committees continues to carry great weight in Congress. And yet events of the last two decades have demonstrated that there is a limit to the degree to which independent and autonomous committees are in the collective interest of the institution and its members. From an institutional perspective, a highly decentralized system of rigid jurisdictions and autonomous committees may handicap Congress in attempting to respond to problems that do not fit within established jurisdictional categories. It may also complicate the task of party leaders seeking quick legislative action and obstruct the development of policy that ties various elements into a coherent whole. If those are the consequences of a rigid, decentralized system, such a system undermines the ability of Congress to compete with a president and the more centralized executive branch. Furthermore, rapidly changing issues and political conditions make it difficult for a complex institution to tailor new structures and procedures to each new feature of its environment. By the time reform proposals have been formulated and adopted, the issues and conditions have changed again. A more elastic process in which party leaders configure procedures and committee responsibilities to meet changing circumstances may yield greater speed and integration in policy making.[4]

From the perspective of individual members, a system of autonomous committees limits members' influence on issues that do not fall within their own committees' jurisdictions. This makes it very difficult both for members to control the influence of parochial interests that might be entrenched in various committees and for newcomers to a policy area to be heard. Members may seek different committee assignments to adjust to new circumstances, but transfers between committees costs them committee seniority. A more floor-oriented process may provide opportunities for all members to raise new issues and influence the direction of public policy.

Thus, as outlined in Chapter 5, there often is tension among members' preferences for autonomous committees, a more floor-oriented process, and a more party-oriented process.[5] Preferences for these alternatives, and for combinations of them, vary over time as members experience successes and failures in their own legislative efforts. Most change in institutional arrangements within Congress can be viewed as a process of relieving recently experienced tensions between the alternative decision-making processes. But the institutional tensions cannot be fully relieved. Each of the processes embodies values that are to some degree incompatible with those of the other two. Consequently, congressional decision-making processes, and the functions of committees, are unlikely to stabilize for very long. Any balance between the alternative processes is quite precarious and easily upset by new political conditions.

In the last two decades, the institutional tensions have been greatest in the House, where committee power was the most entrenched during the middle decades of this century. The opening of committees, the floor, and party caucuses to more meaningful rank-and-file participation undercut the power of committee chairs and reduced the autonomy of their committees. As the majority party began to suffer from this more unpredictable, floor-oriented process, it found ways to restore some of the lost committee autonomy through restrictive special rules and other devices. In doing so, however, the majority party empowered the Speaker to play a more central role in policy making. By the mid-1980s, the tension between committees and the floor had dissolved into a partnership between committees and the majority party leadership. The current relationship between House committees and the majority party leadership is likely to experience increased tension in the future if the cohesiveness of House Democrats weakens or the policy agenda becomes less focused on budget issues.

In the Senate, a traditionally more floor-oriented process has become even more floor-oriented during the past four decades. Like their House counterparts, Senate committees suffered a loss of autonomy from budget constraints during the 1980s and regained some of it through omnibus legislating. But unlike in the House, no partnership between committees and majority party leaders has insulated committees from floor amendments, germane or nongermane, or from threatened or actual filibusters. The protection of individual senators' parliamentary prerogatives in Senate rules limits the extent to which such a partnership could act to preserve committee autonomy. In turn, the relative weakness of Senate committees on the floor limits the incentives for active participation in committees, and certainly does not encourage the development of independent subcommittees.

The current condition of congressional committees is quite mixed. Simple characterizations—a decentralized system or a centralized system—do not fit. Committee members remain the central players in most policy battles and continue to exercise considerable discretion in setting the direction and details of policy in most areas. At the same time they are now less autonomous than they were in the 1950s. Particularly in the House, democratization of decision-making practices within committees helped to guarantee that more members and interests would have a voice. At the same time, changes in chamber and majority party practices made committees more accountable and their policy recommendations subject to closer scrutiny. In both chambers, the repertoire of decision-making processes now appears to be much larger than it was thirty years ago, with committees playing a quite variable role in policy making. For many members as well as outside observers, the place of committees in congressional decision making is now ambiguous.

REFORM PROPOSALS

Since the late 1970s, efforts to reform rules that directly affect committee jurisdictions or powers have been few and unsuccessful in both chambers. Nevertheless, ideas for change continue to percolate. A brief look at some of the reform proposals that recently have been given some consideration will illustrate the continuing differences between the two chambers and the evolving attitudes about the appropriate role of committees. The proposals unique to each chamber are noted first, then an area of common interest is discussed.

THE HOUSE

After several waves of reform in the early 1970s, little interest has been generated recently in meaningful reforms that directly alter the functions of House committees. Part of the reason is the defensive position of the majority party Democrats under two Republican presidents during the 1980s. Rather than expend their political capital fighting battles within their own party to achieve further reform, Democratic leaders have chosen to focus their resources on maintaining intraparty cohesiveness and preserving domestic programs. But, with the exception of concern about the budget process, no sustained demand for reform has been heard within the majority party. Indeed, many Democrats have complained that some of the reforms of the 1970s went too far. For example, one survey of members uncovered considerable interest in strengthening the power of full committee chairs.[6] Instead, Democrats generally have encouraged their leaders to exploit more fully the parliamentary tools already available in order to adapt to new circumstances.

House Republicans are unsatisfied with the current partnership between the majority party leadership and the standing committees. Because of restrictive special rules, expanded use of suspension motions, and omnibus legislating, House Republicans have lost some of their opportunities to challenge committee proposals. For example, restrictive special rules often limit floor amendments, protect committee bills from points of order that the bills violate House rules, and, in areas of overlapping jurisdiction between committees, authorize floor consideration of legislation designed by committee leaders but never debated in committee. And Republicans have complained about the abuse of closed markups, proxy voting, and other aspects of committee procedure. Even committee Republicans are boxed out by some of the parliamentary tricks developed by House Democrats during the 1980s.

House Republicans are quite frustrated about the decision-making practices imposed by the majority party. The frustration is reflected in the nearly routine Republican votes against majority party procedural motions. It also is exhibited in more detailed and well-argued Republican proposals for rules changes. Their proposals touch on many aspects of committee activity.[7] They include:

- Ban joint referral. Republicans would allow sequential and split referral, but dislike the possibility that any one of two or more committees may report a measure, a practice which gives the Speaker great leeway in finding a way to get the measure reported to the floor.
- Prohibit proxy voting. Under conditions that are easy to meet, current rules allow a chair or other members to cast votes in committee on behalf of absent members. Republicans would like to ban this practice altogether, which would make it more difficult for chairs to find majorities to beat Republican amendments.
- Limit subcommittees. Partly for logistical reasons and partly for political reasons, Republicans propose that no committee, with the exception of Appropriations, have more than six subcommittees

and that members be limited to four or fewer subcommittee assignments. Republicans, with fewer members and an interest in scrutinizing majority party actions, have considerable difficulty attending all subcommittee meetings.

- Guarantee minority committee staff. The Republicans would like the House to adopt a rule guaranteeing the minority one-third of the investigative staff as well as of the permanent staff.
- Limit restrictive rules. Republicans would require the Rules Committee chair to give a four-day advance announcement of the intention of the committee to report a rule that restricts germane amendments, which would give Republicans more opportunity to mount opposition to the rule.[8]
- Limit suspension of the rules. Republicans would formally limit the suspension procedure to measures authorizing or appropriating no more than $50 million and require one-day advance notice of an intention to offer a suspension motion.
- Restrict waiving points of order. Republicans recommend that provisions in special rules barring points of order on the grounds that a measure or amendment violates budget guidelines, be subject to separate floor votes. They also would require a two-thirds vote for any rule that waives all points of order.
- Remove inhibitions on limitation amendments. Republicans would eliminate the rule that makes it difficult for them to propose amendments providing for limitations on the uses of appropriated funds.
- Restrict reconciliation. Republicans would prohibit legislation in budget reconciliation bills that is not directly related to a committee's reconciliation instructions to reduce spending or raise revenues.

The Republican proposals have not been given serious consideration by majority party Democrats. Many (but far fewer) Democrats share some of the Republican concerns that underlie the proposals.[9] After all, the opportunities for individual Democrats to influence policy outcomes also are limited by many current rules. But Democrats benefit from chairing subcommittees, proxy voting, and freedom from voting on many Republican floor amendments. Democrats also benefit from a flexible use of bill referral procedures, special rules, suspension motions, and reconciliation legislation. Perhaps most important, many of these practices serve to bolster the power of the majority party's contingents on committees. As long as the vast majority of Democrats associate themselves with the collective interests of their party and the policy recommendations flowing from committees, and Democrats retain majority control, such proposals have little chance of adoption. It is reasonable to predict that Republican attitudes would change if they gained majority control of the House.

The limited scope of the Republican proposals is noteworthy. No proposals to make significant changes in committee jurisdictions were offered in the official Republican package. Republicans are interested in limiting the effect of developments in special rules, suspension motions, and limitation amendments so that they can more freely challenge committee recommendations, but they otherwise would like to see more dependence on committees and less on the majority party leadership in drafting legislation. After all, depending on the issue and the committee, Republicans find that they can shape policy in many committee settings, even when they may lack votes on the floor.

Perhaps most important, Republicans often endorse restrictive special rules, multiple referral, and other practices of recent vintage. They seek only to reduce the chances that these devices can be used to limit their own procedural options. Republicans often support restrictive rules, for example, because they believe that their own amendments will be treated in a fashion that meets their needs. Similarly, Republicans agree that multiple referral and suspension motions are conveniences important to the efficiency and effectiveness of the House.

The limited scope of the Republican proposals suggests that even minority party members do not see a need for more fundamental reforms and recognize the institutional advantages of many of the practices devised by the majority party. In general, members of both parties appear to approve the greater flexibility that has been added to the decision-making process in the House. The prereform House was characterized by a fairly simple, relatively fixed process. Single committee referral was followed by an open rule, relatively few floor amendments and no recorded votes in the Committee of the Whole, and a small conference delegation of senior committee members. Today, however, measures may be referred to more than one committee in several different ways, special rules can be molded to particular circumstances, and conference delegations are structured in a variety of ways. The developments in the budget process even put critical policy choices on the floor before committee deliberations. Referral, floor, and conference practices that were near constants twenty years ago are now quite variable, yielding a remarkable number of combinations in how the House processes legislation. The malleability of the process is now widely appreciated and accepted.

The flexibility of the process conflicts with a system of rigid jurisdictions, fixed sequences, and autonomous committees. That is, it conflicts with committee power of the strength present only two or three decades ago. It is true that House committees have managed to recover some of the autonomy they lost during the 1970s, but they still do not enjoy the degree of autonomy they enjoyed twenty years ago. And little on the horizon indicates that committee autonomy will be much stronger in the near future.

THE SENATE

More serious consideration of reform has occurred in the Senate, where there is a greater frustration with current procedures. At least four major sets of proposals were offered in the 1980s, but none of them achieved significant changes in the standing rules.[10] The most recent effort, a 1988 study conducted by the Committee on Rules and Administration, deserves some scrutiny because it reflects the continuing frustration of many senators with the inability of the Senate to improve its own institutional arrangements. By early 1990, Senate leaders had not lived up to their promises to give the committee's report serious consideration.

Like the House Republican proposals, the Rules and Administration Committee proposals are interesting for what they did *not* recommend. In its executive summary, the committee report explained:

> [T]he Committee believes that solutions to the Senate's problems do not always lie in changes in or additions to its current rules. For example, the Committee has carefully considered issues of committee jurisdiction and referral. . . . Based on its study, the Committee does not find it to be necessary or appropriate at this time for the Senate to undertake the difficult and contentious task of reorganizing its committee system. This matter is important and must be seriously considered in the coming years. Frustration with the three-tier system of budgets, authorizations, and appropriations is growing and must be addressed. To fully resolve this frustration may require a comprehensive restructuring of the committee system.[11]

In the Senate, where multiple referral has not become as commonplace as in the House, jurisdictional tensions continue to give rise to occasional public complaints. As a result, jurisdictional issues have received more attention in the Senate during recent years. But the potential controversy engendered by jurisdictional questions—and certainly by reassigning budgeting, authorizing, and appropriating responsibilities—would make it impossible to overcome the inevitable filibuster of any reform package. The committee chose not to distract senators from more feasible reform proposals.

The two proposals with the most direct bearing on committee power concern two distinctive features of Senate rules: the absence of a rule limiting debate and the absence of a rule requiring that floor amendments be germane to the measure under consideration. Extended debate, or filibuster, gives the individual senator a tool for obstructionism that is not available in the House. Although debate may be stopped by a successful cloture motion, this procedure is cumbersome, is itself time-consuming, and requires a three-fifths constitutional majority (three-fifths of all senators). Nongermane amendments give senators a convenient means for addressing new issues on the floor and circumventing committees. Both features of Senate rules have long been subject to heated debate, but the difficulty of overcoming a filibuster to any rules change (which requires a two-thirds majority of those present and voting) has prevented substantial reform.[12]

To tackle the problem of extended debate, the Rules and Administration Committee recommended that the Senate consider fixing a time limit, or even prohibiting all debate, on motions to proceed to consider measures. Under the current rule, senators may filibuster the motion to proceed to the consideration of a measure as well as the measure itself and amendments thereto. This modest proposal would not eliminate filibusters on measures, amendments, or other motions, but it would make it possible for the Senate to get to the measure before a filibuster could start. It also would speed floor action on some measures even in the absence of threatened filibusters.

Stronger medicine was recommended for nongermane amendments. The committee forwarded a proposal to enable an extraordinary majority vote (a three-fifths majority, for example) to require that amendments to a pending measure be germane. This would give the Senate the option to impose a germaneness restriction without having to gain unanimous consent, as is currently required in most cases. Such a rule could be reinforced, the committee noted, by requiring that measures be read for amendment section by section. Considering amendments one section at a time, it is argued, would lend greater order and predictability to Senate floor debate. It would establish an amending process similar to the one employed by the House and, in doing so, would substantially reduce the ability of senators to circumvent committees by offering nongermane amendments to bills. Amendments still could be considered out of order, and amendments still could address multiple sections, but generally unanimous consent would have to be obtained to do so. Committee members could object when they sought to protect their bills.

Furthermore, the Rules and Administration report suggested that it should be more difficult for the Senate to vote to overturn a ruling of the presiding officer on germaneness questions. The Senate's rules now require amendments to be germane after cloture is invoked and when a general appropriations bill is pending, but the Senate frequently votes, by a simple majority, to overturn rulings of the presiding officer on germaneness questions in order to attach nongermane matters to bills. The reform proposal is that an extraordinary majority, say three-fifths, be required for overruling the presiding officer on germaneness questions.[13] Such a rule would strengthen cloture as a tool for protecting committees from nongermane amendments and reduce the use of necessary appropriations bills as vehicles for circumventing the authorizing committees.

Substantial support for such proposals exists among senators. A 1988 survey of senators discovered that 76.9 percent of the respondents favored limiting debate on motion to proceed to the consideration of a measure. About a third of those in favor offered only qualified support, however, indicating that a strong rule, such as one prohibiting all debate on the motion to proceed, might have substantial opposition. Only 61.5 percent said they favored stricter germaneness rules, less than the two-thirds required to invoke cloture on a filibuster on rules changes.[14] Thus, the prospects appear to be brighter for modest debate limitations than for new germaneness rules.

With respect to the internal operations of committees, the Rules and Administration Committee suggested only one significant reform. The proposal would mandate that all markups be conducted at the full committee level, thereby limiting subcommittees to hearings and investigations. The proposal is designed to reduce the total number of meetings and hearings and alleviate senators' scheduling conflicts. If adopted, it would force a substantial change in practice on only four or five Senate committees, most prominently Judiciary and Labor and Human Resources, from both of which opposition could be expected.

As a package, the Rules and Administration Committee proposals represent substantial reform of Senate decision-making practices. A combination of meaningful limits on debate and nongermane amendments with a neutering of subcommittees would greatly reduce the parliamentary prerogatives and resources of individual senators and enhance the importance of full committee chairs and their staff. As a result, while various components might receive Senate approval in the near future, it is highly unlikely that the Senate will endorse the full package.

AUTHORIZING, APPROPRIATING, TAXING, AND BUDGETING

Congress's system for coordinating policy, spending, and revenue decisions is very elaborate, and it changes frequently. Traditionally, the distinction among *authorization decisions* (establishing programs and their details), *appropriations decisions* (granting spending authority to programs and agencies once authorization decisions are made), and *revenue decisions* (designing tax laws) organized the relations of committees. The budget process adopted in 1974 and modified in the 1980s seeks to coordinate and sometimes orchestrate these decisions through budget resolutions and reconciliation instructions. The complications of making this process work and the frustrations of managing large federal budget deficits have spurred interest in reform. Any alteration of the budget process necessarily affects the relationships among authorizing, appropriating, taxing, and budgeting committees.

Three sets of proposals have received considerable attention. The least dramatic proposal is a change from an annual cycle of appropriations and budget decisions to a biennial cycle. Behind this proposal are members seeking to restore a more autonomous role for authorizing committees and, to a lesser extent, the appropriations committees, which have lost power to the budget committees and party leaders who direct the budget process. They hope that reducing the frequency with which the thousands of discrete budgeting decisions are made will create more time for oversight activities and crafting of new policy and programs, as well as reduce dependence on continuing resolutions, debt ceiling resolutions, and other emergency vehicles for legislating. There appears to be considerable support for a biennial budget and appropriations cycle, although neither chamber has come close to adopting a plan.[15]

As attractive and simple as the move to a biennial budget cycle seems, it could create problems of its own. The stakes in each round of budgeting would be higher in a biennial cycle, which could make stalemate and budget trickery even more of a problem than under annual budgeting. If that happened, decision-making responsibility would continue to flow from committees to central leaders who are in a position to negotiate on behalf of the parties and chambers. And from the point of view of committees interested in new policy initiatives, waiting for the next budgeting round before new policies could be implemented would reduce the ability of Congress to respond to rapidly changing conditions and undermine the value of membership on committees with appropriate jurisdiction. Interim or supplementary appropriations to handle such situations might effectively put Congress back into near constant debates over the budget.[16]

Another proposal addresses the distinction between authorizations and appropriations. The tensions of legislating under budget constraints in the 1980s exacerbated long-standing conflicts between authorizing and appropriating committees. Authorizing committees have complained for decades about appropriations bills providing for unauthorized programs. In fact, until 1977, the Senate had a rule that made certain authorizing committee members ex officio members on appropriations bills related to their committees' jurisdictions. In recent years, the delays caused by indecision and stalemate over the general direction of budget policy have forced more authorization decisions into omnibus emergency legislation, such as continuing appropriations resolutions, which are crafted by the appropriations committees. On the other hand, appropriators have complained about delays in getting authorization bills passed so that they can be guided by them. But because it is possible for the chamber to waive the rule barring appropriations without authorizations, this has been a less serious problem for appropriators than the encroachment of appropriators on the turf of authorizers has been for authorizing committees.[17]

The radical proposal for improving this situation is to eliminate the appropriations committees and grant appropriations responsibility to the respective authorizing committees.[18] Like biennial budgeting, this proposal is designed in part to reduce the number of wholly separate decisions and thereby reduce intercommittee conflict and create more time for other activities. In principle, a single committee would simultaneously consider new authorizations and appropriations, make sure that they are mutually consistent, and report them to the floor so that both elements could be considered in close proximity to each other. Furthermore, entitlement decisions that create nondiscretionary appropriations from the perspective of the appropriators could be made in better coordination with ordinary appropriations decisions in the committees with the consolidated functions.

Needless to say, this dramatic change in process would greatly strengthen the hand of the authorizing committees. The consolidated functions would enhance the bargaining position of committees relative to both other members and the executive branch. In the Senate, however, such a process would not insulate committees from unfriendly floor amendments and might even improve the ability of senators to pursue appropriations issues on authorization measures and vice versa.

Support for the plan is much stronger in the Senate than in the House. The 1988 study of members' views on reforms reported that while half of the Senate favored consolidation of authorizations and appropriations responsibilities, only a third of the House did so.[19] House members are more wedded than senators are to their current committee system and the distribution of power it provides. Moreover, the House has experienced fewer complications than the Senate in relations between authorizing committees and its Appropriations Committee in recent years, in part because the House Appropriations Committee generally has been more successful in reporting and gaining adoption of appropriations bills in a timely fashion. But in neither chamber is there sufficient support for such a radical proposal to be adopted. The authorization-appropriation conflict continues to be a widely recognized problem with no feasible solution in sight.

A third proposal represents a different diagnosis of the problems created by budget decision making. A number of members believe that the entire budget process established in 1974 should be eliminated, preserving the original authorizations-appropriations process without the overlay of budget resolutions and reconciliation bills. Underlying the proposal are the objections of both appropriators and authorizers to the constraints placed on their discretion. They argue that the budget process contributes little to managing the deficit—success or failure in establishing and meeting spending and revenue goals rest on an agreement between Congress and the White House that is not much influenced by arcane congressional budget procedures. In any case, Congress has demonstrated remarkable ingenuity in circumventing budget ceilings and reconciliation instructions, which makes the current process largely meaningless anyway but costs committees a great deal in time and energy that could be put to solving policy problems.

No systematic survey with reliable findings has addressed this specific question, so it is difficult to assess the support for repeal of the 1974 budget process among members of Congress. Nevertheless, many members have noted in public forums their interest in simplifying congressional budget procedures and reducing the amount of effort required to meet somewhat artificial budget deadlines and targets. Certain elements of the argument are inconsistent, of course: the current process cannot both be meaningless and limit the power of authorizing and appropriations committees. Some of the complaints seem to represent frustration with budget policy outcomes as much as with budget procedures.

Repealing the 1974 process would indeed alter the distribution of power in Congress. Most important, much of the centralizing influence of the budget process would be lost. Party leaders could still negotiate with the White House over the shape of the budget, but their ability to enforce the agreement would be weakened. Ready-made mechanisms such as reconciliation instructions, 302(b) appropriations ceilings, and points of order, along with the policing effort of the budget committees, would not be available. In order to make budget agreements meaningful, new mechanisms would have to be devised on an ad hoc basis, and party leaders would have to draft colleagues to assist them in reviewing and sometimes obstructing the recommendations of committees. Both would cost the leadership more in time and energy than current procedures, so neither would be likely to be accomplished frequently or effectively.

A CONGRESS NOT YET RIPE FOR REFORM

As this brief review of reform ideas suggests, there is a reservoir of reform proposals that would change the functions, practices, and autonomy of congressional committees. Nevertheless, reform proposals do not yet seem ripe enough for picking.

Major reform comes only when a substantial consensus emerges in Congress about both the nature of weaknesses in current decision-making processes and the fit of the proposed remedies to both institutional and individual needs. Currently, many members believe that important policy dilemmas, such as how to reduce the budget deficit and meet domestic and international commitments, cannot be resolved by procedural change alone. And even when there is a widely shared view on institutional problems and solutions, overcoming the opposition of members who have a stake in current arrangements is not easy. Usually, only a sustained effort by party leaders is sufficient to push past the obstacles and accomplish significant reform. But, as was true in the 1980s, pressing issues distract leaders from procedural reform and leave reform a relatively low priority. Thus, substantial procedural reform is most likely to occur when it is perceived to be connected to pressing issues, as when conflict between the president and Congress over important issues encourages Congress to improve its own capabilities.[20] As of early 1990, the conditions of consensus about problems and solutions and leadership commitment do not seem close to being met.

Continued incremental change in rules and practices is more likely than comprehensive reform. Of course, the accumulation of numerous changes in rules and practices can have significant consequences for the power of committees, even when the individual changes were not intended to affect committee power. The new features in House special rules and Senate unanimous consent agreements, adjustments in multiple referral practices, innovations in conference committee arrangements, and other small steps will continue to change the legislative functions of committees.

The future direction of the role of the two committee systems is conditioned by factors beyond the control of members of Congress. As outlined in Chapter 5, the nature of the policy agenda shapes attitudes about the best organizational arrangement within Congress. In the 1980s, budget deficits forced party and budget leaders to trade spending (or revenues) in the jurisdiction of one committee for spending (or revenues) in the jurisdiction of other committees, creating conflict between committees and helping to centralize decision making. If the congressional agenda becomes less focused on budget issues, the business of the various committees may again be perceived as more

separable and generally less salient, conditions that enhance the autonomy of committees.

In addition, the size and cohesiveness of the parties, particularly of
the majority party, mold the roles of central party leaders and floor
coalitions, which in turn influence the autonomy of committees. If
majority party Democrats in the House lose some of their current
cohesiveness, because of agenda or electoral conditions, members may
lose their tolerance for assertive central party leaders and demand that
committees be granted more autonomy. Furthermore, differences between the chambers will continue to shape the future of committees. In
the smaller Senate, with its rules preserving individual rights of
effective participation at the floor stage, it is unlikely that either agenda
change or a transformation of the political coalitions in the chamber
will, by themselves, substantially increase the autonomy of standing
committees.

Forecasting the future of the committee systems is a very complex
and error-prone enterprise. Unfortunately, the theory needed to predict
the future of the national political agenda, the size and cohesiveness of
congressional parties, and the procedural context of committee activity is
not well developed. Nevertheless, it is reasonable to think that the
current agenda, party balance, and procedural setting will not remain
the same for long. As a result, the dynamic character of the committee
systems of Congress is likely to endure.

CONCLUSION

We have pursued two general themes in this book and hope that we
have marshaled a convincing case for both.

The first theme concerns variation within and between the two
chambers. Generalizations about committees always come at the risk of
neglecting one or more important counterexamples. The best examples
are generalizations about decentralization and subcommittee government.
The House and Senate have exhibited fundamentally different patterns
that should not be ignored. Another example is the mixed effects of the
budget process for authorizing and appropriations committees. And more
generally, different environments and member goals can be counted on
to produce different decision-making patterns. The committee systems of
the House and Senate are not monolithic, homogeneous structures; they
are richly variegated on most important dimensions.

The second theme concerns change in committee systems. Given
how difficult it is to obtain significant change in the systems, it is
amazing how frequently and quickly major changes in the functions,

practices, and autonomy of committees can occur. At times, the modification of rules and practices not directly associated with committees transforms the context in which committees operate. For example, new functions for party leaders, acquired because of changes in the policy agenda or the coalitional alignments within the parties, often affect committees. Similarly, reform of floor procedure intended to improve efficiency usually has implications for committees. And nearly any change in the sequence of stages in the legislative process alters the strategic setting of committees. But, looking back over recent decades, even direct manipulation of committee structure and procedure is quite common. It seems unlikely that the committee systems will look the same in two decades as they do today.

The somewhat ambiguous status of committee power in Congress today may be unsettling. It certainly is a source of frustration for many members. Two points should be kept in mind. First, the tensions in decision-making processes that produce enigmatic roles for committees are unavoidable. As in any organization, it is difficult to achieve a lasting balance between specialization and integrated policy making, between the division of labor required to manage a large work load and a well-coordinated process to create coherent legislation, or among the legitimate needs of individual members, their parties, and the institution.

Second, tensions are desirable. If Congress uniformly favored a party-oriented over a committee-oriented process, for example, it would be less able to adapt to new conditions that required the advantages of a committee-oriented process to be more fully exploited. That is not to say Congress always and rapidly adjusts to new circumstances; nor is it to contend that congressional procedures should change in response to each new development in the political environment. Rather, it is to argue that members of Congress are, and should be, encouraged to identify and articulate rationales for alternative institutional arrangements when there is some conflict over alternative processes. Even if it produces conflict and some dissatisfaction, the self-conscious specification of alternative institutional arrangements is vital to the independence of Congress, for only then can Congress define for itself when and how to adapt to new and frequently changing conditions.

NOTES

1. See Melissa P. Collie and Joseph Cooper, "Multiple Referral and the 'New' Committee System in the House of Representatives," in *Congress Reconsidered*, 4th ed., ed. Lawrence C. Dodd and Bruce I. Oppenheimer (Washington, D.C.: CQ Press, 1989), 245-272.
2. On the costs and benefits of a division of labor, see James G. March and Johan P. Olsen, *Rediscovering Institutions: The Organizational Basis of Politics* (New York: Free Press, 1989), chap. 2.
3. Formal theorists of legislative politics have begun to consider the importance of motivating members to specialize and gain expertise in the business of their committees. See David Austen-Smith and William H. Riker, "Asymmetric Information and the Coherence of Legislation," *American Political Science Review* 81 (September 1987): 897-918. See also the following papers by Thomas W. Gilligan and Keith Krehbiel: "Collective Decision-Making and Standing Committees: An Informational Rationale for Restrictive Amendment Procedures," *Journal of Law, Economics, and Organization* 3 (1987): 287-335; "Collective Choice Without Procedural Commitment," in *Models of Strategic Choice in Politics*, ed. Peter C. Ordeshook (Ann Arbor: University of Michigan Press, 1989); and "Asymmetric Information and Legislative Rules with a Heterogeneous Committee," *American Journal of Political Science* 33 (May 1989): 459-490.
4. More flexible procedures have costs: reducing incentives for specialization, consuming resources that could be committed to specialized functions, compelling explicit decisions about matters that could be automated, and so forth. See Herbert Kaufman, *Time, Chance, and Organizations: Natural Selection in a Perilous Environment* (Chatham, N.J.: Chatham House, 1985), 75-77.
5. This tension is a common feature of political institutions in democratic systems. More generally, we might characterize the tension as one among preferences for a division of labor and the application of expertise, individual or subgroup rights, and majority rule; or among a confederation, direct unitary democracy, and monarchy. The contrasts are common and can be found in many organizational and political settings. For background and references to the relevant literature, see March and Olsen, *Rediscovering Institutions*, chap. 7.
6. Center for Responsive Politics, *Congressional Operations: Congress Speaks—A Survey of the 100th Congress* (Washington, D.C.: Center for Responsive Politics, 1988).
7. *Congressional Record*, January 3, 1989, H14-15.
8. They also would bar special rules that provide for the adoption of a measure or amendment upon the adoption of the rule (so-called self-executing rules) unless opposed by a two-thirds vote of the House.
9. The 1988 survey of the Center for Responsive Politics found, for example, that nearly all Republicans favored reducing the number of subcommittees while only about half of the Democrats did so. Similar differences were uncovered for the issues of stricter limits on committee and subcommittee assignments. See Center for Responsive Politics, *Congressional Operations*, chap. 6.
10. These include the Pearson-Ribicoff study group of 1982-1983, the Quayle committee of 1984, the Byrd proposals of 1986, and the study of the Committee on Rules and Administration in 1988. See *Report on Senate*

Operations 1988, Senate Committee on Rules and Administration, September 20, 1988 (Washington, D.C.: U.S. Government Printing Office). In addition, of course, several proposals dealing with the various aspects of Senate procedure and structure are introduced during each congress.

11. Ibid., 3.
12. The cloture rule, Rule XXII, has been changed several times since the 1950s. The 1959 rule required a two-thirds majority of those present and voting to invoke cloture. In 1975, the Senate changed the rule to require that three-fifths of the entire membership support cloture, except on measures changing the Senate's standing rules, in which case the old requirement still applied. However, the use of dilatory motions rendered useless the long-standing rule limiting debate to 100 hours after cloture was invoked, so in 1979 the 100-hour limit was clarified to include all action. The 100-hour limit was reduced to 30 hours in 1986, as a part of the package providing for televised floor sessions.
13. The committee suggested that a similar rule apply to rulings on the question of legislating on general appropriations bills. Current precedent allows a legislative amendment to a general appropriations bill only if the amendment is germane to legislative language in the House-passed bill. The Senate occasionally has overruled the presiding officer in order to incorporate legislative language on new subjects.
14. See Center for Responsive Politics, *Congressional Operations*, chap. 3.
15. The investigators conducting the 1988 survey of members found that 85.8 percent favored a two-year budget cycle. See Center for Responsive Politics, *Congressional Operations*, chap. 2.
16. Several other plans to streamline the budget process have been proposed to achieve goals similar to those pursued in biennial budgeting. For example, Representatives Richard Gephardt (D-Mo.) and David Obey (D-Wis.) have sought to move the adoption of the first budget resolution to earlier in the year, require action on authorizing legislation by June, and then stipulate that Congress could not recess until action on appropriations and reconciliation bills was complete. Besides improving the chances that appropriations bills will be enacted before the fiscal year begins on October 1, the plan is intended to separate authorizing, appropriations, and reconciliation actions.
17. For a recent example, see "Appropriations: Turf Fight Develops over Funding Bill," *Congressional Quarterly Weekly Report*, November 4, 1989, 2958.
18. There is a long history to the distribution and consolidation of authorization and appropriation authority. Indeed, it should be noted that severe restriction of appropriations committee power would not be unprecedented. Both chambers consolidated authorization and appropriations power in the authorizing committee during the late nineteenth century—a pattern that lasted until the early 1920s. A useful account can be found in Allen Schick, "The Whole and the Parts: Piecemeal and Integrated Approaches to Congressional Budgeting," report prepared for the Task Force on the Budget Process, House Committee on the Budget, Serial No. CP-3 (Washington, D.C.: U.S. Government Printing Office, 1987). The present-day authors of the proposal to consolidate authorizations and appropriations are Senators Daniel Inouye (D-Hawaii) and Nancy Kassebaum (R-Kan.), who introduced the plan as S. Res. 270 in the 100th Congress. Many less dramatic proposals have been offered to reduce conflict or redistribute power between the appropriations and authorizing committees. For example, Rep. John Dingell

(D-Mich.), the House Energy Committee chair, has proposed that the Speaker be required to appoint to conferences members from the appropriate authorizing committees whenever the Senate adds legislation to general appropriations bills.

19. Center for Responsive Politics, *Congressional Operations,* chap. 2.
20. James L. Sundquist, *The Decline and Resurgence of Congress* (Washington, D.C.: Brookings Institution, 1981).

Index

245